Career Resources for a Life in the Law

Should You Really Be a Lawyer?

The Guide to Smart Career Choices Before, During & After Law School

By Deborah Schneider, JD & Gary Belsky

$21.95   248 pages

What Can You Do With a Law Degree?

A Lawyer's Guide to Career Alternatives Inside, Outside & Around the Law

By Deborah Arron, JD

$29.95   352 pages/5th edition

The Complete Guide to Contract Lawyering

What Every Lawyer & Law Firm Should Know about Temporary Legal Services

By Deborah Arron, JD & Deborah Guyol, JD

$29.95   288 pages/3rd edition

Should You Marry a Lawyer?

A Couple's Guide to Balancing Work, Love & Ambition

By Fiona Travis, Ph.D.

$18.95   168 pages

Running From the Law

Why Good Lawyers Are Getting Out of the Legal Profession

By Deborah Arron, JD

$16.95   192 pages/3rd edition

To order, call (800) 359-9629.

Or order online from www.DecisionBooks.com

To my extraordinary grandparents, Gene and Sylvia Weissman—D.S.

To a mischief maker—G.B.

Should You Really Be a Lawyer?

The Guide to
Smart Career Choices
Before, During & After
Law **School**

Deborah Schneider, JD
& Gary Belsky

DecisionBooks®
Seattle, Washington

DecisionBooks

Published by Niche Press LLC

PO Box 99477 Seattle WA 98139 U.S.A.

DecisionBooks is a trademarked imprint of Niche Press LLC

Cover and interior design by Rose Michelle Taverniti

Authors Deborah Schneider, JD, and Gary Belsky offer keynote addresses, lectures, seminars, and workshops for prospective law students, law students, and practicing lawyers on how to make smart career decisions. For more information, please visit www.shouldyoureally.com

DecisionBooks are available at special discounts for bulk purchases. For more information, write to Special Markets, DecisionBooks, PO Box 99477, Seattle WA 98139, or email info@DecisionBooks.com

Library of Congress Cataloging-in-Publication Data

Schneider, Deborah, 1971-

  Should you really be a lawyer? : the guide to smart career choices before, during & after law school.

      p. cm.

  Authors, Deborah Schneider and Gary Belsky.

  ISBN 0-940675-57-9

  1. Law--Vocational guidance--United States. I. Belsky, Gary. II. Title.

  KF297.S36 2005

  340'.023'73--dc22

                                    2004012959

*W*alk through any legal bookstore and check out all the sections on Reference, Careers, or Graduate School. There, you will find shelf after shelf of books that tell you how to ace the LSAT, how to get into a good law school, how to succeed on law school exams, how to land a legal job, how to manage your legal career. But until now, none helped you answer the basic question—should you be a lawyer at all?

Now, *Should You Really Be A Lawyer?* is the first book intended to help you approach the decision of whether to become a lawyer or to remain one, and how to find the right career for you—whether it's in or outside of the legal profession. From years of research and experience, we know just how difficult such career decisions can be. As one prospective law student told us in exasperation, "I wish there was a website that would just tell me what to do!" It doesn't exist. Nor is there a single book that can provide everyone with all the answers they need. But we believe this book can help prospective and current law students, as well as working attorneys, make satisfying career choices using a method we think you'll find simple, interesting and enjoyable. If, after reading it, you have comments or anecdotes you'd like to share, or questions you'd like to ask us, we would be happy to hear from you. Just email us at <u>authors@shouldyoureally.com</u>.

—Deborah Schneider and Gary Belsky, June 2004

Contents

PART I

Decisions, Decisions

Chapter 1 The New Science of Decision-Making

> "Why did I go to law school?
> Because I didn't know what to do after
> I graduated. I saw law school as a
> way to avoid making any big decisions
> for a while."
>
> — Josh, real estate agent and non-practicing attorney

*S*teve, age 30, is smart, gregarious and talkative, yet pays little attention to detail and has a short attention span. He tells great jokes, makes constant wise-cracks, and loves being the center of attention.

What is Steve's occupation—standup comedian or lawyer?

You might be tempted to say Steve is a stand-up comic. It would make sense, too. After all, comedians are generally extroverted hams who enjoy being in the spotlight. Lawyers, on the other hand, are detail-oriented introverts who are anything but "the life of the party." But those are only stereotypes—which is the point of this exercise. As it happens, there are more than a million lawyers in this country, and fewer than a thousand working comedians. So, while Steve's profile fits our Hollywood-centric view of what comedians are like, our wise guy is—statistically speaking—a *thousand times* more likely to be a lawyer!

So, what does this have to do with whether **you** should really be a lawyer? And, if you are currently in practice, whether you should really continue?

Actually, quite a lot.

This "Steve" hypothetical is just one example of experiments in an innovative new field of decision-making psychology called **Behavioral Economics**. One of the academics who pioneered the field recently won the Nobel Prize in economics, and if you have read *Time, Newsweek* or the *Wall Street Journal* any time in the last 12 months, you know that Behavioral Economics brings together the disciplines of psychology and economics to study how people form judgments and make decisions. No doubt about it, this field has a bright future in universities and academic think tanks. But we think this exciting new science is too important to be left to academia. We strongly believe that, when applied to daily living, this branch of decision-making psychology can help teach the rest of us how to make smarter career and life choices.

Let's be clear about decision-making:

Throughout our lives, all of us become vulnerable to all sorts of psychological traps when making important life decisions. These traps take the form of processes—largely unconscious—that we use to make easier the work of the thousands of choices we face each day. In academic circles, these processes are called *heuristics*. We call them shortcuts. By any name, though, these decision-making processes come into play in every decision we make—from the mundane (*what should I do this weekend?*) to the profound (*what should I do with my life?*). And we often use these shortcuts without realizing it.

Which brings us back to Steve.

His scenario illustrates two concepts that are the bread and butter of decision-making psychology—*ignoring the base rate* and *rules of thumb*. In plain English, the idea is that at one time or another all of us ignore the hard facts in life (like the overall odds in a given situation), and depend instead on shortcuts and soft assumptions to make decisions. This concept is central to the study of how people make choices: Because life is so complex, and so many decisions must be made, we all take shortcuts to simplify our choices. The problem is that these shortcuts, while sometimes helpful, are themselves psychological traps that can get in the way of making the best decisions. In Steve's case, for instance, most people who choose Steve's profession are ignoring the base rate (one million lawyers versus one thousand comics), relying on a rule of thumb (that lawyers are introverts; comedians are extroverts), and failing to ask the right question ("What are the odds of *anyone* being a lawyer or a comedian?")

As you get into the book, we'll demonstrate how prospective law students, current law students and actual lawyers commonly overlook the right questions and instead rely on a dozen key shortcuts when choosing to pursue a JD, or choosing among jobs, or deciding whether to remain in law at all. The result? Too many otherwise intelligent individuals invest tens of thousands of dollars and countless hours in a post-graduate degree only to learn the high price of making a career decision without thinking through the consequences (or without thinking much at all). In fact, too many law students wind up in jobs they dislike, and too many lawyers either remain unhappily trapped in practice or flee the profession without fully exploring their options, and all because they fall victim to some very subtle and insidious decision-making traps.

Luckily, though, there's help.

Reading through one or more parts of this book, there is a better-than-even chance you won't make the same mistakes. Because while the lessons learned from Behavioral Economics initially centered on financial decisions, this subject offers significant insights into your career decisions as well. And by understanding how you're really approaching the decision to become or remain a lawyer (or what to do with your law degree), you can avoid common decision-making traps that have contributed to the indecision, confusion and regret of so many people in law. You'll also learn how to ask and answer the right questions—and how to gather the critical information—that you'll need to decide which career is truly right for you.

We refer to these decision-making traps as **Choice Challenges** and, throughout the book, we will introduce you to 12 of them, we will demonstrate their impact on your career and daily life choices, and we will teach you how to overcome them and make better decisions.

The 12 Choice Challenges

Anchoring—When we attach ourselves to a fixed position regardless of evidence to the contrary.

Confirmation Bias—When we shut out information that contradicts our initial preferences.

Decision Paralysis—When we avoid making decisions because we're overwhelmed by choice.

Endowment Effect—When we place a higher value on things we already have than if they belonged to someone else.

Herd Mentality—When our actions and decisions are weighted by those around us.

Ignoring the Base Rate—When we ignore the odds (the base rate) in a given situation.

Information Cascade—When our actions or decisions are influenced by repeated exposure to a barrage of information.

Mental Accounting—When we treat money differently depending on where we get it and what we want to do with it.

Overconfidence—When we overestimate our skills, abilities or knowledge.

Regret Aversion—When our decisions are based on the fear of feeling bad in the future.

Rules of Thumb—When we adopt intellectual shortcuts to make choices less complicated.

Status Quo Bias—When we resist change and prefer to stay with what's familiar.

Law School: The Movie

To give you an illustration of how these Choice Challenges can affect your career decisions, here's a pretty good story—even better because it's true. One of your authors, Gary, met his future co-author when he was 20 and she was 10. Gary was in college, teaching language part-time; Deborah was one of his fifth-grade students. At some point in the school year, Gary was discussing his career options with Deborah's father. The conversation went something like this:

Deb's Dad—So, Gary, what are you going to do after college?
Gary—Beats me.
Deb's Dad—What do you like to do?
Gary—Write.
Deb's Dad—You should go to law school.
Gary—Why?
Deb's Dad—Because you're a good talker and you're smart.
Gary—But I really don't want to be a lawyer.
Deb's Dad—You might one day, and a law degree is just a good thing to have.
Gary—Um, okay.

Actually, maybe this isn't such a good story. Gary took the LSATs, did well, was accepted to a good law school, got there, hated it, quit in the middle of his second semester and landed a job as a reporter. We tell you this story not to blame Deborah's dad for Gary's wasted $8,000 in tuition, but to point out that Gary decided to attend law school by relying on a rule of thumb supplied by Deborah's dad: *a law degree is just a good thing to have*. **Rules of thumb** are mental shortcuts we use to make decisions simpler, but they can lead us astray when we rely on them and overlook the right considerations about our choice. By using this particular rule of thumb as a shortcut, Gary failed to ask the right questions before he pursued law: Do I know what lawyers do and would I enjoy being one?

Gary is not unique, of course; this happens every year.

In fact, 10 years after Gary deep-sixed his law school career, Deborah began hers. In part, she was influenced by her father (a non-lawyer) who *still* thought that everyone in the world could benefit from a law degree because it was "just good to have" but she was also swayed by watching many of her college classmates take the LSAT and apply to law school. Although she took a job in D.C. right after college, she was anxious to confirm her long-standing plan to become a lawyer, so she consulted several non-practicing lawyers for advice.

Each conversation went something like this:

Deb—I'm thinking about law school, but I don't think I want to practice law.

Lawyer—Get a degree anyway. It's a valuable credential. Everyone in D.C. has one.

Deb—Even if they don't practice law, like you?

Lawyer—Oh, sure. Law school teaches you how to think and how to write. It's good training, and a resume-builder. It makes you more marketable. And, as a woman, a JD will give you more credibility. No matter what, you'll always have your law degree. No one can take that away from you.

Deb [thinking about it]—*Hmmm, I love to write, I'm a very logical thinker. I'd probably like law school. What if I don't get a law degree and then I later regret it? I definitely have to get a graduate degree before I turn 30 and I'm too old to be a student anymore. And that's a good point about being a woman with an added credential. My mom has always said that she regrets not getting a graduate degree. What if I wind up divorced, or a single mom someday!? I don't want to be a bag lady!*

So what happened? Deborah only spoke with non-practicing lawyers who were happily ensconced in non-legal jobs they enjoyed. She didn't do her homework by talking to practicing lawyers, or ex-lawyers who didn't think that their degree paid off. She never set foot in a law firm. She didn't witness what lawyers did on a daily basis. She didn't read any legal documents to see what lawyers read and write. She never did any self-assessment exercises to discover her favorite skills or areas of interest. She never explored other professions or graduate school programs. And three weeks into law school she realized the mistake she'd made. Turns out, Deborah hated legal research and writing. She loathed reading cases. She was bored to tears from studying contracts and property law. After a wrenching first semester she called Gary, who was starting to write a book about how to make better decisions. The conversation went something like this:

Deb [freaking out]—I've never been so stressed and depressed in my life! I hate school! I hate reading cases! I hate legal research and writing! I don't want to be a lawyer! *I hate life!*

Gary—So drop out.

Deb—What will people think? I'm not a quitter! I've planned to get a law degree since I was, like, six! What if I regret it? I'd rather do anything else in the world, but I don't know what I'd do if I actually left.

Gary—Here's an idea. You could do something that you like.

Deb [ignoring Gary]—I wish I had called you *before* I ever started law school! Now it's too late, I've already gotten through one semester. Everyone says the first semester is the worst, but then it goes downhill from there. I may as well stick it out. Thanks. I feel better.

During the next two-and-a-half years, Deborah discovered that law school did indeed go downhill from there. The more real-world legal experience she got—through law review, moot court, lawyering skills classes, internships, externships and clerkships—the more convinced she became that she didn't want to practice law at all and going to law school "just for the credential" had been a huge mistake. She also discovered that many of her classmates had entered law school with the same assumptions and lack of real information.

It might not surprise you, then, to learn that Deborah eventually became a career counselor who helped lawyers, law students and prospective law students make better career decisions. And after years of conversations with hundreds of attorneys, law students and career counselors, Deborah was amazed by the decision-making patterns that emerged surrounding the choices to enter and remain in law. One day, she was in conversation with several law school career counselors (many of them former lawyers). *That* conversation went something like this:

Career Counselor No. 1—I wish people would stop viewing law school as a graduate liberal arts degree! I cannot tell you how many students I counsel who have no business being in law school. Half of the first-years have no idea why they're here, they just came here to avoid deciding what they really wanted to do. By the time they're third-years, they still have no clue and wind up crying in my office. We have more therapists on staff than career counselors.

Counselor No. 2—Same here. The problem is, too many of them graduate and have never spent 20 minutes in a real conversation with an attorney. I did the same thing when I was a student.

[Heads nod in agreement.]

Counselor No. 3—I just counseled a third-year who'd been miserable throughout law school. We discovered that she'd be really happy as a fly fishing instructor. Fly fishing! She was thrilled but I was dying to ask her: "Aren't you upset that you just *pissed away* three years and over $100,000 on a law degree?"

[Group groans]

Counselor No. 4—And what about all the alumni who come back to see you because they want out? They didn't ask any real questions of themselves before or during law school, but after two years of working they come running back for all the self-analysis you can throw at them. Half of them decide they're too deep in debt to leave their jobs. I'm like, "*Helloooo?* Didn't you know about compound interest rates when you were taking out your loans?"

Counselor No. 5—Even the ones without debt feel guilty about not wanting to practice law after they got the degree. They want permission to not practice.

Counselor No. 6—I'm also amazed at what uninformed decisions law students make when choosing summer and post-graduate jobs. They choose their law firm based on what they read on greedyassociates.com, or on what their friends say. And it doesn't occur to them to think: "Gee, if I'm spending 3,000 hours a year at this place, I should make sure that I like the people." By the time they find out what a 2,000 annual billable hour requirement actually means, it's too late.

Counselor No. 7—They should make law school more like an MBA program— require you get a couple of years of real-world work experience first. Law is the only profession without a required internship. Even your *manicurist* had to complete a supervised internship!

[Group laughs; everyone looks at their nails.]

Deb (interrupting]—Wait a minute. Nearly every one of us is a lawyer who made a career change. Who are we laughing at? Maybe we should figure out a way to actually help.

This book is our way to help, to assist you in making better choices about a major life decision. Let's run through some of the principles that we'll cover in this book, those psychological decision-making traps that contributed to Deborah's (and thousands of other lawyers') law-related choices.

When Deborah decided to go to law school, her decision was influenced by rules of thumb recited by her dad and other lawyers—that "a law degree is just a good thing to have," "it's a valuable credential even if you don't practice," and "law school teaches you how to think." These are somewhat misleading and insufficient reasons in and of themselves for getting a JD, but they exist as relied-upon guidelines to this day. By relying on these rules of thumb, Deborah (like Gary) failed to ask the right questions about pursuing law (most importantly, "Do I know what lawyers do and will I enjoy being a lawyer?").

Deborah was also persuaded by the fact that everyone around her was taking the LSAT and going to law school. This is often referred to as the **herd mentality**—making decisions that are heavily influenced by the actions of others around you. The herd mentality is a powerful force that routinely affects people's decision to go to law school, stay in law school, practice law and even pursue certain jobs or career paths. In legal terms, it's called being swayed by a jury of your peers.

Deborah was similarly moved by the advice of non-practicing lawyers, coming under the spell of another decision-making trap—**the confirmation bias**. This simply refers to the tendency to seek out and rely upon facts or opinions that confirm your initial or existing preferences. In other words, once we get an idea in our heads, we tend to avoid asking questions that may challenge our preconceptions. As a result, we make decisions based on information that's inaccurate, incomplete or simply inane. In this case, when Deborah relied on non-practicing lawyers to advise her she received information that would cement her inclination to go. Naturally, these lawyers told her what she wanted to hear: That a law degree would be beneficial, whether or not she ever practiced. Deborah accepted those responses and avoided asking questions that would challenge them. Only later, after law school, did she find a lot of lawyers who never practiced law and did not consider their degree a worthwhile investment.

Deborah was likewise obsessed with getting a graduate degree by 30, an arbitrarily chosen age that took on far too much significance in her decision-making. This common trap is called **anchoring**—attaching great importance to a fact or figure that may have little or no bearing on our judgments or decisions.

When she decided to stay in law school, Deborah was influenced by her fear that she might later regret her decision to leave. Again, this is another power-ful force called **regret aversion**, which means that people tend to shy away from taking an action because they fear they'll regret their decision later. Like a lot of Choice Challenges, the practice of making decisions based on fear of regret sounds obvious when you hear it explained, but the extent to which this tenden-cy affects your decisions is greater than most people think.

Deborah was also overwhelmed by the thought of how to decide what to do if she left law school. This reflects a common Choice Challenge called **decision paralysis**—a reference to the difficulty people encounter when having to select from many options. For Deborah, ruling out law ruled in everything else, and the thought of choosing among all those professional paths was too daunting.

Finally, Deborah resisted leaving law school because she didn't want to "waste" all the time, effort and money she invested into her first semester. Such waste-not-want-not thinking is the **sunk cost fallacy**—the tendency to pay too much attention to resources (money, time, emotions) that have already been spent. The sunk cost fallacy often afflicts unhappy lawyers who yearn to leave legal practice but feel as though they're throwing away their law degree by changing careers.

Each year, many prospective law students, law students and lawyers fall prey to these same Choice Challenges and various others. That explains why it's easy to go to law school without doing your homework, yet difficult to drop out when you hate it. That explains why it's so hard to forgo a traditional legal career path even when you suspect that you won't enjoy it. And it explains why it's so daunting to decide among legal jobs and careers.

So what can you learn from this, and how can our law school saga help you? The bad news is that it's easy to get tripped up when we make career choices if we're not aware of how we're making them. The good news, though, is that once you become aware of those decision-making pitfalls, and learn to ask the right questions, you can make better choices. But sometimes the most obvious questions are the hardest to ask.

Chapter 2

How *to* Use This Book

"" I decided at age 10 that I was going

to law school... and I never thought

about it again. ""

—Helen, attorney at a legal services organization

*G*iven our belief that most people don't really understand how they make choices, we've focused this book on helping improve your decision-making process. We interviewed prospective law students, law students and lawyers— lots of lawyers—about their life and career decisions. We also consulted professionals who work with them: law school career counselors, professors and administrators, undergraduate career counselors and career counselors who specialize in working with lawyers (to give you a small sampling). And because not everyone who has questions about a legal career asked them before they went to law school, we've organized this book into three parts:

Should You Really Go To Law School?
Should You Really Stay in Law School?
Should You Really Practice Law?

You could read just the one part that applies to your circumstances. But we firmly believe that you would benefit from reading most if not all of the book, regardless of which particular camp you find yourself in. That's because many of the decision-making traps that lead people to go to law school in the first place also lead them to stay in law school or to continue practicing, even after they realize that they'd prefer to do something else. In any case, here's a breakdown of what each part will cover.

Part I: Should You Really Go To Law School?—If you're considering law school, this part will help you decide whether pursuing a legal or a non-legal career is the right path for you. You'll learn how to thoughtfully evaluate your reasons for pursuing a law degree, discover what law school is all about, assess whether you would enjoy practicing law, develop a realistic picture of what attorneys actually do, gain real-world work experience in legal and non-legal settings and explore alternatives to law school. If you ultimately decide that a legal path is the right journey for you, we also include pointers on choosing and paying for law school.

Part II: Should You Really Stay In Law School?—If you're a law student who's unsure of whether to remain in law school—or who doesn't know what to do with your law degree—this section is for you. You'll learn how to identify the issues driving your desire to leave, along with the psychological barriers that stand in the way. This section will also help you evaluate the pros and cons of staying versus leaving, and explore alternatives (such as taking a semester off to investigate other career paths). If you decide to stay in school, this chapter will help you make better decisions about summer and post-graduate jobs.

Part III: Should You Really Practice Law?—If you're lawyer who is considering changing jobs or careers—or if you're a law student or recent law school graduate who is considering forgoing legal practice—this section is for you. We'll help you assess the reasons for your dissatisfaction with your current job and determine whether a legal, law-related or non-legal career is the best fit for you.

The Decision Assessments

There's no simple test to determine if entering or leaving the legal profession is the right decision for you. But we have developed a fairly simple device—we call them Decision Assessments—that may go a long way to help you sort out your unique decision-making issues and answer these important questions. Of course, you could simply go through the Decision Assessments and add up your score to help you make your educational or career decision, without reading the accompanying discussions. But we advise against that. It's not that we're in love with our words. We just think it's important that you learn all you can about how to avoid the decision-making blunders that have plagued generations of prospective law students, law students and lawyers before you.

Use it Or Lose it

One more thing: Check out the name of this section—How to Use This Book. The operative word here is "use." Think about this book like a piece of home gym equipment. If you buy a treadmill and only use it as a clothes hanger, you won't benefit much. Similarly, if you buy this book and let it sit on your shelf, you won't make any better decisions. Or if you flip through it, but don't take any of the recommended action steps, you probably won't make better choices about your legal or non-legal career. But use this book thoroughly, and your career, your finances, and your psyche will be in much better shape. Working through the book will not only save you time and money, but also prevent stress, worry, and regret. In fact, we're pretty sure this is the some of the best (and least expensive) legal advice you'll ever get.

One More Thing: Listen to the Devil's Advocate

As we pointed out earlier, we consulted hundreds of lawyers, law students, law professors and law career counselors while writing this book. Their advice fell into two categories—*Conventional Wisdom* and *Unconventional Wisdom*. You can decide which is which because samples of both are interspersed throughout the book under the title, The Devil's Advocate Says.

The Devil's Advocate Says...

Take your time—Many students tell us they chose law school because they didn't have time to research other options—they were too busy cramming for the LSATs and completing law school applications. If they'd spent the same number of hours having informational interviews, they might have chosen a different career path or entered law school with better direction. So before you invest time applying to law school, spend time researching other career paths. (Part 1).

Confess!—One reason that leaving law school is so difficult is admitting—to yourself and to others—you may have made a mistake. Would you rather admit it now to family and friends—or later, to a shrink or career counselor? Many lawyers tell us they wish they'd had nerve to admit their mistake much earlier, and certainly long before they launched their law career. (Part 2).

Cut your losses—People often don't abandon even miserable jobs because they remind themselves how much they've already "put into it"—time, money, emotional investment. Before you make the same mistake (the sunk cost fallacy), remember that you won't get those miserable years back by hanging in there and being miserable for even longer. (Part 3).

PART II

Should You Really Go to Law School?

Chapter 3 *The* **Decision Assessments**

"People always say, 'I'm going to law school because I want to keep my options open.' But I never hear anyone say, 'I'm going to law school because I want to be a lawyer.'"

— John, a writer and former big firm lawyer

*D*id you ever see that Seinfeld episode where Elaine is in her office at J. Peterman's, looking apathetic and bored? She picks up a pen on her desk, removes the cap and sniffs its tip. Her inner thoughts are revealed in the voice-over:

"This pen smells really bad," she muses, *"So, why do I keep smelling it?...Is it too late for me to go to law school?"*

Like Elaine, many people get the idea to attend law school in a moment of career confusion or frustration. Or, as one prospective law student told us: "Applying to law school gives me something to do; to take my focus off the fact that I hate my job, and that I don't know what I want to do." Of course, there are people—you probably know a few—who seem to have planned since birth to become lawyers. Well, maybe it's OK for them, but not for you. So, whatever is prompting you to consider law school, it is very important to carefully examine your motivations.

This chapter will help you analyze your reasons—or lack thereof—for going to law school. This first step is critical because making better decisions begins with understanding your own decision making process. Unfortunately, a lot of prospective law students *don't* examine their decision for faulty assumptions or for misguided reasoning. And while some of you will wind up enjoying law school and your legal career, many others of you will face serious consequences—the law school experience will be excruciating, and only later will you realize you're in the wrong job... maybe even the wrong profession.

Here's the good news. If, after careful research and consideration, you decide to attend law school after all, you'll be far more likely to have a positive experience and land a job you like. Given the money and time a JD requires, it's worth making sure that your investment will be worth it. This chapter will help you assess how you're approaching this decision through a series of four Decision Assessments. When you come to them, please check all statements that are true for you. Don't worry about adding up your overall score right away; you'll do that at the end of the chapter. For now, just tell the truth, the whole truth and nothing but the truth. The more honestly you respond, the more you'll benefit.

We'll score your responses later. For now, let's review the statements you checked, and tell you what they say about your decision-making process:

DECISION ASSESSMENT 1

✓ *Check all statements that apply to you.*

I'm considering going to law school because...

❑ **A** Everyone around me is applying to law school.

❑ **B** I've researched various graduate degree programs, and I've decided that law is best for me.

❑ **C** The economy is weak, so it makes sense to stay in school until the job market picks up.

❑ **D** I think it's beneficial to understand the legal system as it applies to everyday life.

❑ **E** After attending a few classes and speaking with several law students, I think I would enjoy law school.

❑ **F** Most people I know are getting graduate degrees, so I need one to stay competitive.

❑ **G** The intellectual challenge of law school appeals to me.

❑ **H** I'm attracted to the law because of its powerful potential for social change.

❑ **I** I'm ready for a career change, and I think the law offers what I'm looking for.

The Herd Mentality

☑ **A** **Everyone around me is applying to law school.**

☑ **F** **Most people I know are getting graduate degrees, so I need one to stay competitive.**

Did you check either of these two statements? If so, you may have been swayed by a Choice Challenge called the **Herd Mentality**. Here's an example of how this decision-making trap can affect your decisions:

Marge and Homer buy a new car, a Volkswagen Beetle. Inexplicably, over the next six months, numerous strangers began making them offers to buy their car. For some reason, each offer gets smaller than the next. As far as Marge and Homer could tell, the car was in good shape and yet, after six months, they seriously considered selling the Beetle for half what they paid because they worried something might be wrong. Should they have sold the car?

Most people who encounter this question think it's an easy decision—after all, why in the world would they sell the car just because strangers keep offering them less and less money for it? But think of it this way: What if Marge and Homer had bought 1,000 shares of VW stock at $30 a share and, six months later, the share price had fallen to $15? In that case, many people would scream "sell!" After all, that's what investors do when other people start selling the stock they own and the share price drops accordingly. When some shareholders see other people offering them less and less money for their stock, they think: *Gosh, if most investors are dumping VW, they must know something.* So they too sell their stock and push the share price even lower. On Wall Street, this behavior is called "investing with the herd," and it describes people's tendency to conform to the behavior of others when making investment decisions.

Just because law school is right for some people doesn't mean it's right for you.

The *herd mentality*, then, is a powerful decision-making trap that refers to the tendency to allow our actions and decisions to be heavily influenced by those around us. This should sound familiar. After all, herding is a common tendency that begins early in life. We learn at a young age to look to others for clues about everything from how to dress to what to drive. And, in many ways, this is satisfactory. Society functions in part because people conform to the habits and opinions of others around them.

But following the herd is a problem when it causes us to adhere to trends that may not be in our best interest. (Plenty of investors learned this the hard way when they invested in dot coms.)

Taking cues from the herd when you're making career decisions is one of those instances. Yet each year, thousands of prospective law students look around, see lots of smart people applying to law school and conclude that they should do the same. That's because herding often becomes more prevalent during times of uncertainty. Understandably, then, college students near the end of their undergraduate careers—who don't know what they want to do or how to figure it out—are likely to do what everyone else around them is doing. Often that means grad school. Although it's easy to understand why the herd mentality drives so many people to law school, it's equally easy to see what's wrong with following that path:

Just because law school is right for some people doesn't mean it's right for *you*. It's your career, your time, your money and your life. So even if everyone around you is taking the LSAT, you should resist the temptation until you've truly evaluated whether law school is the right choice for you. Otherwise, you may find yourself with plenty of company in law school but riddled with doubt about being there. At the very least, the decision to attend law school should only come after weeks of research into different grad school programs and non-legal careers. The way to decide which ones to research is to determine what jobs interests you, regardless of how much you think you might earn. Maybe your true interest is law, and maybe it's not. But you will be on the right path if you focus on pursuing what sounds genuinely enjoyable to you.

Once you've found a few areas of interest—in addition to law school—you need to explore them in more depth, to see which feel right for you. Talk to students in law school and other graduate school programs. Consult attorneys and non-attorneys to see what different jobs entail, and whether a legal or non-legal job is more appealing. (We'll explain how to do this in the chapters ahead and in the Tool Kit, starting on page 214). Work or volunteer in a job that sounds interesting. Take your time looking off the beaten path for less conventional jobs that intrigue you. So what if most people you know are getting MBAs, JDs and MDs? If you're excited at the idea of doing something unconventional, pursue it. When you make the decision that's right for you, you'll make the right decision. In this way, you'll avoid falling victim to the *herd mentality*.

The Information Cascade

    ☑ C **The economy is weak, so it makes sense to stay in school until the job market picks up.**

If you checked this statement, you may have been influenced by another common Choice Challenge—the **Information Cascade**. It refers to the way our actions or decisions are influenced by repeated exposure to a barrage of information.

It's not a news flash that the media can sway our actions and decisions. But it's not just the media and advertising that set off *information cascades*.

Word-of-mouth can achieve the same result (especially for, say, a hot new restaurant). Trend-setters can do it, too (especially in fashion). Or consider this—think how you react when you see a traffic jam. If you choose to take a detour and others follow, leading others to also follow, you have set into motion your own *information cascade*. In this same way, career decisions are often made.

In the late 1990s, for example, thousands of Americans dropped their so-called "old economy" jobs to join the dot-com startup companies of the so-called "new economy." A few years later, when the dot-coms started collapsing, laid off workers and concerned college grads raced off to grad school in droves to avoid the "lousy economy." Many of them were influenced by widely-reported news about recession, layoffs and a tough job market. As a result, law school applications skyrocketed to all-time highs in 2002 and 2003. As any law school official will tell you, there has always been an inverse relationship between the volume of law school applications and the strength of the economy—when the economy goes down, law school applications go up.

Although it's perfectly understandable why people would prefer security in grad school rather than slugging it out in a tough job market, there are some problems with letting an *information cascade* influence your decision to attend law school:

> First, going to law school out of fear that jobs will be tough to find is simply shortsighted. Too many prospective law students opt for the safety of law school without adequately exploring what being a lawyer is all about. If being a lawyer isn't the right career for you, law school is a bad choice...in good times or bad.

> Second, in a tight economy, the legal job market gets hit, too. So when more people go to law school reasoning "there are no jobs out there," law school enrollment rises. *But the supply of legal jobs does not.* In a weak economy, private law firm hiring may even decline or stagnate, government jobs may become subject to a hiring freeze, and public-interest jobs become more competitive (not only because more people apply for them, but because organizations see funding decline).

In short, the forces behind an *information cascade* can create a seller's market for lawyers and law students in the public and private sectors. So, given that law students must find two summer jobs and a post-graduate job, law school may not be the best way to avoid a challenging job search. And if the market doesn't pick up after your three-year hideout, you run the risk of winding up deep in debt *and* unemployed. You may have been better off contending with a challenging job market without investing all the time and money in a JD.

If you thought it was difficult to ignore the herd mentality, sometimes it's even more difficult to tune out the *information cascade*. What we're saying is, don't go to law school because you're spooked by media reports of a soft economy or corporate layoffs. After all, you can't control the job market, but you can take charge of how you manage your career. If reading news of layoffs makes you nervous, stop reading the news. We're not suggesting you stick your head in the sand. We're just recommending that you ignore unnerving news (the *information cascade*) while you thoroughly assess whether law is the best path for you. Right now—as you consider law school—your most valuable information is an inventory of your personal interests, skills, and career priorities to help you decide whether there are any legal or non-legal jobs that would make a good match.

The way to figure that out is by assessing what you enjoy doing and exploring what different jobs involve.

This worked for one prospective law student—Jordan, a recent college grad—who told us he considered enrolling in law school because, in his words, he "didn't think he could get a good job in this economy." After some self-assessment, though, Jordan realized he hadn't given enough thought to what he really enjoyed doing. When he did, he sought out and landed a job as a reporter for a local newspaper. Thrilled with his work, Jordan is grateful he's getting real-world experience before reconsidering grad school.

If it's tough to get a paying job that interests you, we suggest you get a job that'll help pay the bills while you volunteer part-time with an organization (legal or non-legal) whose mission genuinely excites you. Yes, this will require some juggling, but it beats committing three years—and years of paying off loans—for a degree you're not entirely sure of. Above all, keep in mind that right now your mission is to make the best decision for you...not to please your folks, not to impress your friends, not to revitalize the global economy. Just focus your energy on thoroughly researching several different career paths until you figure out the best one for you. In the chapters ahead, we'll walk you through the process.

☑ **D** I think it's beneficial to understand the legal system as it applies to everyday life.

☑ **G** The intellectual challenge of law school appeals to me.

Did you check either one or both of these statements? In the course of researching this book, many law students told us they entered school not because they wanted to practice law but because they thought it would be helpful to learn how the U.S. legal system works. Well, some of the information is interesting, even useful, but most lawyers we talked to said they didn't think "understanding the legal system" was a strong enough reason alone to warrant the investment of time and money in a JD, especially if they later realized they didn't want to practice law. But don't take their word for it. Seek out any *non-practicing lawyers* on your own, and ask if they apply what they learned in law school in daily life and whether their investment in a JD was worth their time and assets.

Yet another rationale for attending law school is the "intellectual challenge".

Some law students do find the academics challenging...but not terribly interesting. Others discover only after they began practicing law that they spend an inordinate amount of their time doing administrative tasks (like document review), and don't get the intellectual challenge for which they hoped. To be sure, many law students find their legal studies fascinating, and they secure post-graduate jobs that are enjoyable and intellectually satisfying. But that's the point—you want to preview what the law school experience will be like for you before you commit to it. Don't merely assume that law school, or any legal job, will offer the intellectual challenge you're looking for without proper investigation. After all, law isn't the only career that offers intellectual challenge. You might find others you would enjoy more.

> Law isn't the only career that offers intellectual challenge.

☑ **H** **I'm attracted to the law because of its powerful potential for social change.**

☑ **I** **I"m ready for a career change and I think the law offers what I'm looking for.**

If you checked either of these statements, you've identified some positive reasons for pursuing law. But while it's admirable to be drawn to the law because of its potential for change, it's important to be sure that you'd enjoy the work of an attorney. That means finding out if you would enjoy day-to-day lawyering, as well the process of trying to affect change through the legal system. That's because, while the law has the potential for change, being instrumental in it is often slow-going and usually involves compromise. That's why some lawyers who wanted to use the law as a tool for change become frustrated with drawn-out litigation (cases can take years to resolve) and find it difficult to get satisfying results for clients. Yet, other attorneys enjoy their day-to-day work enough and have patience to withstand an often drawn-out process to accomplish change.

All this is to say that, before you decide to get a law degree to help affect change, get some work experience in a legal setting and speak with plenty of lawyers to make sure you'll be more motivated than frustrated. The same advice applies if you're looking to law as a second career. Some who are ready for a new track have thought about what they wanted, have spoken with numerous lawyers about their work, and knew enough to know they'd enjoy it. In other words, their pursuit of law was a well-informed choice. But others chose law to escape a job they disliked and found they didn't enjoy it any better. So be sure to speak with plenty of practitioners and get exposure to their work.

☑ B   I've researched various graduate degree programs, and I've decided that law is best for me."

☑ E   After attending a few classes and speaking with several law students, I think I would enjoy law school."

Congratulations, if you checked either of these statements. You're on your way to making a well-informed decision. You've learned to rely not only on the actions of others—or on information that may or may not have personal relevance—when making your decision. That said, be sure that you thoroughly research a spectrum of graduate schools and the careers for which they prepare you. The following chapters will help you.

DECISION ASSESSMENT 2

✓ *Check all statements that apply to you.*

I'm considering going to law school because...

❑ A   I'm not sure what I want to do, and a law degree will keep my options open.

❑ B   People whose opinions I trust are encouraging me to get a law degree.

❑ C   I've thought about what I'd enjoy in a job, and the law would be a good fit for my skills, strengths, and interests.

❑ D   The people whose jobs I'd like to have in a few years all have law degrees, even though they no longer practice.

❑ E   I've already worked in legal and non-legal environments, and I would prefer a legal setting. *(Continued on next page.)*

(Decision Assessment 2, continued from previous page.)

❏ **F** I was a liberal arts major, so a law degree seems like the next logical step.

❏ **G** Everyone says I would make a good lawyer.

❏ **H** I'm competitive by nature, so I think I'd enjoy law school and the legal profession.

❏ **I** My prior professional experience sparked my interest in law.

We'll score your responses at the end of the chapter. For now, let's review this second set of statements, and tell you what they say about your decision-making process:

Decision Paralysis

☑ **A** **I'm not sure what I want to do, and a law degree will keep my options open.**

People are funny. Not David Letterman funny, but funny in that we say we want "options", when what we really want are "answers". To understand what we mean, consider the following hypothetical:

Situation A—Suppose you want a digital camera, but haven't decided how much to spend or which brand or model to buy. You walk past a display window and see a popular Nikon selling for $318, which you know is below retail. Do you buy it or wait to learn more about other models?

Situation B—Same facts except that next to the Nikon is a popular Olympus camera selling for $399, which you also know is below retail. Which do you buy, or do you wait and research still other cameras?

When people were presented only with *Situation A*, the majority of responses (roughly 75%) still favored the Nikon. A relatively small group (25%) said they would continue shopping for other brands or models. But when faced with *Situation B*, the number of people who said they would wait increased to about 50%. This illustrates a Choice Challenge called **Decision Paralysis**. To better understand it, consider another experiment:

Some years ago, researchers set up shop in an upscale grocery store and handed out samples of jams and jellies. At first, shoppers were offered a choice of six different samples. Later that day, the number of samples was increased to 24. Anyone who came to the tasting table at any time, received a coupon good for $1 off any jelly or jam in the store. Here's what happened: Nearly fifty percent more shoppers visited the table when there were 24 jams as opposed to when there were six. But those shoppers who did visit when there were just six jams were *30 times more likely to make a purchase* than the shoppers who had 24 samples. Conclusion: We're attracted to choice, but the greater the choice, the harder it is to decide.

Have you ever walked into a video store and felt overwhelmed at the selection? Who hasn't? For that reason, some of us head straight to the "New Releases" section. In this way, we narrow our choices to simplify the decision-making process.

This type of default-driven decision making is typical of the way many grads arrive at their decision to enroll in law school. Too often, prospective students gravitate to law school by default to avoid sifting through what seems to be a dizzying array of career choices. This is particularly common among undergraduates who want to have a ready answer to that dreaded question—*What are you doing after graduation?* Of course, *decision paralysis* isn't confined to college students. When older adults reach a career crossroads of their own, they also can feel paralyzed at the many choices life presents.

But just because investigating other jobs or grad school options seems mysterious and time-consuming, and because law school is a well-regarded and clearly marked path, many people—young and not-so-young—often choose law by default rather than devoting the time and energy to exploring in depth legal and non-legal options. Now, relying on a default option is fine when choosing a video. If you don't like the movie, you're out only a few bucks and two hours. Choosing law school by default is risky because at stake is such an enormous investment of time and resources. You don't want to expend three years and thousands of dollars only to discover that there were other careers you would have enjoyed more than law. Another problem with JD-by-default decision-making is that you still have to figure out what you want to do, and where to work, during two law school summers and, again, after you graduate. That means deciding on a practice area (such as litigation or transactional work), a practice setting (private sector, public sector or public interest) and what type of clients you wish to represent (corporate, government or individual). As you can see, choosing to attend law school is not the way to avoid making career decisions.

Like most Choice Challenges, *decision paralysis* is difficult but not impossible to handle. The best solution is the systematic approach.

For example, start by creating a list of, say, 10 career fields to explore (fewer if that feels overwhelming). Then, commit to exploring just one or two at a time. One way to identify a list of potential fields is to focus on those that genuinely interest you. To do this, ask yourself some key self-assessment questions (see Chapter 6), and create a list of things you need to be happy at work. Use this list to identify different legal and non-legal settings that match your preferences. In this way, you're focusing your time and energy on exploring jobs and graduate school programs that interest you most. Sure, there are hundreds of careers in the science, mathematical and engineering fields, but if you have no interest in those areas, why bother? What's the upside here? A few hour's work could save thousands of dollars and a lot of career pain.

Once you've identified some fields of interest, explore them in depth. Do a little web research or reading to see if you're interested in exploring a certain career in more detail. If you are, talk to people working in it. Ask friends or relatives who might know people in that field if you don't. If you're still interested after those conversations, try to get some hands-on experience by working or volunteering in that area.

Doing a little research is a much better approach than choosing law school by default. Remember, this is about making the *right* decision...not the easy decision.

The Confirmation Bias

☑ B **People whose opinions I trust are encouraging me to get a law degree.**

If you checked this statement, you need to be sure you're not falling under the spell of our latest Choice Challenge—the **Confirmation Bias**. To see how this psychological trap might snare you, try this hypothetical:

Imagine your friends are planning to take you out to dinner for your birthday. Rather than surprise you, they give you a choice between two new restaurants:

Restaurant #1 has an award-winning chef, exemplary service and boasts a romantic candlelit setting with a panoramic view. Its specialties include chicken parmesan, rack of lamb, bouillabaisse, and vegetable kabobs.

Restaurant # 2 has a nationally-acclaimed chef and an artfully decorated dining room, sweeping views and gracious service. Specialties of the house include vegetable jambalaya, shrimp scampi, filet mignon and chicken marsala.

Which restaurant would you choose?

If you had trouble choosing, it's because the descriptions were purposely constructed to sound equal. And when both of these like-sounding descriptions are presented to people, most say the two restaurants were too similar to choose between. But an odd thing occurs when people are presented with comparable descriptions one at a time (say, chicken Parmesan versus vegetable jambalaya) and asked to give tentative preferences as they go along. All of the sudden, people have no trouble choosing between the two places. In fact, most everyone has a clear preference, *based on whichever restaurant they had liked after hearing the first pair of attributes*. What this demonstrates is that once we develop preferences— even small ones—we view subsequent information in a way that supports our preference. Or we discount new information that doesn't fit our existing opinions and feelings. That's what the *confirmation bias* is all about—a tendency to seek out and be influenced by information that confirms our initial preference.

In other words, once you develop a feeling about an issue or a person—no matter how unconscious that preference might be—it becomes much harder to overcome your bias. You get it in your head that you don't like something (or someone) based on a first reaction and suddenly you're unable to view its positive attributes as significant enough to make a difference. Or, you get an idea in your head and then avoid asking questions or seeking information that conflicts with your initial preferences. Instead, you seek information that conforms to your preferences, or you seek out people who will tell you what you want to hear.

> **"I** went to law school because my mother said I was diplomatic and would make a good lawyer. I wish she had told me I was diplomatic and would make a good diplomat."
>
> —Susan, former lawyer

Here are some examples of how the *confirmation bias* comes into play with career choices.

Some prospective law students, especially those who know little about the legal profession, are so relieved to have settled on law school that they avoid asking questions that might conflict with that plan. Once they have law firmly planted in mind, they often consciously or unconsciously avoid talking to people who might question the wisdom of their decision or even try to talk them out of it. Some may solicit advice only from people who will back up their decision to attend law school, and refrain from asking those who might offer a different viewpoint.

Some lawyers we've met confessed that once they decided to attend law school they blew off researching what different legal jobs entail. That's because they feared that if they saw something they didn't like, it might cause them to rethink law and they didn't want to go back to the drawing board and find something else to do.

As you might imagine, the *confirmation bias* can be so seductive that one could overlook vital considerations. That's why remaining open to different perspectives is especially important when making major life decisions. In short, if you only ask contented lawyers whether you should pursue law school, you may miss out on important viewpoints. Just because some people enjoy being lawyers doesn't mean you will; just because some lawyers dislike their jobs doesn't mean you will. If you haven't given thorough consideration to what you need to be happy in a job, and if you haven't researched legal and non-legal jobs to know which will be a better fit for you, you're not ready to invest in a law degree.

But let's face it, the *confirmation bias* is difficult to overcome.

We prefer to hear what we want to hear, and it's hard to ask questions when we're afraid we might not like the answers. So, if you haven't already fallen for *the confirmation bias* (or even if you have) do yourself a favor—seek out a variety of contented and discontented lawyers who work in various practice areas, or who have left the field. It's just as important to speak with people in non-legal fields who have jobs that sound interesting to you, so you can make a meaningful comparison. And here's another caution—consult with people who don't have a personal agenda. What do we mean? Look beyond your family and friends. If your parents always dreamed of introducing you as "my son (daughter) the lawyer," they may not be able to help you think critically about your decision to attend law school. Instead, speak to lawyers and nonlawyers who will tell it like it is. If you think you'd benefit from professional advice, consult a career counselor at your undergraduate institution, at a law school near you, or someone in private practice.

What if you discover that lawyering doesn't appear as interesting as you expected? Don't let it throw you—it's better to realize you don't want to be a lawyer *before* you become one! People who are happiest in their careers tend to be those who make honest choices about what they like and dislike.

Now that you've learned how to spot and overcome *decision paralysis* and the *confirmation bias*, let's briefly review the other statements you might have checked in Decision Assessment II:

☑ **D** **The people whose jobs I'd like to have in a few years all have law degrees, even though they no longer practice.**

Take your time—Many students tell us they chose law school because they didn't have time to research other options—they were too busy cramming for the LSATs and completing their law school applications. Later, they realize that if they'd spent the same number of hours having informational interviews, they might have chosen a different career path or entered law school with clearer direction. Take your time. Before applying to law school, research a variety of legal and nonlegal career paths.

☑ **F** I was a liberal arts major, so a law degree seems like the next logical step.
☑ **G** Everyone says I would make a good lawyer.

As you've probably guessed, none of these statements alone are sufficient reasons to invest in a law degree—and they don't add up to much as a set. If you checked any (or all) of these statements, it suggests you may have fallen for the *confirmation bias,* and adopted these notions because other people led you to believe them. Let's take them one at a time:

First, if the people who have the jobs you want someday also have law degrees, that's fine. But don't forget, your own long-term occupational needs are subject to change. Especially at the beginning of your career. So, if it is at all possible you won't want that particular job 5 or 10 years from now, it's a good idea to see if there are legal jobs you'd enjoy in the short run. You might find it helpful to have informational interviews with individuals who have your dream jobs and ask them about their career paths. Did they ever practice law? Was their JD essential to helping them get to where they are? In retrospect, do they think getting a JD was worth it? If they could do it over again, would other degrees or professional experience have prepared them as well? You will discover how many different paths lead to the same job. That's why it's important to see if you'd want to be a practicing lawyer as preparation for your ideal job, or if other paths seem more appealing.

Next, if you're gravitating towards law school because you think your liberal arts (English, poli-sci, etc.) degree "hasn't prepared you to do anything", think again. Law isn't the next logical step for liberal-arts majors; it's only the next logical step if you want to be a lawyer. That's why it's critical to see what law school will prepare you to do. If lawyering doesn't appeal to you, don't worry—your academic and life experience has prepared you to excel in other fields. If you're having difficulty determining what you want to do, we'll give you plenty of pointers in the chapters ahead.

Finally, a warning to all those who have been told, "you'd be a good lawyer:" Consider the source. Those who advocate that you follow a career path in law may not actually know much about lawyering, let alone if it's right for you. Even if they are correct, you still might not be a contented lawyer. According to the American Bar Association, more than half (that's right, more than half) the lawyers in this country would change professions if they could afford to leave. If career satisfaction is important to you, you need to thoroughly evaluate what legal and non-legal career paths are open to you, and to see where you would be happiest.

☑ **H I'm competitive by nature, so I think I'd enjoy law school and the legal profession.**

☑ **I My prior professional experience sparked my interest in law.**

If you checked either of these statements, law may be the right path for you.

But knowing that you're competitive isn't enough to base your decision on. While some personality types find law school and legal practice the perfect outlet for their assertive (aggressive?) tendencies, others turned out not to enjoy law school or the practice of law as much as they thought they might. They didn't relish the legal research and writing, and found the adversarial system too hostile and nasty. That's why it's so important to find out what legal jobs involve, and to assess whether they're a good match—not only for your personality, but for your skills, interests and priorities. That means finding out if you're interested in legal subjects and basic lawyering skills. And it's also important to explore non-legal fields where you can direct your competitive energy, like business or politics (to name just two). Or perhaps you'll learn you don't want put your competitive instincts into work—maybe into after-work activities (like athletics) instead.

The *Devil's Advocate Says...*

Talk to strangers—Speak with all sorts of people who can help with your career decisions. Sometimes this will mean family, friends and peers, but you will also have to ask strangers. It's easier for some than for others because of shyness (i.e., knowing who to ask) and practicality (i.e., knowing what to ask). We can help with the practical (see Tool Kit, page x), but personality issues are trickier. Still, we can promise that most people are willing to give strangers a few minutes or hours of their time if approached with the right pitch in the right circumstances. But you do have to ask.

The same advice—know what attorneys actually do—applies if your prior professional work triggered your interest in law. Some students enter law school because teaching sparked an interest in *education law*, or nursing sparked an interest in *health law*, or technology sparked an interest in *intellectual property*. Some wound up enjoying legal practice; others did not. That's why it's important to see what specific legal jobs actually involve and whether you'd enjoy doing them. If you discover that the day-to-day of lawyering doesn't appeal to you, you can explore other jobs and graduate programs in your fields of interest.

☑ **C** **I've thought about what I'd enjoy in a job, and the law would be a good fit for my skills, strengths, and interests.**

☑ **E** **I've already worked in legal and non-legal environments, and I would prefer a legal setting.**

Of all the statements in Decision Assessment II, these two are the most promising.

Assessing what you need to be happy in a job means a) you know what you're looking for, and b) knowing how to choose a career that meets your needs. Once you've assessed what you want in a job, you can put that to good use by seeing if actual legal jobs have what you're looking for. That means speaking with lawyers and getting some exposure to legal work to see if it provides what you need. If you find specific legal jobs where you'll get to actually use the skills you enjoy most, and the work involves subjects that interest you, you'll be far more confident about pursuing a JD. And that's why getting work experience beforehand—in legal and non-legal settings—is so important: it lets you see the nature of the work itself so you can make a thoughtful comparison. At the end of the day, this will help you avoid relying on the opinions of others, and later regretting not having exploring other options.

---

❿ECISION ASSESSMENT 3

✓ *Check all statements that apply to you.*

I'm considering going to law school because . . .

❑ **A** I always knew I would be a lawyer.

❑ **B** A law degree is a valuable credential even if you don't intend to practice law.

❑ **C** I've spoken with different types of lawyers about their work, and I have identified some legal jobs I think I would enjoy. *(Continued on next page)*

(Decision Assessment 3, continued from previous page)

> ❑ **D**   I want a prestigious career, and the law is a respectable profession.
>
> ❑ **E**   My family is paying for law school.
>
> ❑ **F**   I've worked with lawyers in prior jobs, and I would enjoy the work they do.
>
> ❑ **G**   A law degree opens doors and teaches you how to think.
>
> ❑ **H**   I've spoken with people in a variety of non-legal professions, and I think that law is still the best fit for me.
>
> ❑ **I**   You can do anything with a law degree.

Okay, time to review a few more common reasons for considering a JD.

We'll score your responses at the end of the chapter. For now, let's review this third set of statements, and tell you what they say about your decision-making process:

Rules of Thumb

☑ **B**   A law degree is a valuable credential even if you don't intend to practice law.

☑ **G**   A law degree opens doors and teaches you how to think.

☑ **I**   You can do anything with a law degree.

If you checked any of these statements, you may have been influenced by the next in our series of Choice Challenges—**Rules of Thumb.** These are the shortcuts we all use to make choices simpler and less confusing. We use them every day for all kinds of decisions. Sometimes they're accurate and helpful, sometimes they're misleading and can interfere with the decision-making process. People often rely on rules of thumb when deciding to attend law school.

This is problematic for several reasons:

First, many popular *rules of thumb* are misleading. Let's consider the two most frequently cited by prospective law students—that law school "opens doors" or that it "teaches you how to think." Law students who discovered later that they didn't really want to practice law realized that there may have been a less expensive and time-consuming way to learn "how to think". As for the students whose law degree buried them in debt, law school did not open more doors because they felt obligated to accept the highest-paying law firm job they could to pay off their loans.

Another equally misleading *rule of thumb* is, "a JD is just a good thing to have, regardless of whether you practice." Or that popular variation—"You can do anything with a law degree." To be sure, some lawyers agree that the credential itself—along with the writing, thinking and analytical skills that law school teaches—are beneficial even if you don't practice. But others maintain that you can obtain those skills and credential yourself without attending law school; furthermore, investing thousands of dollars and three years of your life is a high price to pay if all you want is to be a more analytical thinker and writer.

> **"I**t would be helpful for prospective law students to see some sample time-sheets of first-year associates. They have no idea how many hours are spent doing mundane tasks."
>
> —Emily, attorney at a large firm

There's no right or wrong answer about whether to attend law school if you don't intend to practice law. But the right way to decide is to identify your career goals, talk to a lot of practicing *and* non-practicing lawyers, and to expose yourself to legal and non-legal work before deciding whether a JD will assist you in the non-practicing jobs that interest you. We know many non-practicing lawyers who, choking on their student loans, deeply regret not having done this research.

Another problem—*rules of thumb* may be right for some people and not others.

For example, many students claim they're going to law school to give them "a trade, a marketable skill set." While this isn't an entirely bad reason to attend law school, it certainly isn't the best reason for everyone. That's because you might discover that you don't enjoy using the legal skills (legal research and writing) that you learn in law school. You might prefer utilizing different skills when you're on the job. So don't head off to law school in search of "skills" until you figure out what skills lawyers use, and determine whether those are the kind you would like to develop and use at work on a daily basis.

Finally, some people rely on *rules of thumb* instead of asking the right questions about which jobs will be best for them. As we've said, it's vital to check out what law school and legal practice actually entail before you decide to get a law degree. If you identify several different jobs you'd enjoy doing that require a JD, then you'll be a better position to make an informed decision. All this is to caution you that, if you're relying on any of the *rules of thumb* mentioned here, check their accuracy in conversation with several law students and lawyers. Better yet, talk to people in various legal and non-legal jobs about their work and, if you can, spend some time—even as a volunteer—working in legal and non-legal environments.

Anchoring

☑ **A** **I always knew I would be a lawyer.**

☑ **D** **I want a prestigious career, and the law is a respectable profession.**

Did you check either of these statements?

Each year, thousands of students enter law school citing these two reasons among the driving forces behind their decision. If so, they probably have succumbed to the next in our series of Choice Challenges—**Anchoring**.

Anchoring refers to the common tendency to cling to an idea, fact or figure that really should have no bearing on your decision. In the law school context, *anchoring* yourself to the notion that "someday" you will be a lawyer, may prevent you from doing a proper inquiry into alternate careers. In fact, many lawyers told us were "on auto-pilot" when they chose to attend law school, and they described their career selection as a "non-decision." Sadly, law students from the West Coast to the East Coast, from New England to the South, repeat this same experience every year, and face an unhappy surprise when they arrive at school, or on the job, and learn what lawyers actually do. The lesson here is that going to law school because it's something you—or your parents—always envisioned for you isn't a sufficient reason. It's just an *anchor*, a fixed position to which you're attached.

Another *anchor* is the notion that you "must get a graduate degree as soon as possible." So, each year, students race off to law school because they're convinced they must have a professional degree...and the sooner the better. They don't particularly like math, so an MBA is out. They can't stand the sight of blood, so medical school is out. That leaves...law.

Again, the big problem with *anchoring* is that it doesn't give you adequate time to discover which, if any, graduate degree is right for you.

Getting some work experience before you pursue grad school will help you make an informed decision. After all, there's no point in rushing to get a graduate degree that you may not ultimately use. In fact, many lawyers who raced off to law school straight from college later returned to grad school for a second graduate degree because they didn't carefully assess whether law was the best career for them the first time around. That's an expensive learning curve. So the next time someone says you were destined to be a lawyer, or that law will offer money and security, remember: Some students who take out huge law school loans discover later the profession isn't for them, and they wind up feeling more unstable (financially and psychically) than ever.

Some law students struggle to repay their loans, and are less prosperously for a longer period than if they hadn't gone to law school.

Some students who pursued law because they thought it would offer "stability" found it otherwise. Just read any of the professional journals (e.g., *ABA Journal, National Law Journal, Lawyers Weekly*) to see that the legal job market is just as vulnerable to market forces as the non-legal job market. In fact, in a weak economy, law firms can implode, consolidate, and lay off attorneys just like non-legal companies.

Some students (or their parents) may not realize that the legal profession has changed dramatically over the years. As one lawyer put it, "When I started practicing 30 years ago, law firm jobs were for a lifetime. You didn't have to be a rainmaker to make partner or to advance. You didn't have to bill your time in six-minute increments. Today, law feels more like a business than a profession. New attorneys face many more pressures than I ever did."

Next, let's look at the notion of pursuing law for the prestige.

A number of law students say they chose law because they are attracted to the profession's status. There's nothing wrong with wanting a prestigious job. It's only a problem if prestige is the dominant factor in your decision, and if you fail to explore the real work of the legal profession. Many lawyers discovered that the prestige and other trappings associated with their profession weren't enough to keep them satisfied. The attrition among highly-paid large law firm associates (many don't last more than two to three years) bears this out. Regardless of how much money you make, or how prestigious your title or employer, you still have to show up on the job every day. And if you detest the work—or the impact it has on your life—the prestige may be a small comfort. Although *anchoring* is a powerful force, you can overcome it. First, make a conscious effort to set aside your parents' expectations, and whatever "shoulds" you have imposed on yourself. Ask yourself three questions (and don't be afraid to be ruthless in your answers):

Why do I really want to go to law school?

What do I personally need for a satisfying career?

What efforts have I made to learn about the legal profession or non-legal careers?

Do your best to detach yourself from the *anchors* imposed by you and others while you investigate various legal and non-legal jobs to see which ones are more appealing. You can do this by reading about various types of jobs, talking with people who have interesting-sounding positions, and working or volunteering in different environments until you have a clear sense of what you'd enjoy doing.

Mental Accounting

☑ **E   My family is paying for law school.**

If you checked this statement, you may have fallen victim to the next Choice Challenge—**Mental Accounting**. You might also have your parents read this section, too.

Mental accounting is the tendency to treat money differently depending on its origin (salary vs. gift, for example), where it's going (to education vs. vacation), and how much we're spending (we usually make greater efforts to save $25 on a $50 purchase than on a $500 purchase). In short, we tend to make financial decisions inconsistently because of our differing views of the money involved. That's why we tend to purchase more—and pay more for what we purchase—when we use credit cards. We treat the plastic money as somehow being less valuable than hard cash.

In the context of your law school decision, *mental accounting* relates to this question: *Would you still go to law school if you had to pay your tuition?* If your parents or grandparents are paying most or all of the tuition, be honest about whether you would be willing to personally underwrite your legal education. Answer truthfully. It's not that we want to save your family all that money. It's because if you answer no—as in, *No, I wouldn't go to law school if I had to pay for it*—it's a signal that you may not be all that interested in becoming a lawyer. And, if that's true, you would be making a huge mistake to squander your family's money and complicate your own future at the same time. If being a lawyer isn't the best fit for you, then your time and their money would be better spent in other ways.

☑ **F I've worked with lawyers in prior jobs, and I would enjoy the work they do.**

If you checked this statement, you've cited a very solid reason for considering law, assuming you've worked closely enough with attorneys to know exactly what they do on a daily basis. If you've seen what particular legal jobs involve, and you think you'd enjoy doing them, pursuing the legal profession is perfectly appropriate. That said, if a legal setting is the only type of work environment you've ever been in, do consider exploring any possible non-legal careers that interest you. Why? To avoid experiencing regret later about failing to pursue other paths.

☑ **C I've spoken with different types of lawyers about their work, and I have identified some legal jobs I think I would enjoy.**

☑ **H I"ve spoken with people in a variety of non-legal professions, and I think that law is still the best fit for me.**

If you checked either or both of these statements, you're well on your way to making an informed decision. If you take the opportunity to speak with attorneys about their work, you'll be far less likely to fall for the Choice Challenges that lead people to pursue law based on faulty reasoning. If you've also spoken with non-lawyers, you can make an even more informed decision as to whether law is right for you. A note of caution: when speaking with others about their work, don't forget to consider if you would actually enjoy doing that job (just because one person likes her job, doesn't mean it will be a good fit for you.) Once you've researched various legal and non-legal career paths, you need to go one more step—get some hands-on experience in the areas you've looked into.

Would you still go to law school if you had to pay your own tuition?

The *Devil's Advocate Says...*

Less is more—Your legal education will cost less if you work beforehand and save more. The more you save, the less you borrow. The less you borrow, the smaller your loan interest payments will be. And the less you owe, the more options you'll have ... because you're less likely to feel obligated to take a high-paying legal job just to pay off your loans. This reasoning is especially valid if you're interested in a public-interest or public-sector career.

We'll score your responses at the end of the chapter. For now, let's review this last set of statements, and tell you what they say about your decision-making process:

Ignoring the Base Rate

☑ **A**   I want to help people.

☑ **C**   I want to increase my earning potential.

If you checked either (or both) of these statements, you may have been taken in by our next Choice Challenge—**Ignoring the Base Rate**. This refers to the all-too-common tendency to ignore the odds in a given situation. Sometimes we do this willingly, as for example, when we buy a lottery ticket and ignore the slim odds are of winning. Here are a few examples of *ignoring the base rate* as it applies to law students:

> They *ignore the base rate* by assuming they'll get large-firm jobs after graduation (in fact, only about 22% of all grads actually get to work in firms of over 100 attorneys).
>
> They *ignore the base rate* by failing to understand that their salary might not

increase as much as they expect (the median starting salary for all law school grads nationwide is $60,000. Starting salaries for public interest lawyers, government lawyers, judicial clerks, and even small firm attorneys in many cities tend to be considerably lower).

They *ignore the base rate* when they expect to get into sexy practice areas such as international, entertainment or sports law but remain unaware of the limited opportunities in those fields and how difficult it is to get them. Many students don't fully appreciate the price of getting a dream job in these competitive fields—like taking a low starting salary, doing several unpaid internships, or taking temporary contract work until a permanent position opens. Students unaware of the odds may not exert the effort necessary to achieve their goals. Or, by the time they finally realize the odds and challenges involved—*the base rate*—they may simply give up.

And, law students *ignore the base rate* by failing to realize that while nearly half of all incoming law students express an interest in public-interest law only 4% of graduating students wind up in such jobs (25% if you include government jobs and judicial clerkships). Note: once student loans and lower starting salaries become a reality, students discover they cannot afford to take lower-paying public interest jobs and still repay their loans. So they wind up in private sector jobs that are far from what they originally came to law school to do. In fact, a nonprofit public interest legal group (equaljusticeworks.org), issued a research paper on this topic. Called *From Paper Chase to Money Chase—Law School Debt Diverts the Road to Public Service*, it documents several important base rates—for example, that 94% of survey respondents financed their studies through school loans, and that 50% graduated with law school loan debts of $75,000 or more.

The median starting salary for all law school grads nationwide is $60,000.

The point of calling attention to the odds—*the base rate*—of getting certain legal jobs isn't to depress or discourage you. It's to help you plan to achieve your goals. With that in mind, consider these strategies:

If you're interested in being a public interest lawyer, look for law schools with loan-forgiveness or loan-repayment assistance programs. And look into less expensive state schools rather than costlier private schools, and less expensive cities over more expensive ones.

If you want to work in a large law firm, see how many (or how few) law school grads wind up in such firms. See what credentials (e.g., grades) you need to get those jobs. Then ask law firms how many associates are still there after one year, two, three, four or five (plus) years. While you're at it, ask lawyers in large firms, smaller firms, government and public-interest jobs about their job satisfaction (your career services office can connect you to different types of attorneys), and check out attorney job-satisfaction surveys from The American Lawyer magazine, www.Law.com, and the Vault Guide to the Top 100 Law Firms (www.vault.com).

If you're interested in working in some of law's most competitive areas— e.g., entertainment, international or sports law—see how many people wind up in those jobs and learn what is required to get there. Talk to lawyers who have the kind of jobs you want and ask what it took.

Ask for guidance; people are generally helpful because they were once in your shoes.

Again, we want to stress that paying attention to *the base rate* doesn't mean you have to abandon your dreams in the face of discouraging statistics. It simply means you have to use that knowledge to map out a plan to get what you want.

Overconfidence

☑ F **I want to work in a specific practice area, such as litigation, or criminal, entertainment, international, sports, corporate or public-interest law.**

If you checked this statement, here's a little quiz: How do you pronounce the name of the 34th state to be admitted to the Union? Is it *Mis-sou-ree* or *Mis-sou-rah*?

Now, how much would you bet your answer is correct?

Well, whatever you bet, please send your check to us in care of our publisher. The 34th state admitted to the union wasn't Missouri...it was Kansas. Sorry, but the point of this trick question was to illustrate another Choice Challenge— **Overconfidence**. It refers to the tendency to overestimate our skills, abilities or knowledge. Here, most people get Missouri's pronunciation right, but wrongly (overconfidently) assume it was the 34th state without verifying that fact.

While *overconfidence* helps us take risks and try new things that seem unattainable, it can also lead us astray when it causes us to make decisions based on an over-inflated sense of what we can accomplish or overcome. Think about college, for example: Have you ever assumed you could finish a project in a certain amount of time, only to wind up pulling an all-nighter to finish it (or requesting an extension)? Well, *overconfidence* afflicts law students too. Too many prospective law students don't know how little they know about the legal profession when they make the decision to get a law degree. For example, many students don't know why they're in law school or how they'll use their JD. But they're confident—actually, *overconfident*— that they will figure it out before graduation. What often happens, though, is that they get overwhelmed with course-work, law review, moot court, and other activities, leaving little or no time or energy to find a job they like. They wind up unable or unsure of how to find a job that's the best fit for them, and then scramble for any job.

What does all this have to do with you?

Well, if you checked *"I want to work in a specific practice area"*, you need to be sure that *overconfidence* isn't clouding your judgment.

Some students enter law school confident that they want to pursue a specific practice area (say, criminal law) even though they've never set foot in a criminal law setting. If they later discover the field isn't as appealing in the real world, they worry about starting over on another path. Other prospective law students assume that getting a JD is the right way to fulfill certain career goals, whether it's to make money, do good in the world, or whatever. But they often don't consider that there are many ways to achieve one's career goals that don't require a law degree. In other words, there are different means to achieving the same ends. If your primary goal is to make a lot of money, you might explore investment banking or other types of jobs in business. If your goal is to save the world, you might explore nonprofit organizations like the Peace Corps or Teach for America. A non-legal position just might be a better fit for you, but you won't find out unless you explore.

> Too many law students don't know why they're in law school, or how they'll use their JD.

The problem with *overconfidence* is not unlike the peril of *ignoring the base rate*—it can get in the way of gathering critical information. Here's how to overcome it and make career decisions with more certainty:

Play dumb—Get in the habit of assuming you don't know it all and get comfortable with the idea of asking a lot of questions. For example, if you think you know what practice areas interest you, ask yourself: What information am I basing this decision on? What steps did I take to get this information? Then enlist the help of other people to question your assumptions.

Identify what you don't know—Do you know what you're looking for in a job? What your favorite skills and interests are? What different types of attorneys do on the job? What alternatives to law might appeal to you? What you realistically see yourself doing with a law degree? Keep asking questions and be committed to finding the answers.

Educate yourself—Once you've figured out what you don't know, get cracking. Find out exactly what lawyers do in the areas that interest you. If you think you're interested in litigation, speak with and work with litigators. Also, look at salaries and employment opportunities in your fields of interest.

☑ **D I am fascinated by the law.**
☑ **E I enjoy counseling people and problem-solving.**

We're 100% in favor of learning for the sake of learning. But while it's great to take an interest in legal subjects, you still want to be sure there are legal jobs you'd actually find fascinating. So consider:

What exactly is it about "the law" that fascinates you? Is it listening to Nina Totenberg on NPR? Is it watching Court TV, or waiting for the next O.J. Simpson trial? Is it reading Linda Greenhouse's legal coverage in the New York Times? Is it an undergrad course in law? Are there specific areas of law that interest you, or are you interested in the judicial system? Once you've thought about the basis for your interest, investigate what law school is all about, speak with attorneys about their work and get some exposure to a real legal workplace. That way, you'll be able to predict whether you'll enjoy being a lawyer as much as you enjoy learning about law.

As far Statement #2 (*"I enjoy counseling people and problem-solving"*), identify what it is that interests you about the counseling role. Check out legal jobs where client counseling is an important element, and compare them with non-legal jobs where counseling is emphasized (e.g., therapist, financial advisor, school counselor). Speak with a few lawyers and non-lawyers whose work involves counseling and see which is more appealing.

☑ **H Law is a good background for other fields that interest me (e.g., politics, business).**

☑ **I I"m planning to join my family's law practice.**

Both statements reflect perfectly legitimate reasons for pursuing a legal career. After all, many lawyers have parlayed their legal backgrounds into non-legal careers or joined an existing legal practice. If you're thinking of using your

JD to assist you in other careers, it's still important to look carefully at specific legal jobs that might interest you, and whether other degrees or experiences would be better preparation for non-legal fields. For example, would a public-policy degree, or more work experience, prepare you for politics? Would an MBA, or more work experience, prepare you for business? Would you enjoy these paths more than law school? We pose these questions and suggest you answer them because some lawyers later found that a non-legal career path would have provided a satisfactory platform for their non-legal career. It is also wise to see if there are specific legal jobs you'd enjoy because many law students initially say they're getting a JD for other careers but later get swept up in the pressure to practice.

If you're planning to join a family legal practice, you certainly have a good reason to go to law school, so long as you enjoy the work...*and* get along with your future law firm partners. Still, it wouldn't hurt to investigate in what other fields you might thrive so you don't later regret not having pursued them.

☑ **B   I enjoy legal research and writing.**
☑ **G   I"ve worked in legal and non-legal settings, and I prefer the work of a lawyer.**

If you've gotten hands-on legal experience and enjoyed it, you have a sound basis for going to law school. You get big points for these answers because you've discovered what fundamental lawyering skills entail, and that you enjoy them. And because you've worked in non-legal settings as well, you can make an informed comparison. Next, continue speaking with a variety of lawyers in different practice areas until you've identified several jobs you could realistically see yourself doing. Doing so will enable you to enter law school with some career direction and prepare you to make the most of your educational experience.

Adding it Up: If There's Reasonable Doubt, Stay Out

Okay, it's time to score your four Decision Assessments.

Decision Assessment 1 (page 17)

Statements—A & C (1 point each) _____
Statements—D, H & I (3 pts each) _____
Statements—F & G (5 pts each) _____
Statement—B (7 pts) _____
Statement—E (10 pts) _____

Subtotal _____

Decision Assessment 2 (page 23)

Statements—A, B, F, G (1 point each) _____
Statements—D & H (3 pts each) _____
Statement—I (5 pts) _____
Statement—C (7 pts) _____
Statements—E (10 pts) _____

Subtotal _____

Decision Assessment 3 (page 31)

Statements—A, D, E, I (1 point each) _____
Statements—B, G (3 pts each) _____
Statements—C, F, H (7 pts each) _____

Subtotal _____

Decision Assessment 4 (page 38)

Statements—A, C, E, F (3 pts each) _____
Statements—D, H (5 pts each) _____
Statement—I (7 pts) _____
Statements—B, G (10 pts each) _____

Subtotal _____

Total points _____

There were 150 points possible in our four Decision Assessments. While not a perfect predictor, your score will provide a broad sense as to the merits of continuing on with your legal education. So, if you scored...

0 to 50 points—Resist the impulse to go to law school until you know more about it, and know more about actually being a lawyer. If your score falls in this range, there's a pretty good chance you haven't spoken with lawyers and non-lawyers about different career paths or gotten real-world experience in a legal setting. You need to do both to make a truly informed decision. If you haven't yet assessed your skills and interests to see if any specific legal jobs would be a good fit, take the time to do so. That way, you can see if legal jobs match what you like to do.

51 to 99 points—This a gray area. You probably do have some valid reasons for going to law school and a sense of what you want from a JD, and you have done a little research. But you may be reading this book because you're still not sure that law is the right direction for you. That's OK. There's no rush to get a law degree until you're ready. The chapters ahead will walk you through the process of figuring out what you want from work. These steps will give you more clarity.

100 to 150 points—In this range, the chances are you have a solid basis for choosing law school, and you know enough about yourself and the legal profession to make an informed decision. The fact you're reading this book shows you're approaching this career move thoughtfully. So keep up the good work and read the rest of this section for any steps you haven't yet taken. If you ultimately decide to attend law school, read Part II and refer to the Tool Kit (page 214) for pointers on choosing and paying for law school.

Regardless of what you scored, we bet that there are still some steps you need to take in order to make a truly informed decision. The following chapters will walk you through them, and explain how they will help you make the best possible choices for your situation.

"Telling everyone I was planning to go to law school made me feel more directed, and I thought people would take me more seriously. Of course, these were horrible reasons, so I decided *not* to go. But I did get an internship at a law firm. It was supposed to be for three months. But after two months, I left. It just didn't fit my personality, and the daily grind had little to do with being creative. Turns out, lawyering was the last thing I wanted to do. I just wanted all of the *perks* of being a lawyer. I think that if I hadn't interned, I probably would be a lawyer right now, and a hundred-grand in debt.

"Of course, choosing not to go to law school meant facing up to the fact that I didn't know what to do with my life! I figured it out, though. I'm a writer now, and it's as exciting a profession as I thought the law would be." —**Courtney**

"I knew I didn't want to practice law by the end of my first year of law school. That's when I began working with our career services office to see what else I could do that would merge my interest in law with other skills. Over time, I had informational interviews with all sorts of professionals. Eventually, I realized that a position in legal career services and recruiting would fulfill my career goals. That's where I am today! I'm so glad I didn't quit law school—not only did I get a wonderful education, but I made many great friends, was able to do some soul-searching, and I feel proud of my accomplishments." —**Melanie**

"I considered going to law school. I wanted a profes-sional degree, a career that would make me proud, and I wanted to prove that someone from a low socio-economic background could achieve great things. I did work at a law firm for two years, and I had mentors at the firm. But after some soul-searching, I decided to become a teacher. I knew I wanted a family eventually, and that the teaching would allow me to spend time with them. I was satisfied with my decision-making process because it was my own. I've been teaching for six years now, and I've completed my Masters in Education, which enabled me to become an

adjunct professor. I teach and learn all day long! I would not change a thing. These experiences truly make me feel like I am affecting positive changes in my community." —**Mark**

"It was at the start my third year of law school that I questioned whether I'd made the right choice to go to law school. I didn't enjoy the course-work, my taste of law firm life wasn't all that exciting, and working for one of the professors felt too isolating. It's been two years now since I graduated, and—despite my misgivings—I realize that going to law school was the *right* decision for me. Over those three years, I was really challenged. Challenged by my classes, challenged by the grades, challenged by the endless competitions. By the end of law school, I had some successes and some failures. But more than that, I learned how to take on more than I ever did before, and no matter what job I have in the future, I'll be more prepared to step up to the work than I would have without law school. I think that alone made going worth it." —**Carrie**

"When I got to college, I declared myself a political science major because I thought that's what you needed to do to go to law school. From Day One, I told my advisors that I wanted to go to law school, and not once did any of them ask 'why?' Nor was I ever encouraged to explore other options. By the time I graduated, I didn't want to go to law school, but I felt completely boxed in. I wish now I had been shown the other options open to me, and had been encouraged to explore them prior to making a decision." —**Lisa**

"When I went to law school I wasn't at all sure it was the right place for me. For the first time, I felt intimidated in an academic setting, and also I felt oddly directionless even though I was plugging away toward my law degree. Now that I have graduated and have been in practice for five years, I'm thrilled that I persevered and got my JD. My legal education has informed and enriched my view of the world. And my law license has empowered me to help people. I take great satisfaction in advocating on behalf of my clients and in support of worthy causes." —**Samantha**

Chapter 4

The **Real LSAT**

> **"**Ask any junior or senior what they're doing after graduation, and nearly everyone has the same answer—'I don't know, but I'm taking the LSAT.**"**

—Leslie, a college senior

*I*n the previous chapter, we discussed why the decision to attend law school is so often poorly made. One big culprit is the LSAT, the Law School Admissions Test. When making admissions decisions, law schools rely heavily on one's LSAT score and grade point average (other variables include geography, gender and racial diversity). But because the LSAT takes on such great importance, a weird dynamic kicks in. Too many prospective law students take their direction from the LSAT. They view it as an oracle capable of telling them if they're meant to go to law school.

As one prospective law student told us, "I think I'll decide to go to law school if my LSATs are high enough for me to get in anywhere."

We're all for aptitude tests, but the fact that you're good at something shouldn't determine whether you want to spend your life doing it. (You might have a knack for mowing lawns and gardening, but that doesn't mean you want to make a career of landscaping.) That's why your LSAT scores and the time/money/effort you spent on the exam should have no bearing on your decision to become a lawyer. Too many people let their score, and the amount of energy they expend on the test, weigh too heavily on their choice. Some lawyers who made this mistake came to regret it later.

If students get a high LSAT score, they assume it means they should become a lawyer.

As one pre-law advisor observed: "If students get a high score (on the LSAT), they assume it somehow means they should become a lawyer. I make a major effort to try to inform prospective applicants that the LSAT is not, nor ever was, intended as a vocational guidance instrument."

The fact is, too many people preparing for the LSAT questions fail to ask the *right* questions regarding the wisdom of getting a JD. Here's where they go wrong:

They're so busy in the exam's logic games that they don't question the logic of their choice.

They're so immersed in the analytical reasoning section that they fail to carefully analyze their reasons for going to law school.

They're so busy with the reading comprehension that they haven't bothered to read real legal documents to determine if they even want to comprehend them.

They're so fixated on the writing sample that they haven't sampled what real legal writing involves to see if they'd enjoy doing it.

They're so busy with the "experimental" section that they aren't experimenting with real-world experience (legal and non-legal).

They spend endless hours taking practice exams, yet they fail to see what legal practice actually involves.

You see where this is going. People are so focused on getting *into* law school that they don't explore what they're actually getting into when they enter law school and, later, the legal profession.

Take Our LSAT Before You Take the LSAT. Because the LSAT frequently distracts people from the right considerations, we've devoted the next few chapters to our own LSAT:

L is for Law School—What's It All About?
S is for Self-Assessment—Is Law Right For You?
A is for Attorneys—What They Do & Where They Work
T is for Try it Out—Get Some Practice Before Getting Into Practice

The reason you tackle these four questions before deciding to attend law school is obvious: It's important to know what lawyers do—and if you'd enjoy doing it—*before* you jump through all the hoops to become a lawyer. The legal profession is right for some people and not for others. You need to know where you belong before making one of the biggest, most expensive career decisions in your life. One career counselor who has spent two decades counseling law students and attorneys, put it this way: "If people spent as many hours having informational interviews (with lawyers and law firms) as they did studying for the LSAT, they would make much better decisions."

Slow down—Some of you may be thinking, "All this self-assessment takes too much time. I just want to make a decision now!" But consider: Author Richard Bolles, in his popular career book, *What Color is Your Parachute?*, writes— "...Work consumes about 80,000 hours of your time on this earth. Yet, most of us spend more time planning next summer's vacation than trying to figure out what we want to do with those 80,000 hours."

In the following chapters, you'll learn how to determine what law school really demands, and what it can do to your mind, soul...and budget. You'll examine your own reasons for going to law school, and whether there are legal jobs that satisfy what you want in a job. You'll learn how to discover what lawyers do on the job and how to experience it for yourself. By working on our LSAT before you prepare for law school, we guarantee you'll make a much more informed decision.

Chapter 5 L is for Law School: What's it All About?

"Business school seemed too fluffy, and med school would have required extra science. So I took an 'easy' route by choosing law when what I should have done is get a Masters in Journalism or English Lit."

—Jean, editor and former attorney at a mid-size firm

*W*e believe this chapter, and those to follow, will further help you make an informed decision about law school so that you're not influenced by any of the Choice Challenges we just discussed.

Believe it or not, surprisingly few of the lawyers we interviewed for this book had ever set foot in a law school before attending law school. In fact, many of them conceded that the closest they had come to knowing about the experience that lay ahead was reading Scott Turow's classic *One L: The Turbulent True Story of a First Year at Harvard Law School*, or by renting a DVD of *The Paper Chase*. Not only did our interviewees say they underestimated the academic experience ahead of them, most knew very little about how law school stress might ultimately affect them, what their legal education would end up costing, or how their student loans might affect their career plans. In fact, most of the lawyers we talked to never bothered to explore the other avenues they were passing up to attend law school!

In other words, a lot of lawyers practicing today went to law school without doing their homework (or *due diligence*, as they say in law). And, as with any contract, if you don't pay attention to the fine print, the consequences can be devastating and far-reaching.

In their interviews, some lawyers described the academic pressures, the ego-deflating final exams, and the relentless stress of law school as the worst years of their lives. Some racked up far more debt than they anticipated; others lamented not exploring other career fields when, in hindsight, they could have spent their time and tuition more wisely. Still others who went to law school unsure of why they were really there wrestled with uncertainty well into their legal careers. On a happier note, many lawyers truly enjoyed law school, and value it as a stimulating learning experience that led them to fulfilling careers.

So given that law school is clearly the right choice for some people, and the wrong choice for others, the Big Question is whether it's right for you. The only way to know for sure is to research law school as you would research any large investment of time and money.

Think about it this way:

Would you put down $100,000 for a house without having the structure inspected or checking out the neighborhood?

Would you commit to moving to a new city for at least three years without first paying a visit?

Would you invest $100,000 in a single stock without researching it?

Would you shell out $30,000 for a car without test-driving it?

"I went to law school with a vague, idealized notion of using my law degree to save the world. Now I'm graduating $80,000 in debt, so I can't afford to do the work I intended to do." —Rachel

Of course you wouldn't. Yet a lot of people decide to go to law school—an investment of three years and tuition costs running into five and six figures—without doing nearly enough research or asking the hard questions. Deciding whether to enter the legal profession will have major consequences for your career, finances and personal happiness. Yet too many people use a wholly inadequate decision-making process when approaching these important choices. So, while there are plenty of lawyers who love what they do, there are many who don't. And their career dissatisfaction often stretches all the way back to their first decision to enter the law. Educating yourself about the realities of legal education comes down to asking and answering four key questions:

What are law school academics all about?

What psychological experience can I expect from law school?

What is law school really going to cost me?

What in my life am I passing up to pursue law school?

We can guess what some of you are thinking right now: *I don't have time for this.* Oh yes, you do have time for this. Yes, these four questions may take some effort to resolve, but they're small by comparison with the investment of time, money and energy you will spend as a law student and as a lawyer. My co-author learned this the hard way. During her final semester of college, Deborah briefly flirted with the idea of sitting in on some law school classes and working part-time at a law firm to see what it was actually like. She abandoned that plan, though, reasoning that she didn't have time for all that extra work when it was her last chance to enjoy her carefree college days. Years later, of course, Deborah realized that she could have easily made time to explore what law school and lawyering was really like, and would have avoided a lot of unnecessary grief that way. But enough walking down memory lane. Let's address those four questions.

What Are Law School Academics All About?

For some of you, diving into law school course-work will feel a lot like taking a dive into an empty swimming pool. Especially if your only "legal reading" has been John Grishham thrillers. Because the academic workload (especially for first-year students) is often more intense and stressful than most students expect, it will be beneficial to find out what it's all about and whether you would enjoy it (or at least can endure it). Plus, if you ultimately wind up going to law school, you'll be far better prepared to keep the stress in perspective. We recommend three ways to gather the necessary information.

Read what law students read

Cases—These are what you'll read in class and when performing legal research.

Statutes—The laws of the nation, federal, state and local. Many of the statutes you'll study in your first year of law school are contained in the Uniform Commercial Code (UCC) and the U.S. Code of Civil Procedure.

Legal briefs—These are what you'll learn how to write in first year Legal Research and Writing and Moot Court classes.

The Bluebook—A Uniform System of Citation (Harvard Law Review Association). This contains the rules of legal citation used in legal writing.

The Legal Research Manual—A Game Plan for Legal Research and Analysis by Christopher and Jill Wren This walks you through the basics of legal research and writing.

How do you find these books and documents? If you know any law students, ask to borrow their casebooks, and read the briefs they've written in their *Legal Research and Writing* and *Moot Court* classes. If you don't know any law students, the materials read by every law student are located at any undergraduate or public library, law school library or bookstore, or any major book store. You can also find legal documents online. One popular legal web site (www.findlaw.com) has a comprehensive collection of statues, cases, and basic legal forms. Just click on the links to "U.S. Laws: Cases and Codes" and "Legal Forms". The Internet Legal Resource Guide (www.ilrg.com) also has an extensive web-based collection of free legal forms such as business and employment contracts. And the site for the Legal Information Institute (http://lii.law.cornell.edu) offers its own extensive legal resources. Click on its links to federal and state constitutions and laws.

In addition to the material that law students read in class, you would be smart to review the study aids they read outside class. Looking over commercial law school course outlines—for Contracts, Real Property, Criminal Law, and Constitutional Law—will help you get a sense of the subjects studied. In the Tool Kit section of this book (see page 214), you'll also find many resources for finding free course outlines. You can also look through commercial-outline books such as Emanuel Law Outlines (www.lawbooks.com/emanuel.html) and the Gilbert Law Summaries (www.gilbertlaw.com/index.asp). Another way to get a helpful overview of legal subject matters is to glance through the books in the Law-in-a-Nutshell series (e.g., *Tax Law in a Nutshell*, *Constitutional Law in a Nutshell*, etc.). Again, ask to borrow them from friends, go to a law-school bookstore to check them out, or order them online at (

If you find you enjoy reading cases and statutes and reading about legal subjects, that's great. If you don't, well, you're getting a preview of what law school will feel like.

To round out your understanding of the academic experience, check out some books and web sites that explain how to prepare for law school academics. This will further help you get a sense of what the course-work is actually like, and how to prepare for classes and exams. Two helpful resources are www.Findlaw.com, which has plenty of pre-law materials in its Student Resources section, and Gary Munneke's *How to Succeed in Law School* (2003). Munneke's book will help you understand what to expect from the course load, classroom experience, and final exams.

Talk to people about the academic experience of law school. Reading is helpful, but only to an extent. It's also important to talk to law students, lawyers, law professors, and law school career counselors. How do you find them? If you or your family don't have any contacts, call the career counseling office of any law school and tell them you're a prospective law student. They'll be glad to connect you with some of their students. You can also ask your undergraduate career services office to connect you to alumni who are currently in law school. Use the very same process to find lawyers and law professors. If you, your family or friends don't have any contacts in the legal community, call a law school near you and ask to speak with professors and alumni. Here are some of the questions you will want to ask:

> What are the most important things prospective law students should find out about law school before deciding whether to go?
>
> What type of people tend to enjoy law school, and why?
>
> What type of people tend to struggle with law school, and why?

Spend time at a law school. Not surprisingly, the very best way to get a comprehensive preview of what law school is like is to spend time at one. Yet few prospective law students do. At best, most wait until they've been admitted to law school and show up for the official "Admitted Students Day." There's nothing wrong with these orientation programs. The problem with this approach is that sitting in on one or two classes only offers a peek at what it is like to be a law student. More important, once you've been admitted to law school, you're far more invested in the idea that you're going, and less likely to objectively evaluate whether law school is right for you. Even if the course-work and class-room experience doesn't look appealing, you may not be as open minded to the idea that law school is not for you. That's why it's ideal to check out law school before you take the LSAT and apply.

So, what if you're reading this and you've already been accepted? No matter, just try to go in with an open mind and a willingness to find out what it's really like. The following plan of attack should give you the most realistic sense of the experience:

Attend several classes—It's important to understand what the law school teaching methodology entails because it will be very different from your undergraduate experience. Some students find the Socratic and case-study method thought-provoking and fascinating, while others find it nerve-wracking and not terribly conducive to learning. See what you think. And while you're at it, ask students if you can take a look at their homework assignments and read the cases they're reading to prepare for class.

Sit in on a legal research and writing class—In this way you can see what first-year students are learning about the basics of legal writing.

Hang out in a law school library—Ask a student to walk you through basic legal research. Next, ask someone show you what legal writing entails and how to use *The Blue Book* mentioned earlier. It contains the rules of legal citation. In our opinion, you should never decide to attend law school until you've experienced legal research, legal writing and "Blue-Booking." These skills are an integral part of being an attorney, and many unhappy lawyers cite this as one of the main reasons for their dissatisfaction.

Don't even think about attending law school until you know first-hand about legal research, legal writing, and 'Blue-Booking.'

Visit law school during finals—Talk to 1st, 2nd and 3rd year students about the experience of preparing for and taking finals. While you're at it, take a look at some exams. See if any law students have copies of them, or if law professors will show you old ones, or if they're on file in a law school library for you to view. You can also find them online at www.Findlaw.com (click on "Student Resources").

Attend one or two clinical courses—These are designed to help students develop lawyering skills through practical experience. It's one thing to learn about classes and exam-taking, but it's equally important to see how law schools prepare students for real-world legal practice. Clinic students are placed in legal offices (such as organizations that serve low-income clients, or the district attorney or public defender's office) and receive credit for doing real-world legal work. See if you can observe clinical students by calling the law school's clinical faculty and asking if you can shadow students at their placements.

Sit in on courses designed to teach real-world lawyering skills—These include moot court, mock trial and negotiations. Again, this will give you a realistic idea of law as a job, much more accurately than any movie or TV show.

Of course, doing any of the above steps requires you to actually connect to some folks in law school. If you know any law students, ask them. If you don't, here's what to do:

Ask family and friends if they know any law students.
Ask your undergrad alumni relations office or career services office to connect you to alumni who are currently in law school.
Ask a law school near you if they can put you in touch with current law

students. Many admissions offices can arrange for tours for prospective law
students led by law students, and for the chance to sit in on classes.

Ask a law professor or law school clinical faculty to observe their class.

Ask an undergraduate professor or prelaw advisor if they know law students
with whom you could speak.

As important as it is to get a glimpse of law school life, here's a caveat:

If you're turned off by much of what you observe at law school, don't be
alarmed and rule out law just yet. After all, being a law student (going to class
and taking exams) is very different than being a lawyer. Some people who hated
law school loved being lawyers once they graduated and started working in the
real world. Conversely, some students who loved law school hated being lawyers.
Some were in the wrong jobs, others just thrived in an academic environment (so
they became law professors). That's why it's so important to check out both the
law school environment and real-world legal practice (which we'll get to later).

Still, if you visit law school and are turned off by legal research and writing,
or dislike thinking about legal subjects, listen to what that is telling you. You'll
need to investigate whether there are any legal jobs that still might appeal to you,
and also to start exploring non-legal fields to see if there are others you enjoy
more. Don't worry, though. We tell you how to do that later in the book.

What Psychological Experience Can I Expect From Law School?

It's important to understand that law school can do a number on your ego
and psyche if you let it. What's so stressful about it? For starters, just being
uncertain why you're there...not knowing what you want to do with your JD
when you get it...having your entire grade based on one final exam...and
feeling the peer pressure at grade time.

Many of the lawyers we interviewed said law school was intense and isolating, and left them physically and mentally exhausted from academic pressure,
peer pressure and job-search pressure. Others reported that, by the time they
graduated, they lacked self-confidence and felt risk-averse, overly obedient and
unable to think creatively. One law school's study revealed that significant
numbers of its students were emotionally healthy when they arrived, but developed major psychological distress within the first year. Anxiety, hostility and
depression ran eight to 15 times higher in these students than in the general
population, and these symptoms lasted throughout law school and into their
careers! In other studies of lawyers, 20% to 35% reported symptoms of being

clinically distressed at a level found in only about 2% of the general population.

Here's the good news: It is possible to have a positive law school experience and plenty of students do. For a career investment of this magnitude, it should be at least somewhat enjoyable, so keep the following pointers in mind:

If you enter law school confident of your decision to be there and with a clear action plan for your legal education, you'll be better able to withstand the various pressures, to think for yourself and to pursue course-work and jobs that most interest you. Although some burdens, like grades, can't be eased, one of the best ways to withstand the pressures of law school is to enter knowing what you want to get out of it, what to expect from it, and how to plan accordingly. Asking the right questions will prepare you to deal with law school stressors and capitalize on your experience.

Here are three ways to gather information about the psychological experience of law school:

1. *Read about it*—There are a number of books and web sites that detail common law school stressors and what to do about them. Some good online sources include Vault.com's Law School Channel, which includes online discussions among law students. If you go to www.Vault.com, type 'law student' in the search engine and check out the law student discussion. Findlaw also offers prelaw and law student resources. Go to www.Findlaw.com and explore their own Student Resources section. Finally, check out Law.com's "Law Students Channel" at There are also plenty of books that explain the law school experience, including Robert Millers, *Law School Confidential: The Complete Law School Survival Guide by Students, for Students*, and Jeremy Horwitz's *Law School Insider: The Comprehensive 21st Century Guide to Success in Admissions, Classes, Law Review, Bar Exams and Job Searches, for Prospective Students and Their Loved Ones.*

2. *Talk to law students and law school counselors about common stressors*—Nothing can replace candid conversations with 1st, 2nd, and 3rd year law students; lawyers and recent law school grads; law school professors, and administrators, and career services counselors. Speak with people who had positive and negative experiences. Get them to discuss common law school stressors, such as final exams, grades and job searching. Questions to ask include:

What are the most common law school stressors?

What can law students do to reduce their stress levels?

What can students do to make law school a more enriching and enjoyable experience?

3. *Try it out*—Spend a week or a day or just a few hours at a nearby law school. Ask yourself how you feel when attending classes, reading cases, and soaking up the vibe. Do you feel stimulated? Psyched? Stressed? Sleepy? Pay attention to your answers.

What Will Law School Really Cost Me?

In interviews, lawyers often told us that they chose law school because they hated math.

Like it or not, though, doing the math and adding up your financial costs is an important part of the law school decision. It's vital to understand what law school will mean for your finances, because student debt can dramatically impact your lifestyle and career options when you graduate. Many attorneys underestimate what they will spend during law school, and overestimate how much money they will earn afterward. For some, that translated into staggering debt, limited job options and the prospect of repaying their loans for far longer than they expected. The reason to do these calculations is to get a reality check about the financial implications of getting a JD, and to decide if the investment will be worth it. If you ultimately decide to go to law school, you can better prepare for how to pay for it. Law school is expensive, and getting costlier every year. Planning ahead will help prevent you from unwittingly limiting your job options.

Here are three ways to get information about the financial commitment of a law degree.

Do your homework—Check out www.EdWise.com (among other similar web sites) for a basic understanding of how student loans work, and what they mean for your specific situation. You'll find additional resources in our Tool Kit (see page 214). "I wish I could wave a magic wand to go back and actually see a career services person or financial aid officer," says Kristen, now a twenty-something attorney at a big national law firm. She had wanted to work in public-interest law but couldn't afford it with her loan payments. "(If I had done my homework)," she said, "I would have really understood how much debt I would have and the choices this decision would force me into."

Ask around—Don't try to figure this stuff out alone. Speak with law school financial aid officers, as well as law students and lawyers. Questions for law school financial aid officers include:

What are the most common costs students overlook?

What are the best ways to reduce my borrowing and loans?

What are the most common mistakes law students make when borrowing money?

Ask lawyers and law students what they wish they'd done differently when it came to managing their debt and finances, and to what extent their student loans influenced their career choices. Ask law school career services counselors to discuss how debt can impact job options and how to locate realistic starting salaries for attorneys in private- and public-sector jobs.

Add It Up—You don't have to be a Harvard economist to figure out your finances; you just have to perform a few basic calculations. How many people actually perform them? Not nearly enough. At the most, it will take a couple of days to gather the information and do the math. That's not so bad, considering it could take 10 or more years to repay your loans! So while this exercise might seem like a pain right now, it could be infinitely more painful in the long run if you don't do it. That's why we've tried to make this as easy as possible by walking you through the calculations, and explaining where to get help with the answers:

> Together, my husband and I have student loans totaling $200,000. That's like having a mortgage without a house or a tax write-off.

Step One—Start by calculating what law school will cost you. The best way to get this information is (not surprisingly) from a law school. Contact the financial aid office of a law school you're considering and ask for the estimated cost of attendance, including tuition and living expenses. Write that dollar amount here: $_____. In our example, we'll assume the estimated cost of attendance (including living expenses) is $50,000 per year, or $150,000 for three years.

Step Two—Estimate how much money you have to contribute towards your law school education. Such funds could come from your own savings, your family, and scholarships. Write that dollar amount here: $_____. In our example, we'll assume the student has $50,000 to contribute towards three years of law school.

Step Three—Determine how much money you'll need to borrow in student loans. To estimate this number, subtract the sum in Step Two from the sum in Step One. Write that figure here: $_____. In our example, $150,000 minus $50,000 means that our student will have to borrow $100,000 to cover law school expenses.

Step Four—You need to determine what your monthly post-graduate loan repayments will amount to and how many years it will take to repay your loans. Check our Tool Kit on page x for several online loan calculators. These sites will ask you to plug in how much money you're borrowing, the interest rate you're paying and how many years you're taking to repay your loans. Write those figures here: $_____ over _____ years at _____ interest rate. In our example, we'll say this student is borrowing $100,000 at an 8.25% interest rate (the maximum interest rate possible for government Stafford Loans) and plans to repay it over 10 years. At this rate, she will pay $147,120 over 10 years. If she repays the same amount each month, she'll repay $1,226.00 per month. (Note: If you extend your loan repayments beyond 10 years, you can pay a lower amount each month. However, you'll wind up paying more overall because of interest rates. Conversely, you can repay a larger amount each month and pay off your loans more quickly and repay less overall.)

Step Five—Next, figure out the median salaries for several types of jobs you would enjoy doing, and that you could realistically get. In other words, don't assume you'll be making a six-figure salary (few students do). As we mentioned earlier, the median starting salary for recent law school grads is $60,000, and the median starting salaries for public interest, government, judicial clerkship and small firm jobs can be considerably lower. To determine what salary to plug in here, call a law school career services office in the city you want to live in after law school and ask for the average starting salary in the type of practice that interests you (public interest, public sector and private firms of varying sizes). After designating a median annual salary, calculate your monthly take-home by dividing by 12. Post that figure here $_____. In our example, we'll use a median salary of $55,000 per year. That means our law grad earns $4,583 per month but actually takes home $3,750 per month (after taxes and other deductions).

Step Six—Subtract your anticipated monthly loan repayments and post-grad living expenses from your estimated expected monthly salary to see what your post-law school lifestyle and finances will look like. Again, the budget calculators at Nellie Mae (www.nelliemae.com,) EdFund (www.edfund.org), and Finaid (www.finaid.org) can help you figure this out. Law school financial-aid and career service offices often have budget work-sheets to help you calculate your monthly living expenses. In our example, we'll say our law graduate's monthly, after tax take-home salary is $3,750. Her monthly living expenses total $2,000 and she owes $1,226 in monthly loan repayments. That leaves her with $524 per month for savings and investing (or whatever).

Now you have a realistic idea of what law school will mean for your finances. In our example, the student will spend up to 10 or more years repaying close to $750-$1,000 per month for their education.

What Am I Passing Up To Pursue Law School?

Many people who contemplate law school don't consider their *opportunity costs*—that is, what they are passing up by going to law school. Law students are fond of declaring they're going to law school to "open doors," and yet their decision inadvertently closes many doors as a result of their staggering debt. So it's important to understand your *opportunity costs* and explore other career options to ensure you don't overlook a better match.

> "**M**y law school loans were much more than I expected. What I want to know is how will I pay for my children's education when I can't pay f or my own?"
>
> —Jennifer, law firm administrator

Many lawyers we've spoke to deeply regret not exploring non-legal fields, and later changed careers at great cost. Have you looked into other graduate degree programs or non-legal fields that sound intriguing? Have you looked into working or traveling abroad? Or the chance to pursue a dream, like starting a business, or becoming a recording star or making a difference in politics? (Both George Stephanopoulos, former Clinton advisor and host of ABC's *This Week*, and Jon Stewart, host of Comedy Central's *The Daily Show*, once considered attending law school but opted to pursue their passions for politics and comedy. They never looked back.)

If you haven't explored other avenues, the effort will make a huge difference. Think about it: how can you honestly decide law is the best path if you don't compare it to others? And when you're comparing legal and non-legal careers, consider finances. You may discover that law school may not give you the professional or financial benefit you expected. Some folks who went to law school largely because they wanted to "boost their earning potential" did not ultimately make more money than they would have in the non-legal career they might have chosen. In their case, they would have made more over time had they simply worked for three years at something they enjoyed.

When thinking about *opportunity costs*, another consideration is the cost of time. At the risk of sounding like a Hallmark commercial, time is precious and the older you get, the more you realize it. If you invest three years (at a minimum) pursuing a career that's not a good fit, you incur the cost of delayed gratification and career growth, as well as the psychic cost of being in the wrong profession. To illustrate, we'll tell you a story about Kelly. Like a lot of students, Kelly went to law school because she didn't know what else to do after graduating from college, and she was horrified at the idea of working in "some entry-level job for $20,000 a year." She figured law school would help her land a better job by making her more competitive. When Kelly graduated from law school, though, she wasn't sure law was the right profession for her and didn't know what else she wanted to do. Meanwhile, more than a few of her friends who took those $20,000-a-year jobs right out of college were now making $50,000 a year. After a few exasperating years of legal practice, Kelly concluded that she didn't want to be a lawyer any longer. She decided to move to Hollywood and get a job that sounded genuinely fun—as a movie production assistant. Suddenly, Kelly was making $20,000 a year, while her friends who had been working in the film industry since college were making six figures. The moral? Be sure to investigate careers you might like more than law so you don't waste time and money on a legal career you don't truly enjoy.

> Ask yourself, 'What would I regret passing up if I went to law school?

With that in mind, here are three ways to evaluate your opportunity costs:

Search other careers that interest you—Check out such web sites as www.Wetfeet.com and www.Vault.com (and other resources in the Tool Kit, page 214), and read the career guides published by both of these companies.

Speak with people in non-legal jobs that sound appealing— Once you've identified a few career fields that sound interesting, talk to people who work in them to see what they're actually like. Such conversations are known as *informational interviews*. We'll walk you through this discovery process in Chapter 7, and in the Tool Kit (see page 215).

Try it out—The very best way to explore non-legal career paths is to get hands-on work experience. You could do this by working or volunteering, full-time or part-time. If you don't have time, *shadow* someone. Shadowing means that you accompany someone to his or her job and observe what the work entails. Another way to learn about different fields is to take a class, or attend conferences or workshops in an area that sounds interesting. You can find classes offered through university extension programs, community colleges and a variety of for-profit and non-profit organizations. For example, if you're interested in starting your own business, attend a seminar offered through your local chamber of commerce or other groups that support entrepreneurs. You can also read local publications and search online for classes and events in your area.

As you research different non-legal and legal fields, ask yourself the following questions:

Are there non-legal careers or jobs that seem more interesting than law?

Are there people who have jobs or careers that I'd like who don't have law degrees? (What steps did they take to get to their position? Am I willing to do the same thing to get there? How long would it take to have my dream job if I didn't go to law school?).

What are my prospects for advancement if I remained in my current field and didn't go to law school? Would additional training, education and mentoring help me advance into positions I'd enjoy?

What is the likelihood that a law degree will bring the salary and satisfaction I desire versus another career path?

What will I regret passing up if I go into law?

Chapter 6   S *is for* Self-Assessment: Is Law Right for You?

"One day Alice came to a fork in the road and saw a Cheshire cat in a tree. 'Which road do I take?' she asked. 'Where do you want to go?' he said. 'I don't know,' said Alice. 'Then,' said the cat, 'it doesn't matter.'"

—Lewis Carroll, *Alice in Wonderland*

*I*n the previous chapter, we posed four questions to help you understand what law school is all about. In this chapter, we raise four additional questions... this time to help you determine if law is right for you. Why bother with all this introspection? Because if you don't actively steer your own career, you—like Alice and millions of unhappy job-seekers—will never know where you will end up until you actually get there. In fact, some people never stop to think about what they want in a job; others ignore the signs even as they plunge ahead in the wrong direction. So, before you decide to embark on a legal career path, let's see if law is the right destination for you.

This chapter will help by identifying the characteristics of your ideal job so you can explore the Big Question—whether a legal or non-legal position is a better match. How to begin? By tackling some questions of basic self-assessment. Don't worry, we wouldn't dare ask you some of those weird, touchy-feely, Larry King-like questions such as, *If you could be any type of tree, which tree would you be?* When we talk about self-assessment, we're talking about smart questions that can help define what is essential to your job satisfaction. Self-assessment will also help you see through your own personal Choice Challenges. After all, going to law school just because your friends are, or because your parents are leaning on you, or because you got great a LSAT score, or because it's 'just something you always thought you would do,' does not qualify as sound decision-making.

Incidentally, if, in this self-assessment process, you do identify some future goals for yourself, it will help you focus your energy if you choose to enroll in law school. You will also make far better use of your time and tuition. For example, if you figure out beforehand that you want to work in criminal law, you can use your time in law school to take criminal law courses and clinics (for-credit placements in legal offices) and work or volunteer with a criminal lawyer. We're not suggesting that you have to figure out exactly what kind of law you want to practice before you decide to attend law school. But at the very least, you should know that there are some legal jobs that will be a good match for you…and some that won't. Unfortunately, many prospective law students who don't make this effort realize years later that they could have found a more compatible career if they took the time to ascertain what they want in a job. Consider this example from our decision-making archives:

> "Everyone winds up answering self-assessment questions sooner or later. If you do it sooner, you're more likely to find a job you like than one you want to escape from."
>
> —Rachel, law school career counselor

Years ago, my co-author moved to San Francisco, and was offered a job with a startup company. When Deborah interviewed, she was attracted to many aspects of the work environment—great people, short commute, cool office space, pets at work, humane work hours, generous salary and stock options (when they meant something). Still, she didn't find the work itself, or the company's mission, terribly interesting. But did she ever ask herself, *"Can I be happy in a job that might bore me…can I tolerate working on projects that don't excite me?"* No, not once. Despite her misgivings, Deborah took the job, thinking, "it's a nice group of people…they're not going to run out of money anytime soon…and, anyway, I have no idea what I want to do instead. Plus, there are all those stock options!" A week into her new job, Deborah realized her mistake. A month later, she was consulting a career counselor. The counselor helped her ask the right questions—*What did she like to do? What did she enjoy thinking about? Which of her past jobs and activities were the most fun, and why? How would she prefer to spend her time at work? What would her ideal work environment look like? What were her priorities when it came to her career?* Once Deborah started thinking about her favorite skills and interests, the type of work environment she was happiest in, and what really mattered to her, she began to identify jobs and career paths that matched her personality and interests. She's been in the right jobs—and happy about it—ever since.

This story illustrates two important points: asking the right questions *can* help you find the right career, and it's better to ask them as early as possible.

If you don't like using the skills that most lawyers use, you probably won't enjoy being a lawyer. If you dislike thinking about legal subjects and reading legal documents, it doesn't bode well for your happiness in law. It's better to find out before starting law school whether you would enjoy working in a legal environment, and whether legal work is in line with your priorities. If you don't consider these questions now, you may wind up confronting them later when the stakes are higher—*after* you've invested three years and a ton of money on a JD.

That's why it's so important not to skip (or even skim) the questions we've included here. And if you're concerned that this self-assessment process will take too long, then commit just a single hour and see what you learn. Seriously, just spending 60 minutes could save you a tremendous amount of time and effort down the road. What's 60 minutes compared to the time you'll spend applying to law school, not to mention being an unhappy law student or lawyer? If you get stuck or tempted to give up in this phase of self-assessment, enlist the help of a friend who knows you well or make an appointment with a career counselor.

So, here are the four basic questions we'll explore in this chapter:

What skills do you most enjoy using?
What subjects genuinely interest you?
What do you want in a work environment?
What are your career priorities?

One by one, we'll walk you through these questions and help you create a list of the *skills* you most enjoy using, the *subjects* you most enjoy thinking about, the elements that would make a satisfying *work environment*, and what are your *priorities* when it comes to work. After you've made some comprehensive lists, you'll pick your five favorites in each category. That will give you an outline to help you find the types of jobs you'd enjoy, and you can use that criteria to look for legal and non-legal jobs that have what you're looking for. In other words, once you've completed your chart, don't leave it in the book—your answers won't do you any good there. Keep your criteria handy to help you identify the most meaningful legal and non-legal job opportunities.

Okay, let's take them one at a time...

What Skills Do You Most Enjoy Using?

By skills we mean the day-to-day activities that you do on the job—the way you spend your day at work. Some of the skills you would use as a practicing lawyer include writing (briefs and other legal documents), researching (legal issues), interviewing (clients, witnesses, experts), advising (clients and colleagues) and negotiating with others (opposing counsel). That said, it's important to realize that all legal jobs are not created equal; different types of lawyers utilize different skills. For example, one important skills question to ask is whether you prefer to spend more time working alone or in the company of others. If you're a people person, you may be miserable in a job where you're often working alone all day. If you're not a people person, a job that requires constant interaction with others could be a real drag. If you're clerking for a judge or working as a new associate at a large law firm, your job is likely to involve more legal research and writing and less interaction with other people (like clients). On the other hand, if you're a district attorney or a public defender, you're likely to spend more time dealing with people and less time consumed with legal research and analysis. The point is, because there are so many ways to work as a lawyer, it's important to see what legal jobs emphasize the skills you enjoy using.

Skills Preference Exercise #1

This chart is the first in a series of self-assessments intended to help identify your preferred skills. Take a few moments to recall specific work or volunteer experiences, and circle the skills you most enjoyed using. Feel free to add any skills not listed here.

Advising	Managing people
Analyzing	Managing projects
Auditing	Negotiating
Brainstorming	Organizing
Budgeting	Planning
Coaching	Presenting
Coordinating	Persuading
Counseling	Programming
Designing	Problem-solving
_____	_____
_____	_____

(Continued on next page)

(Continued from previous page)

Drafting	Public speaking
Editing	Publicizing
Legal writing	Recruiting
Interviewing	Reporting
Investigating	Researching
Leading	Selling
Lecturing	Teaching
Lobbying	Training
Mediating	Writing
_____	_____
_____	_____

Skills Preference Exercise #2

Draft two short paragraphs identifying your *most-preferred* and *least-preferred* skills, and the circumstances in which you used them. One law student wrote the following:

"One of my favorite experiences was organizing a non-profit fund-raiser. I coordinated the entertainment, invited guest speakers, sent out invitations, recruited and managed a team of volunteers, solicited local businesses for donations, publicized the event and served as master of ceremonies. The skills I most enjoyed were public speaking (as emcee), promoting and marketing (publicizing the event) and brainstorming (conceptualizing and planning the event). I enjoyed using these skills because I love interacting with people, performing to a crowd and filling a room for a cause I believe in.

"One of my least-favorite experiences was researching and writing a legal memo about a civil procedure issues. I had to research case law, read cases and analyze the relevant legal issues, and write a memorandum presenting and analyzing the legal issues. The skills I least enjoyed using were legal research (researching cases that presented a similar legal issue), reading legal cases (for case law on the same issue), and analyzing a civil procedure issue (to see how different courts have handled a similar legal issue). I didn't enjoy this project or the skills I used because it meant working alone in a library and thinking about subjects that didn't interest me."

Skills Preference Exercise #3

Imagine you could have any job in the world without regard to education or training. Now, draft a series of responses to this question: "I would be absolutely thrilled if I could get paid to _____". List as many jobs or occupations as you like and describe the skills most likely required for each (refer to the list in Exercise #1 if you need help).

Skills I Most Enjoy Using

Of all the skills you identified in the previous three exercises, list the five you do really well and would potentially want to use on the job.

1. _____
2. _____
3. _____
4. _____
5. _____

When identifying your favorite skills, be as specific as possible. For example, if you listed *writing,* consider what it is you like to write—poetry, research papers, fiction, non-fiction? If you listed *working with people*, think about how you most enjoy working with others. Do you like interviewing people? Counseling people? Negotiating with people? Collaborating with others? And while you're at it, think about whether you'd enjoy using your favorite skills in a legal or non-legal setting. For instance, you don't want to commit to law school because you like "writing," only to discover that you're not crazy about legal writing. Maybe you'd prefer reporting, or writing advertising copy, instead. Note: A word of caution to those who would say, "I've never worked before, so I feel like I don't have any skills. That's why I'm going to law school." Hold on. Think about the *inherent* skills you use in college course-work, extracurricular activities, volunteer experiences and hobbies.

What Subjects Genuinely Interest You?

By this we mean, what subjects would you enjoy thinking about on the job every day? For example, in the legal profession...

Tax lawyers spend their day studying tax regulations and clients' financial information.

Divorce lawyers think about divorce laws, marital property and client issues.

Corporate lawyers immerse themselves in contracts, mergers and acquisitions, and the legalities of assorted business matters.

Litigators think about the specific legal issues in dispute, as well as pre-trial procedural matters like deadlines, court filings, witnesses, settlement negotiations and trial preparation.

It's easy to see why it's so important to consider what subjects you enjoy thinking about when you're deciding whether or not to become a lawyer. Because if you're bored by what you have to think about at work, the profession itself will probably come up short. Sadly, many current practitioners discover this too late. So before you commit yourself to law (or any field), ask yourself what you enjoy thinking, reading and talking about.

Subject Matter Exercise #1

This chart will help you get started identifying favorite subject areas. Start by circling your favorites, or add your own:

Art	History	Medicine
Aviation	Labor	Real Estate
Business	Media	Science
Cars	Music	Space Travel
Education	Personal Finance	Sports
Entertainment	Politics	Tourism
Environment	Publishing	Travel
Food	Religion	Wine
Foreign Affairs	Science	Women's Issues
Health	Legal Affairs	Zoology
_____	_____	_____
_____	_____	_____

Having trouble thinking of areas yourself? Just go to a bookstore and walk around. What subjects sound interesting? Or look through an online course catalogue from a large university and note what departments, majors and courses intrigue you.

Subject Matter Exercise #2

Draft a series of short responses to the following questions:

What are your favorite hobbies or interests?

What subjects could you discuss for extended periods without getting bored?

What topics interest you when you open a newspaper or magazine?

What subject-matter web sites do you visit most often?

What undergraduate course did you most enjoy…or wish you had taken?

Subjects of Greatest Interest

Of all the subjects you identified, list the five of greatest personal interest in order of their importance:

1. _____
2. _____
3. _____
4. _____
5. _____

What Do You Want in a Work Environment?

By work environment, we mean the type of work setting you would most enjoy—the type of coworkers, the physical surroundings and office culture, the hours, the dress code, the level of formality, the bureaucracy, commute, etc. In short, the overall environment in which you'd feel most comfortable. Our appreciation of work environments differs from one person to the next. Some prefer formal environments; others find them stifling. Some love fast-paced offices; others a laid-back atmosphere. Some thrive on 60-plus hour work-weeks; others hate working longer than 40. Some people like formal attire; others prefer Friday-casual every day.

As you speak with various lawyers and non-lawyers about their work, you'll discover that different practice settings have different work environments. In fact, it's fair to say that the differences in workplace culture between, say, a large corporate law firm and a public-interest organization are like the cultural differences between New York City and Salt Lake City. Work environments vary among non-legal jobs as well. Just compare the difference between a large insurance company and a small ad agency. Or a large tech company and a nonprofit arts organization.

Unfortunately, many lawyers learn too late that work environment can be just as crucial as the work itself. So, what if you're not sure what kind of work environment you're best suited for? Yet another reason for getting work experience that allows you to sample different settings. At the very least, you should *shadow* people in different types of legal and non-legal offices. That is, spend a day (at least a few hours) with them in a large corporate environment, a small business, a nonprofit organization, a government agency or any other type of organization that sounds interesting. Compare workplaces that are formal versus casual; workplaces where 12-to-14-hour days are typical versus the traditional eight-and-go-home; workplaces that feel high-pressured and caffeinated versus relaxed and laid-back; workplaces that have plush set-ups and lots of support staff versus sparse surroundings and fewer resources. An investment of no more than a few days will give you an eye-opening sense for the most satisfying work environment for you.

The lowdown on billable hours. In law, the one work-environment issue cited by lawyers again and again as having the greatest impact on their lives is *billable hours*. We cannot overstate the surprise that most new lawyers feel when confronted with the pressure to produce 1,500, 1,800, even 2,200 annual billable hours (hours your firm can bill to the client). So, what's the big deal about billable hours? Billable hours are the way private law firms make money—by billing clients for each hour an attorney works on their legal matters.

Many firms require attorneys to track their time in six-minute increments. Imagine this—you must stop every six minutes to record what you've done, or wait until the end of the day and try to remember. Of course, not every minute you spend at work is billable. Yes, doing legal research, taking a deposition, or having a phone conversation on a client's behalf, is billable. But there are all sorts of personal activities that have nothing to do with clients. So, it means that while you may spend 10 to 12 hours at work each day, perhaps only six to eight of them are billable.

Many firms have billable-hours requirements in which associates are expected to bill a certain number each year. This varies, often depending on the firm's size. Currently, the largest firms require new associates to bill a minimum of 1,900 to 2,200 hours per year, while mid-size firms require around 1,600 to 1,900 per year. If the number of hours you spend at work are an issue for you, it's important to ask about a firm's billable requirement before you commit to working there. Many firms list their billable requirements in the *Directory of Legal Employers*, published by the National Association for Law Placement (www.nalpdirectory.com). Better yet, ask new associates how many hours they're required to bill and—just as important—how many hours they spend at the office each week to hit that quota. For example, if they're required to bill 2,100 hours a year (not uncommon), but must actually work a total of 2,900 hours per year, a little arithmetic will tell something about their work day (e.g., if you divide 2,900 by 365, it translates to an eight-hour work day—*if* you worked 365 days a year). So, is one's work environment important? You bet it is.

The exercises below should help define what kind of setting is appropriate for you.

Work Environment Exercise #1

Circle the aspects of a work environment that appeal to you

Large organization	Traditional 40-hour work week
Small organization	Work week of 50+ hours
Fast-paced	Plush environment with many resources
Laid-back	No-frills environment
Casual	People work in groups
Formal	People work individually
Clearly defined rules	Colleagues socialize
Flexible	Colleagues not especially sociable
Short commute	Emphasis on training and mentoring
Access to public transportation	Emphasis on autonomy and independence

Work Environment Exercise #2

Identify three previous jobs—paid or volunteer—and specify some of the qualities you liked or disliked about those work environments. Be specific.

This is an important exercise, and if you wish to make the most of it, draft a short paragraph describing what appealed to you (or not) about one particular work place. One law student wrote: "In one of my favorite jobs, I liked the 9-to-5 work day, the friendly colleagues, the casual dress code, the ability to work independently, the laid-back environment, and the short commute. In one of my least-favorite jobs, I disliked the harried pace, the formal dress code, and the intensity of some coworkers. However, I loved the plush office setting."

Job: _____   Job: _____

1. _____   1. _____

2. _____   2. _____

3. _____   3. _____

4. _____   4. _____

5. _____   5. _____

Job: _____

1. _____

2. _____

3. _____

4. _____

5. _____

My Preferred Work Environment

By now, you should have a pretty good sense about what sort of work environment appeals to you. Rank those five criteria below:

1. _____

2. _____

3. _____

4. _____

5. _____

What Are Your Career Priorities?

By priorities, we mean what is truly important to you when it comes to a job? Is it a huge salary, even at the expense of having a life outside of work? Is it a strictly 9-to-5 job with no weekend work?

Many people don't realize the importance of having a job that's in line with their priorities until they're in a job where their priorities collide. Being in a job that doesn't mesh with your priorities may be tolerable for some but for others utterly intolerable—as in, I don't want to even get out of bed to work today. For example, if it's important that your work is personally meaningful, you may be unhappy with a job that doesn't provide a sense of purpose. Or if you're representing clients whose issues or whose behaviors raise ethical conflicts, you may

---

Career Priorities Exercise #1

Circle the priorities with the greatest appeal. Feel free to add others not listed here.

Career advancement	Making a difference in the world
Family-friendly policies	Meaningful work
Professional growth	People with whom you enjoy working
Entrepreneurial work	Work/life balance
Ethically compatible	_____
High salary	_____
Leadership opportunities	_____

Priorities Exercise #2

Identify five career priorities from this list (or add your own criteria), and draft a paragraph (or a few sentences) for each that provides additional detail and why it's important to you:

1. Priority: _____
2. Priority: _____
3. Priority: _____
4. Priority: _____
5. Priority: _____

not be comfortable advocating on their behalf. Think carefully about what will motivate you to get up in the morning.

You might also skim the Help Wanted section of a large national paper, like the New York Times, and scour major online job listing sites such as www.Monster.com, www.HotJobs.com, www.JDPost.com, www.AttorneyJobs.com, or www.PSLawNet.org. Keep a running list of the jobs that sound appealing, based on your personal priorities.

As you can see, we've constructed a Self-Assessment Grid. So, in addition to filling in your career priorities, fill in the other three boxes based on your answers to the skills, subject and work environment exercises you completed on the previous pages.

Self-Assessment Grid

This grid brings together the results of the previous four exercises regarding skills, subjects of interest, preferred work environment, and career priorities. So now it's time to transfer the results of those exercises to the grid.

Skills

1

2

3

4

5

Subjects

1

2

3

4

5

Work Environment

1

2

3

4

5

Priorities

1

2

3

4

5

For some of you, this self-assessment exercise may be the first time your work preferences have been displayed together. For others, self-assessment will only raise more questions. For example, "Why can't I answer these basic questions... why am I having trouble identifying my skills... why are my priorities so hard to define... why don't I know myself better... what am I going to do with my life? This is natural, and there's no cause for panic. Still, if you filled in most, if not, all of the Grid, we recommend that you make an appointment with your undergrad career services office, and bring the Grid along. Or make an appointment with a private career counselor (see the Tool Kit for tips on finding a career counselor). Of course, we'd like to assure you that the self-assessment process is a formula for career happiness, and for knowing if the law is the right path for you. We'd like to assure you of that, but we can't. Still, what you have done here is to put in capsule form the single most important elements you need for job satisfaction. The next step is to use the information to explore various legal and non-legal jobs to see which ones offer a better fit. Hopefully, by using what you learned here, you will have a better idea of whether legal or non-legal jobs will meet your needs.

"**O**h boy, if I could do my job search again, I'd do things very differently. For one thing, I would have informational interviews with different types of attorneys so I could see what areas appealed to me and based my choices on what I liked. I really regret not pursuing legal jobs that were in line with my interests. I always loved art, but it didn't occur to me to pursue art law, or to speak with museum curators or to get involved with local arts organizations. I wish I had done all of those things during law school."—**Mimi**

"**I** decided to spend one law school summer at a public interest organization and the other at a corporate law firm so I could see the view from both sides. At my law school, there was a lot of pressure to join a big firm, so I was curious as to what all the fuss was about. That experience taught me how important it is to consider your personality before choosing a law firm. I really don't like a big bureaucracy, so I didn't like the big firm atmosphere. I think I would have been better off splitting a summer to really understand life at a big firm versus a small firm."—**Michael**

"**I** took my first post-law school job at the firm I worked for during law school. I had been a part-time clerk there, and they had an opening when I graduated. Had I known more about the firm, I wouldn't have taken the job. There were zero female partners, which wasn't a good sign. And I thought I'd get a variety of cases, but they stuck me in one practice and refused to give me other work or to let me switch practice groups. I recently left that job. When I was interviewing for a new job, I made sure to speak with new associates and former attorneys of the firm to find out if the partners truly cared about their associates' long-term happiness."—**Cara**

"**I**t's embarrassing to admit this, but I chose my first post-law school job by following the herd. I didn't know what I wanted to do, and OCI was incredibly seductive. I'm surprised I succumbed to the pressure, but OCI was the biggest game in town and it was nice to be wooed by those high-paying firms. In retrospect, I would have approach my job search, and all of law school, quite differently. I would have been more diligent about pursuing academic courses and extracurriculars that helped me find my true interests. Had I done that, I would have pursued public interest and quasi-governmental jobs. My classmates who invested their time in law school to making connections with practitioners and deepening their knowledge in a particular practice area fared a lot better— they knew what they wanted and were much more competitive candidates for the jobs they pursued."—**John**

"**W**hen I was a law student, the job search felt like a well-oiled machine—you cranked it up,

stepped right in, and got carried along. I really didn't have any specific ideas of what I wanted to do, so it was easy to do the obvious—work for a large commercial law firm. It would have been nice to hear back then, before I graduated, that there are alternatives to firm practice and alternatives to practicing as a lawyer at all. Instead, the choice seemed like "Which firm?"

"My second summer, I decided against the summer associate game and went to Paris to work for an eight-person branch office of U.S. firm Turned out to be kind of dull (they had no idea what to do with me) but it felt good to do something slightly unconventional and step off the treadmill. Of course, if I could do it all again, I would've chosen a different firm to join after graduation. I hated the one I picked. I probably should have chosen a much smaller firm with an emphasis on media/First Amendment work. And if possible, I wish I had tried to convince a publishing company to take me on in their legal department."—**Emily**

Chapter 7   A *is for* Attorneys: What They Do & Where They Work

"I'm embarrassed to admit this, but I chose my first
post-law school job by following the herd. Some of my
classmates who made a point of knowing about different
practice areas, and who made connections with working
lawyers, did a lot better. They knew what they wanted,
and were much more competitive candidates for
the jobs they pursued."

—John, attorney in a mid-sized firm

*I*n this chapter, we will explore the work that different types of lawyers do every day. Along the way, we will present what we call the Discovery Process, by which you will be able to contact members of the legal profession before deciding whether law school is right for you. To begin, we've put together a simplified overview of the legal profession, in terms of practice settings and practice areas. *Practice settings* refers to the types of organizations where lawyers work. *Practice areas* refers to the types of legal subject lawyers think about. From this information—and the information you gleaned from the Self Assessment Grid—you will begin to learn how to identify different types of lawyers.

Practice Settings

Check the settings that interest you most.

❑ **Private Law Firms.** Private law firms come in all sizes: *large* (generally, 75 or more lawyers), *medium* (25 to 75 lawyers), *small* (fewer than 25)—and, of course, solo practice. Most lawyers practice in firms of 10 or fewer attorneys. Whatever the size, some law firms handle a wide variety of legal matters for clients, while other "boutique" firms specialize in a certain practice area (such as employment law, patent law, land use and so on). In private practice, lawyers generally work in litigation or transactional practice groups. In general, large firms tend to have a more formal and intense environment than smaller firms, though some small firms work their attorneys just as hard as large ones. New lawyers in small firms often (but not always) have more responsibility and client interaction than those in large firms. If you're in private practice, billable hours and responding to clients' requests will be a big focus of your life.

Litigation attorneys are involved in lawsuits from beginning to end. They spend their days preparing for trials (poring over legal documents, deposing witness, filing motions), handling the trials themselves and negotiating settlements before or during trial (the vast majority of civil cases are settled without trial).

Transactional attorneys handle legal issues other than lawsuits, counseling clients on business and legal issues, drafting contracts, handling legal matters resulting from corporate activities such as mergers and acquisitions or drafting legal documents (such as trusts and estates) for individuals.

❏ Corporations

In-house counsel—Lawyers who work for corporations are known as *in-house counsel* or *general counsel*. They serve as internal legal advisors on a wide range of business and legal matters, handling business transactions, negotiations, drafting legal documents, and reviewing business contracts and other agreements. The larger the company (and the more complicated its business activities), the larger its legal staff. A company like IBM might have 100 or more in-house lawyers, while a start-up may have just one or two. Large corporations tend to have more formal corporate cultures, while smaller ones are often (but not always) more laid back. In-house attorneys generally manage to enjoy a better work-life balance than their law firm counterparts because they do not have billable hour requirements.

❏ Government.

Government. There are myriad roles for government lawyers at the local, state, and federal levels. Some of the main areas include:

Administrative Agencies—This includes federal, state and local government agencies such as the U.S. Department of Justice, the Environmental Protection Agency, or state securities administrators. Working on legal, policy and legislative issues, these lawyers develop expertise in specialty areas, such as tax, environmental, communications and securities law. Their responsibilities include drafting regulations, briefing agency heads and researching and monitoring legislative and policy developments. The level of formality or informality will vary from office to office, but government lawyers generally enjoy a better work-life balance than those in private practice.

The U.S. Military—Being a lawyer in the U.S. military means working for the Judge Advocate General's Corps (JAG Corp). Each branch of the military (Army, Navy, Air Force, Marines, Coast Guard) has it's own JAG Corps. JAG attorneys enjoy the opportunity to get solid hands-on trial experience and often derive a sense of meaning from working closely with their clients.

Legislative—Many lawyers in legislative practice at the federal level work on Capitol Hill, for a Member of Congress or for a congressional committee. At the state level, they work for elected officials or legislative committees. Their work typically includes drafting legislation, writing speeches, organizing and managing legislative hearings, meeting with advocacy groups, and briefing elected officials on issues. The work environment—fast-paced, highly-politicized and filled with strong personalities—isn't for everyone, but it is an exciting arena for political junkies who enjoy dealing with a variety of issues and constituencies.

❑ **Criminal Law.** At the federal level, U.S. Attorneys (as part of the U.S. Department of Justice) prosecute those accused of federal crimes. Federal public defenders represent those same individuals. At the state level, Attorneys Generals prosecute those accused of state crimes, and at the city or county level, criminal lawyers work for District Attorneys (who prosecute people accused of violating state or local criminal laws) or the Public Defender (who defend suspects). They spend much of their time dealing with clients in difficult situations and appearing in court. Most criminal law offices are fast-paced with long hours during trials.

❑ **The Judiciary.** In addition to serving as a judge, roles for lawyers in the judiciary include working as judicial law clerks or permanent staff attorneys. A judicial clerkship entails working directly for a judge for one to two years. A clerkship involves extensive legal research and writing, from drafting judicial orders to writing bench memos (a summary of the case intended to provide the judge with a picture of the legal issues presented and the proper disposition of the matter). Permanent staff attorneys can work in the courts for years, primarily involved in legal research and writing for one or more judges. Judges are everywhere, at the federal, state and local levels. Most hear a wide variety of cases, but some specialty courts are devoted to one area, such as bankruptcy, tax or family law. Working in the judiciary is a great fit for those who enjoy legal research and writing, who don't feel the need to deal with clients and who want to work closely with a judge. In general, the judicial environment tends to be formal (at least when the judge is around) and people tend to work an eight-hour day (though some judges work their clerks harder than others).

❑ **Public Interest.** Public-interest lawyers represent the indigent, elderly and disabled, and they may also advocate for public-policy changes. They generally practice in non-profit public-interest organizations, such as Legal Aid, the American Civil Liberties Union or the EarthJustice Institute. They may also work in for-profit firms that practice civil rights law, union-side labor law and plaintiff-side employment-discrimination law. These groups tend to focus on one or two areas, such as children's issues, women's issues, civil rights, immigration or the environment. Some public-interest lawyers work directly with clients (counseling them or representing them in court) while others are engaged in issue advocacy, lobbying, public education, and litigation. Most (but not all) public-interest organizations are relatively small, have a fairly casual work environment, and they are generally run by people with a shared sense of mission who want to make a personal difference in the world.

❑ **Academia.** Lawyers who work in academic settings hold a variety of positions such as teaching (full-time or as adjunct faculty members), managing an administrative department (such as student services or career services), or working as an in-house attorney for the school. Academic environments tend to be relatively casual, 9-to-5 workplaces that are great for individuals who enjoy working with (or at least being surrounded by) students. An added benefit is having access to visiting speakers and interesting programs for faculty and students.

❑ **Law-Related Positions.** Some typical law-related positions include: mediation, employee relations, alternative dispute resolution (ADR), lobbying, government relations, non-lawyer positions in law firms (recruiting, human resources, marketing) or working for a company that provides products or services to the legal profession. These and other law-related jobs are good for individuals with an interest in some aspect of the legal profession but who don't want to practice law. For example: they might use their counseling and negotiation skills in alternative dispute resolution or mediation; use their oral and written advocacy skills in lobbying; or use their business skills in a company that serves the legal market.

Now that you're familiar with the kinds of settings lawyers can work in, take a look at your five favorite subjects and begin to assemble a list of attorneys

1. _____

2. _____

3. _____

4. _____

5. _____

who work in related practice areas (e.g., tax, intellectual property, family law, corporate law, estate planning). The following chart provides an overview of major practice areas:

Practice Areas

Check the areas that interest you most

❑ **Admiralty.** *Admiralty law* involves the body of laws governing navigation and shipping. So *admiralty lawyers* deal with litigation when disputes or accidents arise (think: Exxon Valdez). They also advise clients on legal issues (such as the use of bodies of water) and draft and review contracts and other legal agreements. Lawyers in firms or in-house handle legal matters for clients in the shipping industry (like a cruise line) or for the government (like the U.S. Navy or Coast Guard). Admiralty law is great for people with an abiding interest in the seas and it's role in commerce.

❑ **Aviation.** *Aviation lawyers* deal with legal issues that arise in the not-always-friendly skies. Some handle litigation related to plane crashes, injuries to people or property incurred during flights, or in enforcement proceedings with the Federal Aviation Administration (the agency that oversees aviation laws). They also advise clients on legal issues related to purchasing and operating planes and building airports. Their clients could be individuals (think: John Travolta) or major airlines (Southwest). The happiest aviation attorneys have a genuine interest in the air-travel industry.

❑ **Bankruptcy.** When an individual (think: M.C. Hammer) or an organization (like Enron) can't meet it's inancial obligations, *bankruptcy lawyers* get involved.

Whether they represent debtors (who owe money) or creditors (who are owed money), bankruptcy lawyers try to work out a way for the debtor to repay the creditor (at least in part). Failing that, they initiate bankruptcy proceedings. Bankruptcy attorneys may work in firms, for corporations or banks, or for the government (think: Internal Revenue Service). Bankruptcy is a good field for those who relish financial problem-solving and client counseling.

❑ **Corporate.** *Corporate attorneys* handle a variety of different legal issues for business. They represent clients in litigation (think: Microsoft), draft legal documents related to business transactions (like mergers and acquisitions) and advise clients on myriad legal issues (such as employment and safety). Two key differences between working for a firm versus working for a corporation are that in-house attorneys have just one client (the company) and don't have billable-hour requirements. Corporate law is a good field for those interested in all facets of a company's business dealings and who can work well with various corporate departments and personalities.

❑ **Criminal.** *Criminal lawyers* prosecute or defend those accused of crimes against people (think: murder, assault, rape), drug crimes, organized crime or economic crimes (such as securities fraud). Unlike civil litigators, criminal attorneys spend a good deal of time in court. They also devote a substantial amount of their workday to counseling clients (who are usually stressed), conducting factual investigations and interviewing witnesses. Criminal law is a good fit for someone who's comfortable with counseling highly agitated clients, making frequent court appearances and handling pressures inherent in cases when an individual's personal freedom is at stake.

❑ **Entertainment and Sports.** Some *entertainment* and *sports lawyers* represent "talent"—actors, singers, conductors, musicians and athletes. They assist with a wide range of legal matters, such as drafting and negotiating contracts, advising on tax and estate planning, and intervening if a client gets in trouble (think: Mike Tyson). Many entertainment and sports attorneys work as solo practitioners or in entertainment- or sports-law boutique firms. Others work for entertainment or sports companies, handling legal issues related to sporting and entertainment events, or the distribution of albums and films. This field is good for those who enjoy negotiating and reading the fine print and who can adeptly handle high-profile clients with colorful personalities.

❑ **Environmental.** *Environmental lawyers* in government agencies (like the Environmental Protection Agency) are responsible for drafting and enforcing environmental laws. Lawyers in private firms may advise corporate clients (say, a logging company) on how to comply with environmental regulations, or they may represent groups seeking to enforce environmental laws toward a specific end (say, saving the spotted owl). Lawyers in public-interest organizations (like EarthJustice Legal Defense Fund) engage in policy advocacy, public education and litigation related to various environmental issues. People who thrive in this field have a deep interest in environmental issues, and enjoy reading regulations and working in a field with zealous advocates on both sides.

❑ **Family Law.** *Family-law attorneys* generally work as solo practitioners or in small firms. They assist individuals with their most personal and important life issues, such as divorce, custody, property division, prenuptial agreements and adoption. Not surprisingly, family-law attorneys spend a great deal of time counseling clients, drafting documents, making court appearances and negotiating with opposing counsel. Family law attorneys who are best-suited for this work are adept at counseling clients through some of life's most challenging events and are able to shoulder their clients' emotional baggage without carrying it home with them.

❑ **Immigration.** Some *immigration lawyers* who work in private practice or for public-interest organizations serve clients who want to leave one country and move to another, or who want to become a citizen. They draft all legal documents and counsel them through the proceedings involved in their case. Other attorneys who represent global corporations (like GM) advise clients on issues such as employment practices relating to foreign workers. Lawyers who work for the government (say, at the Immigration and Naturalization Service) draft and oversee the enforcement of immigration laws. Immigration law is a good match for those who enjoy using language skills and are interested in immigration policy.

❑ **Intellectual Property.** *Intellectual Property (IP) lawyers* are involved in the protection of inventions and artistic and scientific creations (such as music, art and computer software). In law firms and corporations, IP lawyers counsel clients, and draft and file documents such as contracts, patents, trademarks and copyrights. When the provisions in any of these documents are infringed, IP lawyers start suing. In government, IP lawyers work in agencies—such as the U.S. Patent and Trademark Office—reviewing patents and enforcing regulations. IP law is particularly suitable for people with technical backgrounds or, at the very least, a strong desire to learn about technology.

❏ **International.** In the private sector, *international lawyers* in firms represent corporate clients (like McDonald's) who do business overseas. They advise on legal issues relating to their business activities (such as mergers), and negotiate and draft legal documents. In the public sector, government attorneys work for agencies (the U.S. State Department, say, or the United Nations) that handle international policy issues. In public-interest organizations, attorneys advocate, educate and litigate around international public-policy issues (like human rights or landmines). International law is a good fit for people with strong language skills and a strong interest in international business or policy issues, and who don't mind working while in a foreign country.

❏ **Labor and Employment.** *Labor lawyers* working for firms, corporations or unions represent either workers or management, and handle various issues like plant closings, wages, work hours and on-the-job safety. *Employment lawyers* generally handle litigation surrounding claims like employment discrimination, sexual harassment and breach of contract. Both types of lawyers in private practice advise corporate clients on how to avoid employee lawsuits, draft legal documents, negotiate contracts, conduct collective bargaining agreements and resolve employer-employee disputes. Government labor lawyers, in agencies such as the National Labor Relations Board or the Equal Employment Opportunity Commission, draft regulations, ensure compliance with labor laws and evaluate individual employee or union complaints against employers. Lawyers who thrive in these areas are skilled at counseling stressed-out clients whose livelihood may be at stake (or who are accused of wrongdoings like sexual harassment) and have a deep interest in civil rights and other legal issues in the workplace.

❏ **Litigation.** Litigators are *trial attorneys* who handle all aspects of a lawsuit for their clients. That includes researching and drafting legal documents, taking depositions, interviewing witnesses, reviewing case documents (lots of them), conducting trials (sometimes) and negotiating and settling cases before trial (again, 90% of cases settle before trial). Some litigators in firms and government agencies handle a wide variety of matters, while others specialize in niche areas such as patent, employment or business litigation. Litigation tends to be a good fit for those who can handle adversarial proceedings, meeting deadlines, juggling voluminous amounts of documents, counseling clients involved in lawsuits and negotiating with opposing counsel. Not surprisingly, litigation isn't for everyone.

❑ **Public Interest.** *Public-interest attorneys* who represent individuals (such as indigent clients) assist them with their legal matters, which can include drafting legal documents (like orders of protection or wills), appearing in court or at hearings, and counseling them through any legal proceedings (eviction, say, or child-custody). Other public-interest lawyers do not work with clients, engaging instead in advocacy and public education on behalf of issues such as women's rights, children's welfare or the environment. Their work centers around research and writing, policy analysis and lobbying and litigating on behalf of the "good guys." Public-interest law is a fit for mission-driven individuals with a commitment to championing causes and serving individuals.

❑ **Real Estate.** *Real estate attorneys* mostly handle transactions, such as the sale or purchase of residential or commercial real estate. They are responsible for negotiating the terms and drafting all documents related to these transactions, and counseling clients throughout the process. They may also advise corporate clients (think: Donald Trump) on issues involved with real-estate development projects (think: casinos). Real estate is great for those with an affinity for reading the fine print, and a talent for counseling people through major transactions.

❑ **Securities Law.** *Securities lawyers* handle legal issues related to stocks, bonds, mutual funds, limited partnerships and other investments. In private practice, lawyers involved with litigation may represent individuals (think: Martha Stewart), corporations (like IM Clone) or financial institutions (such as Merrill Lynch). Or they may represent shareholders who are suing a company in which they hold stock. Transactional lawyers (who don't do lawsuits) negotiate and draft all legal documents related to the sale of securities, public offerings and other transactions. Government lawyers work for agencies like the Securities and Exchange Commission, which enforces securities laws and investigates securities fraud. This area of law is a good fit for those with a curiosity about the securities industry and legal issues concerning individuals and institutions, and who can like reading the *Wall Street Journal*.

❏ **Tax Law.** *Tax lawyers* in private practice counsel individuals (think: Willie Nelson) or corporations (like MCI Worldcom) on a variety of tax and business planning issues. They assess with clients' financial affairs, create tax-planning strategies to lower clients' tax burden and analyze the tax consequences of various business decisions, advising clients accordingly. Tax lawyers may work in law firms, corporations, accounting firms or for everyone's favorite government agency, the IRS. Tax law is a good field for those with the interest (and stamina) to learn the ins and outs of tax law and enthusiasm for counseling clients regarding financial matters.

❏ **Trusts and Estates.** *Trusts and estates attorneys* help clients structure their financial affairs so their assets are distributed as they wish after death. This entails consulting with clients and drafting estate-planning documents such as wills and living trusts. They work for individuals (think: Bill Gates) or institutions (like the Bill and Melinda Gates Foundation). Lawyers who enjoy their work in trusts and estates have a deep interest in, and a knack for, financial and tax planning and have a good bedside manner when dealing with strong personalities and family politics.

In the previous chapter, you identified your skills, interests, career priorities and preferred work environment. Now, by identifying the practice settings and practice areas of greatest interest, you begin to close the circle. If you pay special attention to your Preferred Work Environment and your Career Priorities, nothing should prevent you from beginning to making contact with lawyers in settings, and in jobs, that interest you.

Here are some considerations regarding preferred work environment:

If you would prefer a casual or non-bureaucratic environment, or a small organization, you'll want to talk to lawyers in public-interest organizations, small law firms or small companies.

If an intense, formal, deadline-driven environment is more your speed, you'll want to seek out lawyers in large law firms and large corporations.

If you prefer creative environments, your target should be lawyers who work in creative entities like entertainment, the arts, or in technology companies.

And if you like entrepreneurial environments, seek out lawyers in small companies and law firms, and any type of not-for profit organization.

Here are some considerations regarding career priorities:

> If you listed a large starting salary, don't waste too much time seeking out lawyers who have public-interest, government or academic jobs (though these jobs pay substantially more over time). Instead, focus on lawyers in big firms and corporations.
>
> If you prefer a 9-to-5 work schedule, the kinds of lawyers you want to interview are those who work in government agencies, public-interest organizations or small firms that make work-life balance a priority.
>
> If you have a need for autonomy, your ideal targets are solo practitioners, or lawyers who work for small firms or companies.

These are generalizations, of course, so you'll want to investigate specific organizations to see if they meet your needs.

Now, you're ready for the next step: Make a list of specific individuals who work in the practice settings that interest you. Of course, unless you happen to know a lot of lawyers, it's important to get help. So ask yourself:

> Do any of my family members or friends know lawyers?
> Do any of my undergrad professors or advisers know lawyers?
> Are any of my former employers lawyers, or do they know lawyers?
> Can my local law school connect me with alumni who are lawyers?

We're willing to bet that the answer to a few of these questions is yes, and we'll further bet that many of these "strangers" will be more than willing to give you a half hour of their time. From this process, you should be able to find attorneys with whom you will want to have an informational interview. What is an *informational interview?*

The Discovery Process

Speaking with lawyers and non-lawyers is absolutely essential to helping you make a well-educated decision about whether to become a lawyer, or something else. For some of you, your only exposure to legal practice will have been *The Practice,* and the only lawyers you know are Ally McBeal and her short-skirted colleagues. Many students enter law school professing an interest in, say, criminal law, but have never had a single conversation with a criminal lawyer.

Informational interviews are what they seem—conversations with subject-matter experts in and out of the legal field who can provide information about their job or field. Informational interviews are all about mining for information, not—repeat, not—a veiled attempt to get a job. In addition to helping you make an informed decision about becoming a lawyer, informational interviews can also provide less obvious benefits. For example, if you find out what lawyers do, and you identify several different jobs you'd think you'd enjoy, you can enter law school with a greater sense of direction and a game plan for pursuing jobs that excite you. Informational interviews can also help generate more creative ideas of things you might do in a legal or non-legal profession. Too many prospective law students don't look at career-building broadly enough, overlooking terrific jobs by limiting themselves to a handful of obvious paths. So, think about your passions (food, travel, sports, politics) and speak with people in legal and non-legal jobs in those areas.

For example, if you love wine, seek out attorneys who represent vineyards, or with non-attorneys who manage wineries, or handle public relations for them, or who work in other non-legal capacities. Remember, if all this seems like a lot of work, keep in mind that informational interviews can also help you make contacts that can be very valuable in landing your ideal job. Think about it—the more people you speak with and who know what you're interested in, the more likely it is someone will help lead you to a future job whether or not you decide to attend law school.

Here's a real-world example of what we're talking about:

When my co-author was in law school, she was passionate about politics, particularly campaign-finance reform. Deborah decided she wanted to work for a campaign-finance reform organization during the summer after her first year of law school. Somehow, she mustered the courage to ask for an informational interview with Ellen Miller, then-executive director of a national campaign-finance education and watchdog group. Deborah sent an email to Ellen, explaining that she was a law student with an interest in learning more about campaign finance reform organizations, and requested a 15-minute telephone conversation with her. Their conversation went something like this:

Deb—Hi Ellen, thanks for your time. I'm a first-year law student with a political background and I'm interested in working for a campaign-finance-reform advocacy group this summer. Given that you're a guru in this field, I thought you'd be the perfect person to ask for ideas of organizations to contact regarding internships.

Ellen—Wow, what great timing! I'm actually starting a new campaign-finance-reform organization right now, and we'll need help for the summer. You should come work for me. Send me your resume and then let's talk.

Deborah ended up getting the job and having a terrific summer. She also learned an important lesson—you can create valuable opportunities simply by contacting people for information. Although this scenario may not happen every day, it's more typical than you think. So if you're complaining that informational interviews take time, you're right. But they also just happen to be one of the smartest ways you can use your time before deciding to invest in law school and a legal career. Spending, say, two or three weeks conducting informational interviews with 10 lawyers and 10 non-lawyers is easier than putting in three years in law school and joining the bar when you have serious doubts about both.

Here are some pointers for getting started: First, refer back to your Self-Assessment Grid. Use the results to help you brainstorm the various types of lawyers and nonlawyers whose jobs and work environment meets your own needs. In our experience, the key to successful informational interviews is to seek out individuals whose jobs you might enjoy yourself. Besides, you'll have more fun speaking with people who have jobs you're excited to learn more about. So, flip back to your Self-Assessment Grid, and see what your preferences can tell you about how to kick-start your informational interviews.

For example:

Skills—If you listed negotiating, talk to mediators and litigators. If you listed legal research and writing, talk to judicial law clerks and law firm associates. If you listed client counseling, talk to attorneys who work directly with clients (such as legal services or estate planning lawyers). If you listed drafting contracts or other legal documents, talk to transactional attorneys.

Subjects—If you listed environmental issues, talk to people at non-profits, government agencies, or law firms with environmental practice groups. If you listed international issues, talk to Peace Corps volunteers, and people in think tanks, government and non-profit organizations.

Working environment—If you listed a creative work environment, talk to someone at an advertising agency, a cultural organization or public relations firm. If you listed a formal work environment, talk to someone at a corporation, government agency, think tank or foundation.

Career priorities—If you listed work-life balance, talk to people in government agencies, non-profits, academia or anywhere else where people seem to have a life outside of work. If you listed making a lot of money, talk to people in investment banking, business or real estate. If you listed public service, talk to people in non-profits, government agencies and foundations.

Now that you understand informational interviewing (see page 207 of the Tool Kit for additional pointers), it's time to move on to the next chapter and the final step: obtaining real-world work experience in legal and non-legal environments.

Chapter 8

T is for Try it Out:
Get Some Practice Before Getting Into Practice

"I never set foot in a law firm before

I became a lawyer. Anyone thinking

about law school should definitely work

at a law firm for a year. I had no idea

so many boring details would be a part

of my life.**"**

—Josh, publishing executive and former attorney at a large firm

*I*t's hard to get lawyers to agree on anything. But nearly every one we interviewed did agree on this: prospective law students need real-world work experience in legal and non-legal jobs *before* deciding whether to attend law school. Although it seems like a total no-brainer, relatively few people actually do it. Of course, some college graduates take a day-job they dislike—or go skiing for an extended period—and then persuade themselves that "taking a year off" in this way has somehow prepared them for law school. Sorry, it doesn't work that way.

By "work experience," we mean actually working in legal and non-legal organizations that interest you. In fact, unless you've actually worked in a legal setting—or worked very closely with attorneys—you have no idea what a legal job is really like. That doesn't mean you won't eventually thrive as a lawyer; it just means you're clueless right now about what a legal education trains you to do. That's why one of the most important pieces of advice in this book is to put yourself in a position to do what lawyers do so you can see if you like it.

You can work full-time or part-time, paid or volunteer, but the key is to get at least some experience in some legal environment. In an ideal world, you would get multiple jobs in multiple settings so you could make the best evaluation. But we're not dreamers. Even one job on the support staff of a diversified law firm will help clarify what you really want to do with a law degree...if anything—by giving you a realistic picture of what different practice areas involve. Here's how it worked for a friend of ours:

Julie gave a great deal of thought to attending law school. But it was a huge commitment, and she didn't want to burn through her parents' money without getting a look at the profession first. So, soon after graduation, she went to work as a legal assistant in a private law firm. She hated it—the hours, the people, the work itself. But something about the law—the intellectual stimulation, the potential for doing good in the world—inspired her. That one insight helped Julie understand that if she was still enthusiastic after her law firm experience, the legal profession might still be the right one for her. Because she was interested in public-interest law, Julie eventually left her law firm job to work at a domestic-violence shelter, and later for a legal aid society. By the time she entered law school a year later, Julie understood the legal community much better, and had developed an awareness of the niche in which she was interested. For Julie, law school turned out to be a relatively easy experience because she knew what she was getting into, and what she wanted out of it. We should add that, as a law student, Julie helped several public-interest legal groups raise thousands of dollars so they could help other students finance their public-interest jobs. After she graduated, she landed a two-year public-sector fellowship and now happily works in a U.S. Attorney's Office.

Imagine what *you* could accomplish if you pursued what truly excited you. We understand the inclination to start law school immediately, and to not wait a year or two. But consider how much more time, energy—and money—going to law school requires. That's why working in law *before* law school is a win-win proposition. If you like the profession, you won't regret having worked for a year or two before school. "Working in a legal environment was the deciding factor in my going to law school," says Kristin, a first-year law student. "I interned at a public defender's office and loved it. I saw great lawyers in action who were passionate about their work and about helping people. I also got exposure to what lawyers actually do—the reading and writing—and liked the work itself."

> **"I** wanted to get into criminal law. But once the OCI process got going, I went with the flow. Before I knew it, I was a corporate lawyer. I had no idea that the firms that interview at school are only a small slice of the legal work out there."
>
> —Seth, attorney at a large firm

On the other hand, if you find that you really don't like the profession—or those who practice it—working for at least one year will have saved you several grueling years and tens of thousands of dollars. "I got an internship at a law firm the summer before I was to begin law school," says Caren, a journalist. "After two months I realized that lawyering was the *last* thing I wanted to do. If I hadn't done that internship, I'd still be repaying student loans for a career I wish I had never pursued."

We'll hope we've convinced you to *date* the law before marrying it—that is, to work in the field for a couple of years (or even a couple of months) before you commit to law school. But what kind of job should you look for? Well, the answer depends on what skills you have now, what you're interested in doing, and where you look. In the previous chapter, we explored various practice areas. In the section below, we want to show you the myriad jobs you might pursue in various legal settings. You'll be surprised at how many options you have.

Where You Can Get Legal Experience

Check the jobs that interest you most

❏ **Private Law Firms.** *Paralegal (small firm)*—Small firms have fewer non-lawyer support-staff positions, so you have the potential to play multiple roles and have a greater range of responsibilities. From firm to firm, your title may vary (paralegal, legal assistant, law clerk, legal secretary), but in this role you would handle all sorts of administrative tasks (e.g., filing, administrative work, managing attorneys' calendars), as well as more substantive projects such as organizing documents, drafting letters and other documents, assisting with research, interviewing and communicating with clients and preparing trial exhibits. One advantage of working in a small office is that you're more likely to interact with clients and work closely with attorneys than would be possible at a large firm. To get a job with a small firm, call the firm directly and speak with the office manager or legal secretary, or an attorney there.

❏ **Large firm.** In contrast to a small firm, where you can be a jack of all trades, large law firms have more defined roles for non-lawyer support staff. To land a job with a large firm, start with the human resources department. Here are the most common jobs for people who want to check out law:

Paralegal—Paralegals assist lawyers with various administrative projects such as filing court documents, proofreading documents, organizing, cataloging and collating documents, and with more substantive projects such as drafting correspondence and legal documents and assisting with research. They are generally assigned to one practice group (corporate, litigation, bankruptcy, etc.), so they'll assist lawyers in that department with a variety of cases. Even the more administrative tasks will give you a sense of the documents that lawyers read and write and what it's like to work on a lawsuit or transaction. If you wish to become a paralegal because you're thinking about law school, it's not necessary to take a professional paralegal course. Those are for individuals who intend to make a career as a professional paralegal.

Litigation Assistant—Although the title may vary from firm to firm (file clerk, case assistant), the role of the litigation assistant is largely administrative, helping lawyers manage documents relating to a particular case. Often, litigation assistants are assigned to one major lawsuit that involves a tremendous number of documents (from depositions and discovery) and they are responsible for their organization. Although spending months, or even years, working only on one case can give you a limited perspective and may not be a great fit for people who need a lot of variety, it can still offer a valuable picture of what a major lawsuit involves.

Library Assistant—If you work in a law firm's library, you'll help the library and lawyers function smoothly. Your duties may include re-shelving books, responding to basic research requests, assisting lawyers with online research and suggesting resources to them with their research. This position is good for someone who enjoys combing through shelves and databases, offering both a sense of what legal research entails and exposure to the substantive topics lawyers deal with.

Proofreader—The proofreader reads over law firm documents until they are error-free. These jobs tend to have flexible hours and need not be full-time, so it's possible to do this job along with another one. Proofreading offers a good exposure to the types of legal documents that attorneys read and write, and could be interesting if you enjoy what you're reading. However, if don't enjoy reading legalese, or if you prefer having a lot of interpersonal contact in your work, proofreading could become tedious quickly.

Litigation Support—The job of litigation support is to create and manage systems that keep track of large volumes of documents. For example, it might require setting up a database to track documents in a class-action lawsuit involving hundreds or thousands of plaintiffs. Although this job isn't as useful as being a paralegal—because you won't work directly with lawyers—it could be a good way to get your foot in the door if you have a technical background.

Legal Temp—If it's challenging to get hired by a law firm, or if you don't like commitment, you can always sign on with a legal temp agency. These agencies are responsible for sending you to law firms or corporate legal departments where you will work on a temporary basis (several days to several months) and assist the lawyers with various administrative projects. The work of a legal temp is similar to what paralegals do. You might work solely on one case, or on a variety of cases, but this can be a good way to get an overview of different aspects of practice and different environments and meet a lot of lawyers.

❏ Corporations

Assistant to the Contracts Administrator—Many corporations have contracts administrators whose responsibility it is to handle the company's legal documents (contracts, government filings, etc.) As the administrator's assistant, you might get to assist in the drafting, proofreading and organizing of various corporate legal documents, offering exposure to the scope and nature of corporate legal affairs. To get such a job, try contacting the contracts administrator directly.

Legal Department Assistant—Many corporate legal departments have assistants who help the General Counsel and other in-house lawyers with administrative tasks such as organizing and drafting correspondence and other legal documents, and communicating with various corporate departments. Even if your projects are largely administrative, you would become familiar with the matters that in-house lawyers handle. If you work for a large corporation, you may get to work with more lawyers and get exposed to a wider array of issues. If you work at a smaller company you may very well get more responsibility and could work more closely with the General Counsel. Don't worry if a company tells you it doesn't have a formal intern program. Many people have successfully created their own internship opportunity. Again, contact the General Counsel or another attorney in the legal department, before going through HR.

❏ Government

Agency Intern—If you want to check out government work, there are plenty of internships (paid or unpaid) at the federal, state and local levels. Like most agency internships, you would be involved in both administrative projects and more substantive assignments, such as preparing for hearings and other agency events, drafting public education materials, monitoring legislative and policy developments, and research and writing. To get a job, try using a back-door approach first (by directly contacting the agency that interests you and speaking with a staff attorney) before you try the front-door approach (the official job site for the U.S. Federal Government, www.usajobs.opm.gov).

Legislative Intern—If you're an intern in the legislature, you could work for an elected official or a legislative committee. Although you'll likely do your fair share of administrative work, you would also get involved with research and writing projects, drafting correspondence, responding to constituent requests and planning press and political events. Contact the member of Congress' Chief of Staff or, if you're contacting a committee, the Chief Counsel.

Criminal Law Intern—People who want to get exposure to criminal law generally work in the office of a District Attorney, Public Defender, a state Attorney General, or a defense attorney in private practice. In addition to standard administrative projects, such as organizing trial documents, you may get involved with interviewing witnesses, gathering and evaluating evidence, and observing depositions and court proceedings. To get a job, simply contact the government agency or firm that interests you.

Judicial Intern—Landing an internship with a judge when you're not yet a law student is unlikely because few judges accept interns who aren't studying to be lawyers. That said, we know some prospective law students who did manage to land a judicial internship because they had some sort of personal connection. These interns did mostly administrative work, but also got exposure to legal research and writing, and to court proceedings. But even if you don't have an inside track, you can always write a few judges and ask to intern on a short-term basis, or ask to shadow one of their clerks for a few hours or a full day.

❏ Public Interest Organization

Staff Assistant—People who work for public interest groups tend to wear a lot of hats and juggle multiple responsibilities. So, as an entry-level staff assistant (or program associate), you're likely to handle a combination of administrative and substantive projects. If your organization provides direct legal services, you'll be interviewing clients, assessing their legal issues and needs, and drafting corre-spondence and other documents on their behalf. If your group engages in advocacy and public education, you'll assist with research projects, track legisla-tive and policy developments, and handle public outreach. If the organization is involved in litigation, you'll assist the lawyers with organizing and drafting documents, pre-trial preparation, and research and writing. To get the job, contact the organization directly, ideally by connecting with a staff attorney.

❑ Academia

Teaching Assistant—If you think you'd enjoy being a law professor, try for a job as a teaching assistant at a college or community college, ideally working for a professor who teaches a law-related course. You would assist the professor with planning lessons, grading papers and responding to student questions. Another way to immerse yourself in legal academia is to get a job in a law school, either working in the law library or as a research assistant for a law professor. On a personal note, a friend of ours got interested in legal studies while working as a sign-language interpreter at a law school. After a year "signing" Constitutional Law classes, reading class assignments, and discussing course materials with the professor, Samantha decided to attend law school herself. Three years later, she became a public-interest lawyer.

Legal Intern at an Academic Institution—If you're interested in an academic environment, but not in working as an instructor, you could intern in the legal department of an undergraduate or graduate school. Aside from administrative duties, you could assist with research and writing projects. This job can offer exposure not only to traditional legal areas but also government regulation and public policy issues.

❑ Law-Related Fields.
Some typical law-related options include mediation, lobbying, alternative dispute resolution, government relations, non-lawyer positions in law firms (recruiting, human resources, marketing, etc.), or working for a company that provides products or services to the legal profession. As with any entry-level job, you'll probably do a lot of administrative work, but you can also get substantive projects that will give you a sense of the work. For example, if you work for a lobbying firm, you can assist with monitoring legislation, research and writing projects, attending legislative hearings and meeting with interest groups. If you work in corporate human resources, you could be involved

with researching and drafting documents, and educating employees about their legal rights.

Internships—Whatever law-related job you pursue—in the public, private or public interest sectors—it may be an uphill battle to get a paid staff position. But if you can afford to work for little or no money, do so. You may as well work somewhere whose work excites you. Some prospective law students we know have done internships with their favorite sports teams, publishing companies, television networks, even at the White House and the United Nations. If you cannot afford to work for little or no salary, see if you can combine a part-time unpaid legal internship with part-time paid work (for instance, three days unpaid work and two days paid work). Or, if you're still in school, try to get academic credit for your internship experience during the summer or school year.

Once you've lined up a law-related job or internship, it's important to make the most of it. That means making sure your job helps you answer two questions—Will I get a clear picture of what lawyers do, and would I enjoy doing similar work?

The Legal Jobs that Interest You Most

1. _____
2. _____
3. _____
4. _____
5. _____

Choice Challenges Revisited

Remember anchoring?

If you still feel *anchored* to the notion that you must be a lawyer, then working in the law beforehand will provide a necessary reality check. Better still, it will help you learn about the legal job search process that puts so many law students in panic mode. And, beside the contacts you make, your pre-law work experience will provide you with an insider's understanding into the way firms operate, and what they look for in summer associates. Of course, if you find after working or volunteering in the law that the profession is not for you, that insight will be invaluable. It will help fortify you against the herd mentality that drives so many people into law school.

Some of you are probably still protesting, *"Why can't I just wait until I get to law school, and then figure out what I want to do? After all, I'll have two summers and three years to think about it?"* You could, but the risk would be great. Look at it this way—it might take two summers to finally realize you don't want to be a lawyer. By then, it will be too late to get your time and money back. In addition, some pretty powerful forces in law school could sway you to choose the wrong jobs.

So, we'll say it once more for emphasis:

If you are not absolutely, positively, totally, genuinely sold on law school (but your parents are leaning on you to get a JD), then working first is your best defense. Getting experience in a legal setting can help you make the case to your parents that law isn't the right track for you, or help you discover that it is. It worked for Molly. She faced tremendous pressure from her lawyer-father to attend law school. Molly enjoyed research and writing, but she felt the law was just too adversarial for her taste. Instead, she was passionate about education. So, for the first time in her life, Molly ignored her dad's advice, and consulted a career counselor. How did things turn out? Molly taught for a couple of years in the Teach for America Program, and went on to write a book about education while getting a Ph.D.—at the ripe old age of 26.

Imagine what you could accomplish if you pursued something that truly excited you.

Regret Aversion

One final, but important, point: It's not good enough to just get law-related experience before you make your decision about law school. You need non-legal work experience, too. Now, if you're thinking that sounds totally unrealistic or impractical, hear us out. It's not just about finding what suits you better, and it's not just about saving you a fortune in tuition. Getting legal *and* nonlegal work experience can help you avoid one of the most common causes of unhappiness later in life— regret. To illustrate, we offer a short hypothetical, a version of one of the more famous experiments in the field of Behavioral Economics and Decision Science.

Imagine two people, Mr. A and Ms. B:

Mr. A goes to the movies and, upon arriving, wins $100 as the theater's 100,000th customer.

Ms. B goes to another theater on the same night. When she arrives, she wins $150 as the millionth-and-first customer. The woman right before her won $1,000 as the millionth customer.

Who would you rather be . . . Mr. A or Ms. B?

More of us would choose Ms. B. After all, she wins $150 against Mr. A's $100. Amazingly, though, almost as many people say they would rather be Mr. A. Why? Because they put themselves in the place of Ms. B and think, "*If I had only arrived at the theater a few seconds earlier I would have won $1,000 instead of $150.*" And rather than face those feelings, they choose Mr. A over Ms. B. The issue here is a powerful force in life called Regret Aversion. It refers to a tendency to make choices that help us avoid feeling pangs of regret or responsibility for negative outcomes.

Research shows that in the short run people regret actions, but over the long run they regret *inactions*. That is, if you ask people what they regret over, say, the past year, they will tell you things they did (action). But if you ask them what they regret over the past 10 years, they will talk about things they didn't do (inaction). Here's the point: Any regret you might feel as a lawyer later in life will only be compounded if you don't give yourself at least a year to pursue whatever dream you might have, however unrealistic. Many of the unhappy lawyers we interviewed for this book explained that when they were entering law school, they never considered pursuing other careers. And they regret it today.

Now, you may ask: What if I choose to not to go law school and regret that in 10 years? Yes, there's always that risk. But if you skip law school because you've tried working in a law-related job for a year, we're pretty certain that regret won't be a factor later. Why? Because you will have tried the law, or at least a version of it, so you won't be consumed with what-ifs. And if you later develop an overwhelming desire to get a JD, law school will always be there. In fact, law students who enter the legal profession later in life (and law schools these days *are* seeing more students in their 30s and 40s) generally tend to be more focused in law school, and more fulfilled once they get out.

One of the best stories we know about pursuing your dreams happens to involve a pair of twins we know—Jason and Randy Sklar, both of whom are stand-up comics. When the twins graduated from college, they had been admitted to law school but were more interested in moving to New York City to pursue comedy. Naturally, their parents were more interested in them going to law school, but the twins managed a plea bargain: they would try comedy for a year and go to law school if things didn't work out. Jason and Randy certainly didn't achieve overnight success, but their year in the comedy trenches convinced them that they were on the right path. After a couple of years of day jobs and nighttime comedy gigs, they landed their own series on MTV and their careers took off. Since then, they've had regular standup gigs, TV, film, and commercial work, their own Comedy Central special, and are currently developing and hosting a show on ESPN. There are no guarantees in show business except one—in the case of Jason and Randy Sklar, they're definitely not going to law school anytime soon.

Hopefully, you see our reasoning and will be open to checking out some non-legal careers that interest you. With that in mind, here are several suggestions:

Work for a year each in a legal and non-legal job That's a two-year commitment; hardly a lifetime.

Work in one setting and get part-time experience in the other. For example, if you snare a job as a paralegal, volunteer once or twice a week (or a few times a month) in a non-legal organization that sparks your interest. At the very least, take a class in a field that excites you, or attend an industry seminar.

Check out legal and non-legal roles in the same organization. If you land a job in, say, the marketing department of a company, ask (after being there a while) if you can spend one day a week or a few hours a month in the legal department.

However you approach your pre-law school work experience, consider the words of John Greenleaf Whittier, the famous 19th century poet who wrote, "*For of all the sad words of tongue or pen, the saddest are these . . . what might have been!*"

The Devil's Advocate Says...

Talk to strangers—Speak with all sorts of people who can help with your career decisions. Sometimes this will mean family, friends and peers, but you will also have to ask strangers. It's easier for some than for others because of shyness (i.e., knowing who to ask) and practicality (i.e., knowing what to ask). We can help with the practical (see Tool Kit, page x), but personality issues are trickier. Still, we can promise that most people are willing to give strangers a few minutes or hours of their time if approached with the right pitch in the right circumstances. But you do have to ask.

Take your time—Many students tell us they chose law school because they didn't have time to research other options—they were too busy cramming for the LSATs and completing law school applications. But many realized later that if they'd spent the same number of hours having informational interviews, they might have chosen a different career path or entered law school with better direction. So before you invest time applying to law school, spend time researching it and other career paths.

Get psyched—Many unhappy lawyers say they wished they hadn't buckled under parental pressure to go to law school. The best way to deal with parents is to find some other career path you're genuinely excited about. If you can argue with conviction that another path is better, your parents are more likely to back off about law.

Less is more—Your legal education will cost less if you work beforehand and save more. The more you save, the less you borrow. The less you borrow, the smaller your loan interest payments will be. And the less you owe, the more options you'll have ... because you're less likely to feel obligated to take a high-paying legal job just to pay off your loans. This reasoning is especially valid if you're interested in a public-interest or public-sector career.

Slow down—Some of you may be thinking, "All this self-assessment takes too much time. I just want to make a decision now!" But consider: Author Richard Bolles, in his popular career book, What Color is Your Parachute?, writes, "... Work consumes about 80,000 hours of your time on this earth. Yet, most of us spend more time planning next summer's vacation than we do in trying to figure out what we want to do with those 80,000 hours."

Wait—Every lawyer and career counselor we interviewed reached a unanimous verdict: get some work experience before law school. Ideally, get a job working with attorneys, as a paralegal or in some other support role. Why? Because you'll have a better idea if law school is really worth the time and money, and you'll enter school with a clearer direction than your peers. Real-world experience—in a legal setting or not—will help you avoid following the herd, seeking the same types of jobs everyone does. You'll also have a better sense of the job setting that works for you. You may even find a career you love and avoid grad school altogether, or learn that you want a different degree entirely.

Who would you hire?—Not only will entering law school with work experience give you career direction, it will make you infinitely more marketable when looking for a job. To see things from an employer's perspective, consider two real-life law students and decide who you would hire. Dan, in his mid-30s, has 10 years of experience as a financial journalist. Covering the securities industry for several years sparked his interest in securities law, and it prompted him to get a JD to become a securities lawyer. He entered law school with a deep knowledge of the securities industry and the legal issues relating to it, plus a Rolodex of contacts in the field. Earl is a 22 year-old college grad who has never worked in a law firm. Who would you hire?

PART III

Should You Really Stay in Law School?

Chapter 9 How *Did You* Get Here?

"All my friends were going to grad school after college. I couldn't imagine not joining them. I thought I'd be working in Starbucks if I didn't."

—Jennifer, a recent law school grad

*T*his section of the book is for you if...

> You haven't made up your mind about whether to stay in law school or not.
> You've made up your mind, and you wish to leave to pursue other interests.
> You've decided to stay, and want to make the most of your experience.

Whichever scenario fits, the next few chapters are devoted to helping you match your skills, interests and personal values with a career that's right for you. Don't worry if you're experiencing career-confusion; you're not alone. Over a three-year period, many law students tend to stumble into a variety of decision-making pitfalls that impair their judgement and influence them in ways not in their best interest. Throughout the book these *psychological traps* are referred to as **Choice Challenges**. We introduced nine of them in Part I, and they're summarized below. In this particular chapter, we'll explain how these, and other, Choice Challenges may be influencing the decisions you're working on now:

> **The Herd Mentality**—When our actions and decisions are weighted by those around us.
> **Information Cascade**—When our actions or decisions are influenced by repeated exposure to a barrage of information.
> **Decision Paralysis**—When we avoid making decisions because we're overwhelmed by choice.
> **Confirmation Bias**—When we shut out information that contradicts our initial preferences.
> **Rules of Thumb**—When we adopt intellectual shortcuts to make choices less complicated.
> **Anchoring**—When we attach ourselves to a fixed position regardless of evidence to the contrary.

Mental Accounting—When we treat money differently depending on where we get it, and what purpose we have for it.

Ignoring the Base Rate—When we ignore the odds (the base rate) in a given situation.

Overconfidence—When we overestimate our skills, abilities or knowledge.

In their own way, Choice Challenges present a psychological minefield made all the more treacherous because they operate at a near-unconscious level. The aim of this section is to make you more aware of how they may be affecting your career choices, and to learn how to navigate as you make decisions about the future of your legal career. But first, a few words to those who might be uncomfortable that they've even opened this book:

You have nothing to feel bad about. At some point in their law school career, almost all students seriously question the wisdom of becoming a lawyer.

> **"I** thought about leaving law school after my first semester. But I got really good grades, and I figured that was a good reason to stay. Boy, was I wrong."
>
> —Jolene, event planner and former attorney at a mid-sized firm

If anything, you should pat yourself on the back for exploring any dissatisfaction you have. After all, if you decide to quit, your decision saves you time, money and career dissatisfaction; if you continue, at least you will have peace of mind that the law is the right path for you.

During the first year (especially near final exams or after grades come out), it's typical for law students to wonder what they've gotten themselves into. Some of you are terrified of being called on in class; others are frightened of bombing their finals; still others suspect that going to law school was a huge mistake. Such doubts can persist into second and even third year. Yet, for many students, the only thing scarier than the thought of staying in law school is leaving. No matter how strongly they are tempted to drop out, pulling the rip cord and actually leaving law school is incredibly difficult for most unhappy students. That's why the first step in deciding whether to remain in law school is to examine the roots of your dissatisfaction and indecision. So let's start there. We promise it will be helpful.

When Law School Sucks

One reason students question their presence in law school is because they're unhappy with the rigor and discipline of the law school experience. But law school is supposed to be hard, so it's important to distinguish whether the sources of your pain are the unavoidable but short-term "inconveniences" of school, or if your uncertainty is about whether to pursue a law degree at all. It's understandable if you're not totally enthralled with your law school experience—it is a grind. But it's important to understand that being a lawyer is not the same as being a law student. If your unhappiness is limited to the law school experience itself, the good news is that you can take steps to make your time in law school more bearable, even enjoyable. Let's take a closer look at some of the possible sources of your dissatisfaction and some constructive ways to think about them.

You're afraid you're going to bomb your exams. Let's say it's early in your law school career and you're afraid of failing your exams and getting booted out of school. If that's the case, you're in good company. Most of your peers are concerned they'll flunk their finals—and the ones who say they aren't are lying (either to you or themselves). But even if you don't do as well as you'd hoped academically (most students don't), keep in mind that you're not going to have to take four-hour essay exams once you're a lawyer. (Keep in mind also that law schools are businesses, and businesses don't survive if most of their customers fail; law schools have a vested interest in making sure that the overwhelming majority of their students pass) Success on finals has nothing to do with success as a lawyer. But if you don't believe us, speak with successful lawyers who had low law school grades, and ask them if their marks were any predictor of their career success. Your law school's career services office can help connect you with such alumni, or at least share anecdotes about them.

Still, no one wants to do poorly. And there are things you can do to ease your finals-phobia: speak with professors and upperclassmen about how to succeed on exams, use your school's academic-support resources, take practice exams, read books about test-taking (check your law school's bookstore). But whatever you do, don't let looming exams interfere with your decision to become a lawyer. Finals are a necessary evil that you have to face on the road to becoming an attorney, but they'll have no place in your life once you become one.

You hate the law school teaching style. If you loathe the case study and Socratic teaching methods, you're not alone. But as with finals, you likely won't have to deal with them once you're an attorney. About the only time a Socratic give-and-take occurs in the practice of law is during a high-court appeals process, as in the state or U.S. Supreme Court. That's not something you need to think about at this stage. That said, if you detest reading cases, legal research and legal writing, that might be a clue that you'd be happier either in a non-legal job or a legal job that entails very few of those tasks. So if academics are getting you down, get out of the library and into the real world. Work or volunteer in a legal setting that sounds interesting and see if you enjoy interacting with real attorneys more than law school professors. We'll bet most of you will.

You dislike the law school vibe. If the chief source of your unhappiness is that you dislike your classmates, or the attendant peer pressure, or the law school atmosphere in general, don't blame law school. There are lots of medical, MBA and engineering students who hate the vibes in their schools, too. To be honest, any place where hundreds of ambitious, intelligent people are competing for grades (and, ultimately, jobs) is going to be a place that many (if not most) students find unpleasant. So the first thing to do is spend less time at law school. If school is becoming a nerve-wracking and all-encompassing experience, just show up for classes. Study outside of the law school and find non-law students to hang out with. Again, remember that being in law school is different from being a lawyer in the real world. Some legal jobs are definitely stressful and competitive, but many won't have the same atmosphere as school. Plus, working lawyers are generally older and more mature than law students; many actually have lives and play nicely with others. And while you're spending less time at law school, make time to do things you like— drumming, dancing, cooking, working out—anything, as long as it's fun for you.

> "**W**hen it came to leaving law school, my friends, family and fellow students really turned on the pressure to stay. They couldn't understand why I'd give up just when I was getting over the hardest part."
>
> —Jared, management consultant and law school drop-out

A second remedy is to get (and maintain) some perspective. If you're absolutely clear about why you're in law school and what you want to accomplish with your JD, it becomes easier to deal with the pressures of school without abandoning your dream of becoming a lawyer. One simple but overlooked way to recall why you came to law school in the first place is to reread your admissions essay. If you still don't know why you're in school, ask a career counselor for help. Better yet, attend professional events in the legal community (panel discussions, seminars, brown bag lunches and such that are often sponsored by your local bar association). Not nearly enough law students do this, so you'll distinguish yourself from your classmates. Each year, some students land jobs because they showed up to a program and hit it off with an attorney there. What if the event costs money? No problem, call and see if they'll let you in for a reduced student fee, or for free if you volunteer with the event. They'll likely say yes. You can also make valuable contacts with attorneys by attending career panels and programs at your law school. Once you identify a few areas of law that sound potentially interesting, it'll be easier to remember that law school is simply a means to an end.

The rest of your life is falling apart. Finally, it's important to isolate whatever other personal issues are distracting you now, and whether they—or law school itself—is the source of your doubts to continue. In the vaccuum of law school, it's often easy to forget that life still happens outside. People get divorced, parents get sick; other calamities occur. And some law students are unhappy not because of school, but because they have an undiagnosed form of clinical depression. The best way to determine if law school or some other personal issues (or both) are responsible for your unhappiness is to make an appointment to see a licensed therapist or other professional who can help you sort things out. Your law school may offer this as a free service, or they may be able to refer to you someone who provides free or low-cost counseling services. Once you start addressing these other life issues, you can better assess what factors are really responsible for your unhappiness.

Choice Challenges Revisited

Of course, it's quite possible that law is not right for you. And the source of your stress and uncertainty is the knowledge that you will have a ton of debt when you graduate even though you're not sure it's worth it. Or you suspect there are other things you'd rather be doing than pursuing a law degree. Whatever misgivings you have need to be addressed…soon. One reason some students question their career choice is because they got into law school under the sway of one or more Choice Challenges, *and* didn't do adequate research into law school or the profession itself. We discussed this thoroughly in detail in Chapter 3, so perhaps going over that section again will give you insight into the forces that landed you where you are today.

In any case, here's a recap of those Choice Challenges and how they may have contributed to your present indecision:

If you're like a lot of law students, you may have come to law school under the sway of the **Herd Mentality**. It refers to the tendency to let our decisions be unduly influenced by the actions of others. It explains why many trends and fads take hold—in the stock market, in fashion, in dieting—because we often adopt the habits and activities of those around us. Sometimes there's nothing wrong with this form of decision-making. The herd mentality is one reason why motorists don't cross a double-yellow line, or why so many people buy homes rather than rent. So, yes, "because everyone else is doing it" can be a perfectly logical and reasonable basis for decisions. But when it comes to career choices, the urge to herd is even more powerful than you think. People often decide to go to law school when they see many of their peers taking the LSAT and busily filling out law school applications. The problem with following the herd is that just because law school is a good path for some people, it may not be the best for you. If you relied on the herd for guidance, you might have skipped researching what law school is really like or what legal practice actually entails. That could be one reason you're now questioning whether law school is truly the right path.

If you were influenced by the *herd mentality*, you may also have been swayed by a related Choice Challenge called the **Information Cascade**. This refers to the way our decisions can be impacted by a barrage of information and news. After all, the advertising and public-relations industries are built around this phenomenon. And the various news sources we look to can influence us just as significantly. So, if you were constantly exposed to news that the economy sucks and the job market is weak, you may have been more inclined to seek refuge in law school. Or, if you spent too much time watching *The Practice* or cable reruns of *Ally McBeal*, you might have been more inclined to think being a lawyer was a great way to meet thin, quirky, beautiful people. The problem with letting the information cascade drive your decision is that going to law school largely to escape the job market is not a sufficient reason to go. If being a lawyer isn't the right career for you in general, you won't enjoy being a lawyer in a good or bad economy. So, if the bad news of a bad job market figured heavily into your decision, and you didn't assess what lawyers do and whether you'd enjoy being one, it's understandable if you're now questioning your decision to pursue law.

The Devil's Advocate Says...

Do something—Law students often tell us they don't have time to explore different legal jobs. So they do nothing at all. But doing even one thing a day toward your career search—even spending an hour a week—is better than blowing it off entirely. If you devote as much time to career exploration as you do on one course outline, you would make infinitely better job decisions.

Information cascade can also contribute to another Choice Challenge called **Decision Paralysis**—which occurs when faced with multiple options, we become paralyzed and avoid making a decision. It's no different than being in the breakfast cereal aisle of any supermarket—it's tough to choose when faced with hundreds of choices. Decision paralysis explains why many students are in law school—they didn't really know what they wanted, so they enrolled to "keep their options open." Translation: When it seems too time-consuming and arduous to wade through hundreds of career possibilities, grad school is an appealing way to simplify their choice. Law school is a particularly attractive option because it doesn't require the prior course-work, training or work experience as other graduate programs do. Sound familiar? That's why law school has become a default option for otherwise intelligent, well-educated and ambitious people who can't decide how to channel that intelligence, education and ambition. If decision paralysis influenced your decision, you may have entered law school knowing little about the legal profession. No wonder you're wondering if other paths might have been a better fit.

Another Choice Challenge that may have cemented your decision to attend law school is the **Confirmation Bias**. This refers to our tendency to selectively seek information and advice that supports our original preferences, and to avoid seeking information that contradicts them. (Asking a sales person, rather than a friend, if an item suits your needs is an example of the *confirmation bias*.) So, if you only asked happily practicing lawyers about the merits of law school, you may not have gotten all the information you needed to make an informed decision. And once you decided on law school, you may have avoided seeking information that would conflict with your plans. In fact, you probably avoided talking to any unhappy lawyers or law students—anyone who might have challenged your reasons for going to law school—because you didn't want to stray from your path. As you may be realizing now, the problem with the *confirmation bias* is that you can miss some important perspectives. Someone might have pointed out holes in your reasons for going to law school, and someone else might have advised you to sit in on a few law school classes, or to work in a legal environment, or to speak with lawyers who left the law.

Similarly, you may have gone to law school relying on **Rules of Thumb**. These are the mental shortcuts we all use to make decisions simpler. Each year, tens of thousands students flock to law schools all over the country because they were persuaded by classic rules of thumb such as, *you can do anything with a law degree*, or, *a law degree opens doors* or, *law school teaches you how to think*. The problem with relying on *rules of thumb* is that we fail to check out their validity and whether they apply to our situation.

And, for those who are in law school largely because you "always knew you'd be a lawyer," you may have fallen for a Choice Challenge called **Anchoring**. It refers to the way we are influenced by ideas or notions that should have no bearing on our decisions. When it comes to law school, many people simply decide at an early age that they're going to be a lawyer, and never let go of that idea. The problem with *anchoring* is this: even though you always planned to be a lawyer, you may not have adequately investigated what it's actually like to be one, or if you'd enjoy it. You also might not have explored any non-legal paths to see if there were ones you'd enjoy more. So if you're not enjoying your legal studies, it can be doubly disconcerting because it conflicts with your longstanding vision of yourself as a lawyer.

Some of you no doubt entered law school with a specific idea of what you wanted to do with your law degree: public-interest lawyer, sports agent, large law firm attorney and so on. While it's admirable to have a goal, you may have fallen prey to another Choice Challenge called **Ignoring the Base Rate**. This refers to our tendency to pay little or no attention to important odds and statistics related to a particular situation (for example, people who buy travel insurance *ignore the base rate* because—statistically speaking—almost no one ever dies in an airplane crash.) If you entered law school thinking you wanted to be a public-interest lawyer, you probably ignored (okay, never knew) the fact that only 4% of recent law school graduates wind up in public-interest organizations. Or if you came to law school thinking that you wanted to be a sports agent, you might have ignored the fact that there are practically more sports agents than professional athletes. If you were drawn to law by visions of pulling down a six-figure starting salary in a large law firm, you may not have paid attention to the fact that only 22% of law school grads work in firms of over 100 attorneys (and only 12% in firms of over 250), and many don't last more than two or three years in them. So if you're in law school and beginning to recognize those long odds, you may be questioning if you want to contend with them.

Last but not least, you may have been drawn to law school because you were confident that you wanted to pursue a specific legal practice area, or that you'd simply figure out what you wanted to do with your JD during the course of law school. If that's the case, you may have been suffering from a Choice Challenge called **Overconfidence**. It refers to our tendency to overestimate our skills, ability, or knowledge. (For example, amateur investors who dabble in the stock market are a classic example of individuals suffering from overconfidence.) Now that you're in law school, you may realize that you overestimated how much you know about the specific legal job you thought you wanted to do, or you were overly confident about your ability to figure out what you wanted by the time you graduate.

Now What?

If you recognize yourself in any (or many) of these scenarios, don't despair. While one or more of the above Choice Challenges may very well have influenced your decision to attend law school—leaving you questioning why you're there and what you'll do with your degree—there's still hope. The next few chapters will walk you through the process of deciding whether or not to remain in law school, and what to do with your law degree if you do.

Chapter 10

The **Decision Assessments**

"For me, leaving law school was absolutely the right decision. Once I made it, a huge burden was lifted. I felt as though I had re-taken control of the direction of my life."

—Andrea, management consultant

"Law school was a challenge, but I'm so glad I didn't quit. Not only did I get a wonderful education and made great friends, but I was able to do some soul-searching. I feel proud of my accomplishments."

—Melanie, legal recruiter

*T*his chapter is designed to help you sort out the central question: whether to stay in law school…or not. As you work through the three Decision Assessments, please answer each as honestly as you can. The more candid you are, the more likely you will learn about your decision-making process, and be able to make the necessary corrections. After each assessment, we'll explain what your answers mean:

DECISION ASSESSMENT 1

✓ *Check every statement that reflects your thinking about law school.*

☐ **A** I'd hate to waste the time and money I've already spent on law school by dropping out.

☐ **B** I'm looking into what legal jobs would be a good match for my favorite skills and fields of interest.

☐ **C** I'm concerned about leaving law school without a backup plan.

☐ **D** I'm rethinking my reasons for being in law school and what I really want to do with a JD.

☐ **E** I've already gotten through _____ semester(s), so I might as well finish.

☐ **F** What I like about law school is the ability to develop my analytical skills and learn how to see both sides of an argument.

☐ **G** I'm afraid that if I leave law school now, I'll regret it later.

☐ **H** I enjoy reading cases, as well as writing and doing legal research.

☐ **I** I'm not happy, but I can't imagine leaving law school and doing something else.

We'll score your responses at the end of the chapter. For now, let's review the statements you did or did not check, and tell you what they say about your decision-making process:

The Sunk Cost Fallacy

☑ **A** **I'd hate to waste the time and money I've already spent on law school by dropping out."**

☑ **E** **I've already gotten through ____ semester(s), so I might as well finish."**

If you checked these statements, you may have fallen for a Choice Challenge called **The Sunk Cost Fallacy.** To understand what we mean, consider the following hypothetical:

> *Situation A*—Imagine you are a huge Rolling Stones fan, and a friend gives you a free ticket to one of their concerts. Just before leaving home, you hear that Mick Jagger won't be performing that night. On top of that, a severe storm warning is in effect, and the drive to the concert could be risky. Would you attend?
>
> *Situation B*—Now imagine the very same scenario, except that you have paid a small fortune for your own concert ticket and there's no chance of selling it to someone else. Would you still attend?

More people say they would risk traveling in a dangerous storm—despite Mick's absence— if they had paid for a ticket themselves than if they had gotten it for free. So, why would paying for the ticket ourselves make it any more thrilling or less dangerous to attend the concert? It wouldn't. But for most of us, the money we've already spent on the ticket compels us to justify our expenditure by attending the concert. It doesn't matter that the money is already spent—or *sunk*. We can't allow ourselves to waste what we have already invested. That explains why people often make decisions to rationalize previous choices. Here's an example. Once upon a time, a friend's mom owned a car that frequently needed repair. But she refused to trade it in, reasoning that she didn't want to see all the money she had already put into the car "go to waste." By this same reasoning, we finish bad novels and stay in bad relationships. We don't want to "waste" the time we've invested in them.

For our purposes, the *sunk cost fallacy* comes into play when law students grapple with the question of whether or not to remain in law school. It explains why some unhappy students stay put—they believe they have too much invested to drop out...even if law isn't the right career path for them.

The first year of law school, and especially the first semester, is a rigorous and demanding experience that feels like a rite of passage. So even if you want to bail out after surviving the first semester/year, you might resist leaving because of an unwillingness to see all your time, effort and tuition—not to mention blood, sweat and tears—go down the drain. On top of that, older law students or family members might be on the sidelines, convincing you of the foolishness of dropping out because of what you've already expended. If you are swayed by this reasoning, you may end up *sinking* two and a half more years of time and money to get a law degree you may not want or need.

> "**I** never quit anything in my life before, so the decision to leave law school was the hardest decision I ever made. I struggled not to see it as a personal failure but as an honest realization that it (law) just wasn't right for me."
>
> —Andrea, healthcare executive and law school drop-out

Here's the fallacy in the *sunk cost*:

If you're convinced after *one* semester that being a lawyer isn't right for you, then spending *five more* semesters to justify that one semester isn't a great way to make a decision. That's because you won't get your original investment of time and money back by investing even more time and money. While this may sound rational enough, knowing whether to quit is easier said than done. Moreover, the *sunk cost fallacy* is nearly impossible to overcome once law students complete the first semester of their second year. Once most students reach the halfway point of law school, they feel it's too late to drop out. Chris, now a non-practicing attorney who works in human resources, explains:

"At least once in each of my first three semesters I had a major meltdown and considered quitting. But I talked myself out of it. After my third semester, I gave up the idea of dropping out for the simple reason that I was past the mid-point and thought I might as well finish."

We've heard the same story from hundreds of former lawyers and current practitioners unhappy in their work. But as difficult as it is to overcome the *sunk cost fallacy*, it can be done. Here are a few suggestions:

Put your imagination to work—Pretend that you haven't already spent one semester (or one year) at law school. And ask yourself, "If I could make a decision about law school again, knowing what I now know, would I choose to get a law degree?" If the answer is no, begin looking into what it would take to cut your losses and get out.

Handicap your happiness—Start speaking with lawyers and non-lawyers in different jobs that sound interesting to you to see if there are any you'd enjoy doing. Better yet, start shadowing lawyers on the job and volunteering in a legal environment so you can see what attorneys do. The point is to find one or more good reasons to justify continuing rather than staying because of what you had already sunk into it. Then look at all your future options, legal and non-legal, in terms of their potential for career satisfaction. List them and grade them—high (H), medium (M) or low (L). Go with your gut.

Retrain your mind—Try not to see leaving law school as a waste of the time and money you've already expended. Quite the opposite. After all, you've already picked up some useful analytic skills and—most important—you've learned that you don't want to be a lawyer. Before you take action, though, speak with law school dropouts about how they overcame their reluctance to leave.

Accentuate the possible—Think of the decision to leave law school as a way to cut your losses, preventing yourself from sinking more time and money into a career path that apparently is not right for you. Then think about the possibility of pursuing a career that's a better match for who you are and what you want.

Consider Jill, who finished her 1L year seriously questioning whether law was the right career for her and concerned about racking up more debt. She spent her summer trying to answer that question by working in a law firm while volunteering with a nonprofit organization, and taking an improv class on the side. "I feel like a person again," she told us. "I began the summer completely burned out but I regained my enthusiasm by doing activities I liked." Jill enjoyed her

The *Devil's Advocate Says...*

Confess—One reason that leaving law school is so difficult is admitting—to yourself and to others—you may have made a mistake. Would you rather admit it now to family and friends—or later, to a shrink or career counselor? Many lawyers tell us they wish they'd had nerve to admit their mistake much earlier, and certainly long before they launched their law career volunteer work so much she decided to take a year off from school to work part-time at her firm, volunteer with nonprofits and have informational interviews with various lawyers and non-lawyers until she either found a good reason to continue law or another job to pursue.

Regret Aversion

☑ G I'm afraid that if I leave law school now, I'll regret it later.

☑ C I'm concerned about leaving law school without a backup plan.

If you checked either of these statements, you may be suffering from a Choice Challenge called **Regret Aversion**. Here's how it works:

> *Situation A*—Ms. Green is in line to see the latest Harry Potter movie. She gets to the ticket window and is informed she has won $100 for being the theater's 100,000th customer.
>
> *Situation B*—Mr. Blue is in line at another theater. The woman in front of him turns out to be the millionth customer and she wins $1,000. Mr. B is the millionth-and-one customer, and he wins $150.

Who would you rather be, Ms. Green or Mr. Blue?

Believe it or not, when researchers ask groups to choose between the two scenarios, many people report they would prefer Ms. Green's position (winning $100) to Mr. Blue's (winning $150). Why? Because they would feel worse about missing out on the $1,000, and they're willing to sacrifice $50 more in winnings to avoid feeling pangs of regret. That is an example of *regret aversion*—the tendency to avoid a decision or action for fear you'll later regret it. It influences our decisions because most people want to avoid the pain and responsibility for negative outcomes. This particular Choice Challenge helps explain why many unhappy students hesitate to leave law school despite major doubts—they fear they will live to regret their choice. Or they worry the decision to do without a law degree will somehow hurt them "professionally". Or they worry that they may want to be a lawyer at some point in the future, and they will be unable to because it'll be "too late" or they'll be "too old."

Regret aversion certainly played a role in preventing Deborah from leaving law school even though she had a suspicion that would be the wisest choice. "What if I regret leaving when I'm in my 40's?" Deborah remembers asking. On the other hand, her friend, Gary, never regretted leaving law school. Certain that law wasn't the right path for him, he took the time to find out what he enjoyed doing and pursued journalism instead. Like Gary, almost all of the other law school dropouts we interviewed for this book said they never regretted their choice. But many of the lawyers we talked to had regrets alright. They regretted not following their instinct to drop out of law school earlier, and to pursue something that interested them more.

The problem with letting *regret aversion* sway your decision is that you're largely basing your choice on the fear of feeling bad in the future, rather than on a clear and present desire to be a lawyer. It's like staying in a relationship because you're afraid to be alone. The way to overcome this particular psychological trap is to begin gathering information about what legal practice is really about. That way, you can stop speculating about whether you'll regret not being a lawyer and decide based on whether you want to be one. In other words, if you make a well-informed decision in the present, you won't have to fear regret in the future. And if you do leave, law school will always be there (and happy to collect your money) should you later decide to return.

Another way to overcome *regret aversion* is to remind yourself that the choice to leave law school isn't black or white—that is, you don't have to make a final decision right away. You can take a semester or a year off to explore legal and non-legal jobs in depth. When you get a better sense if there are other careers or jobs that excite you more, you won't have to fear regretting your choice to leave law school. One student who did this was Craig, who finished his first year with doubts about returning. Curious about classroom teaching, he took a year off from law school to teach high school; meanwhile he was still arranging informational interviews with a variety of lawyers. After gathering more information, he decided to stick with teaching and has no regrets about leaving law school.

The Devil's Advocate Says...

Do the math—If you're thinking about leaving law school, focus on what you'd save now (e.g. time and tuition), rather than on what you've already spent. You can beat the sunk cost fallacy if you really understand what's at stake. Some students rationalize staying in law school because "it's only two more years." But it's just not true. If you factor in the bar exam and a few years of practicing, you will have sunk much more time and money into the law just because you didn't want to see that one semester (or year) go to waste. So when you're thinking about leaving, calculate what's really at stake.

Status Quo Bias

☑ **I** **I'm not happy, but I just can't imagine leaving law school and doing something else.**

One of the Choice Challenges related to regret aversion is the **Status Quo Bias**. It refers to our inclination to resist change; to stay with what's familiar.

If you just consider how difficult and frustrating it is these just to switch from one cell phone or long-distance provider to another, you understand something fundamental about change. Change often requires more effort that we're willing to invest, so we persuade ourselves that it's easier to stick with what we have. That's why the *status quo bias* is so seductive, and that's why it is one of the main reasons law students who don't belong in law school decide to stay—because leaving threatens to take too much time, energy and risk. In much the way that people stay in difficult relationships because they feel comfortable, many students stay in law school because being a student feels familiar (even if it feels lousy), and they resist having to face the working world. The problem with the *status quo bias* is this—in love, life, and law school, the devil you know often feels safer than the one you don't. Translation: remaining in law school because you fear choice, change or regret may mean you're sticking with a bad decision that isn't getting you closer to a career or job that you will truly enjoy. Bottom line—at some point, we all have to figure out what we want to be when we grow up, and it's smarter to address this *before* spending thousands on a JD.

☑ **F** **What I like about law school is the ability to develop my analytical skills and learn how to see both sides of an argument."**

☑ **H** **I enjoy reading cases, as well as legal research and writing.**

These two statements go to fundamental aspects of being a lawyer, and, if you checked one or both, you have sound reasons to consider pursuing law. Still, the fact that you picked up this book suggests you have questions regarding what to do with your JD. So, the next step is to investigate whether there are specific legal jobs you'd enjoy doing, or whether there might be any *non-legal* jobs you'd enjoy more. If you enjoy using analytical skills, look at specific legal jobs that emphasize analysis, and see which you'd prefer. Maybe you'd enjoy being a law professor. Or if you enjoy legal research and writing, and reading cases—start identifying legal jobs you think you'd enjoy. Pay a visit to your law school's Career Service Office to help identify potential areas of interest. The CSO staff can also help connect you with lawyers in various jobs so you can speak with them in depth about their work.

☑ **D** **I'm rethinking my reasons for being in law school and what I really want to do with a JD.**

☑ **B** **I'm looking into what legal jobs would be a good match for my favorite skills and fields of interest.**

These are the best answers you could have checked in Decision Assessment #1. Both statements suggest you probably will make an informed decision about whether continuing law school is the smartest investment of your time and money.

> **"**(I stayed in law school) because I didn't know what my other options were. But I knew one thing—I didn't want to move back in with my parents, flat broke and under a cloud of disappointment.**"**
>
> —Eileen, marketing consultant and non-practicing attorney.

Revisiting your reasons for attending law school and your plans for your JD will help reconnect you with the reason you are there. It's easy to lose sight of your goals when you're immersed in briefing and outlining. You start getting swept up in the *herd mentality*, and it's easy to question whether the pain will be worth it. So, to help recall what motivated you to attend law school, re-read your admissions essay, and speak with a law school career counselor. Remembering why you're there can help motivate you to endure the aspects of law school you dislike and focus on what you'll do when it's over. If you can't identify any strong reasons for pursuing law, it's important to start investigating whether there are legal jobs you'd actually want to do. Finding jobs where you'd enjoy applying your legal training can provide much-needed reassurance that law is the correct path for you, and remind you that law school is merely a means to an end

Now that we've discussed reasons people find it hard to leave law school—either because of what they've already invested or because they value the security it offers—let's turn to Decision Assessment 2, and address some further issues surrounding the choice of staying or leaving.

We'll score your responses at the end of the chapter. For now, let's review the statements you did or did not check, and tell you what it says about your decision-making process:

✓ *Check every statement that reflects your thinking about law school.*

- ❑ **A**   I don't want to look like a quitter or a failure by dropping out.
- ❑ **B**   I'm speaking with people in various non-legal careers so that I can compare them with legal jobs and see which I prefer.
- ❑ **C**   My family is encouraging me to stay in law school.
- ❑ **D**   I always thought I would be a lawyer.
- ❑ **E**   I've started speaking with lawyers in various practice areas to see what jobs I would prefer over others.
- ❑ **F**   Everyone is telling me to stay in law school because it gets better after the first year.
- ❑ **G**   My family is paying for law school so I might as well get a free graduate degree.
- ❑ **H**   I like being a student, and I enjoy the academic qualities of law school.
- ❑ **I**   The skills I'm learning and the JD I'll get may be beneficial even if I don't practice law.

Anchoring

- ☑ **A**   **I don't want to look like a quitter or a failure by dropping out.**
- ☑ **D**   **I always thought I'd be a lawyer.**
- ☑ **C**   **My family is encouraging me to stay in law school.**

If you checked these statements, you may be letting a Choice Challenge called **Anchoring** exert too much influence on your decision. *Anchoring* is a mental trap that occurs when we put too much weight on notions or factors that should really have no bearing on our decisions. This explains why some law students, despite their misery, resist leaving law school. They cling—*anchor* themselves—to an expectation that "someday" they will be a lawyer.

Such expectations can be particularly intense if you're the first in your family to pursue a graduate degree, or if you come from a family of lawyers. All the more reason to understand that *anchoring* yourself to others' expectations is no reason to spend five more semesters in law school when you know after the first semester that the law is not for you. After all, your family and friends don't have to wake up every morning and attend class (and eventually go into law) You do. So it's important to make the decision that's best for you, because only you must live with your decision.

Of course, you could just put your head down and push on.

That's what Jeff did.

A non-practicing lawyer who works for a bank, Jeff told us he had hated law school and found it boring and completely uninspiring. "I almost quit after my first semester and again after my first year. The biggest reason I stayed...I simply didn't want to quit." But that's one student's response. Guy Kawasaki, one of Apple Computers co-founders, had a completely different reaction: "It was my father's dream to be a lawyer, but he only had a high school education. I went to law school for him, but I quit after two weeks for me. I view this as a terrific validation of my inherent intelligence " And then there is Carly Fiorina, now Hewlett-Packard's CEO. "When I quit law school," she said, "My dad told me he feared I wouldn't amount to anything." Or listen to the words of novelist Amanda Brown, who dropped out of law school to write a book that later became a pretty good movie—*Legally Blonde*. We're pretty sure she doesn't regret leaving school to pursue her passion for writing.

Now, some of you may be thinking: "OK, but these are famous people." They are now, but they weren't when they left law school; they were students like you, students who made a choice to pursue something that excited them more than law rather than stick with a decision that didn't feel right. Leaving law school didn't hamper their careers and it probably won't impair yours. If your departure from law school ever comes up in a job interview, you can say that the experience strengthened your analytical, research and writing skills, and provided valuable self-knowledge. You can also promise that if you get the job, you won't ditch it later to go to law school

Although it's difficult, freeing yourself from the *anchor* of parental expectations can be accomplished. The best way to understand that you can be successful and fulfilled in a non-legal field is to speak to others who left law school and who achieved career satisfaction. You aren't likely to get Carly Fiorina or Guy Kawasaki on the phone, but you can easily find others by asking your law school's CSO, or your family and friends, for referrals. Try asking in law school chat rooms on some of the web sites we list in the Tool Kit (see page 214). Even more important, focus on finding another field you're genuinely excited about. Once again, the way to overcome *anchoring* is to focus on the right question—"Is there something I want to do professionally that requires a law degree? The key to answering this question is to identify what you like to do and see if there are any attorneys who are doing it. Don't worry, we'll help you with this at the end of this section.

Finally, remember that your only obligation is to make yourself happy and professionally fulfilled. Even if you disappoint others initially by leaving law school, they'll be happy for you in the long run if you are satisfied in your career.

The Confirmation Bias

☑ F **Everyone is telling me to stay in law school because it gets better after the first year.**

If you checked this statement, you may be falling for **The Confirmation Bias**. This occurs when we selectively seek advice and information that confirms our initial preferences. Here's a demonstration:

> On a table are four index cards, each has a letter printed on one side, and a number on the other. The sides facing up show—A, B, 2, 3. Your goal is to assess the validity of the following statement, while turning over the fewest cards possible: "All cards with a vowel on one side have an even number on the other." Which card(s) would you turn over to see if that statement is true or false?

Most people choose Cards A and 2, or Card A alone. Why? Because they instinctively try to prove the statement true. They look at a vowel card to see if there is an even number on the flip side, and then look at an even number card to see if there is a vowel on the other side. In other words, they try to confirm that the statement is true rather than false. Here's the problem—even if both cards turn out to support the rule, there could be a vowel on the other side of Card 3, which means *not* all cards with a vowel on one side have an even number on the other. So the correct response is to choose Card A (to see if there's an even number on the other side) and Card 3 (to make sure there's not a vowel there)

Here's the point of the card trick:

When we face hard decisions, it's natural to solicit input from people who will back us up and who will tell us what we want to hear. That's why we do it. But the toughest decisions require viewpoints that question our reasoning. As a rule, we make better decisions by having others challenge our assumptions. That's why it's not a good idea to seek advice only from happy lawyers, happy law students, professors or parents—they might encourage you to stay in school simply because law was the right path for them.

By way of example, let's examine how the *confirmation bias* contributed to my co-author's decision to stay in law school:

During winter break after her first semester of law school, Deborah solicited advice from other lawyers about the merits of sticking it out. Everyone she consulted was relatively satisfied in the legal profession and encouraged her to stay, saying, "It gets better from here." Instead of calling others who might offer a different view, Deborah went to lunch with her uncle, a law firm partner with a good career. "Maybe I should get a public-policy degree instead," Deborah said. "It sounds so much more interesting." Her uncle scoffed, waving a french fry to make his point:

"Yeah," he said, "but what would you actually *do* with a public policy degree, anyway? That's not practical at all."

Once her uncle rendered his verdict, Deborah didn't consult any people who left law school or lawyers who wished they had, and she didn't consult a career counselor. She didn't bother to explore public-policy school or other graduate schools or careers. In hindsight, Deborah realized that although her uncle's advice sounded somewhat logical, it was too limited a viewpoint upon which to base her decision. And just because law was the right career for her uncle, that didn't mean it was the right career for her. Had she asked different people, they might have encouraged her to explore other paths that sounded more interesting, and to think for herself.

As you've probably concluded, the way to overcome the *confirmation bias* is to seek a variety of perspectives. In addition to consulting your law school career services counselors, you might also see a private career counselor outside of your school—particularly one who specializes in working with lawyers (for a national network of such counselors, go to www.DecisionBooks.com and click on Law Career Experts). Mind you, you're not looking for people to make your decision for you, you're looking for people to help you make the right decision for you. Because in the end it's your choice, from which to reap the joy or heartache.

See your school's Career Services Office, or make an appointment with a career counselor who has experience working with lawyers.

"Ultimately my decision to leave law school was about whether the law excited me," says Gareth, a law school drop-out who now runs a small company. "The issue was whether I could picture myself in this profession 10 years down the road, and whether that could inspire me thought the next two years of law school and bar exam studies. No one else could have those answers for me except for me."

By the way: the flip side to the *confirmation bias* is an equally powerful force called the **Disconfirmation Bias**. It occurs when we ignore or discount information or opinions that conflict with what we want to believe.

Let's say, for example, that soon after you start dating someone new, friends point out some potential red flags. If you don't want to believe anything negative about your new love interest, you might simply explain away (or ignore) your friends' questions. Deep down, you may know that your pals have raised legitimate concerns. But if you don't want to believe they're true you may consciously or unconsciously discount what they say and create your own explanations to counter their arguments. The same thing happens to law students who are concerned that law may not be the best match for them. If they're scared of leaving law school and figuring out what to do next, they'll find a way to ignore the fact that they detest legal research and writing or that they're disinterested in their legal studies and not enthused about being a lawyer. Instead, they'll try to rationalize why staying in law school is still the right choice. That's the problem with the *disconfirmation bias*—it prevents you from gathering all the information you need to make an informed decision, and from exploring other careers that might be a better fit. The way to overcome it, of course, is to seek out disconfirming information—for example, exploring non-legal jobs or other graduate programs that sound more appealing than law.

Mostly, though, you should pay attention to your gut.

If you have concerns that law may not be the right path, note them. Don't ignore that gnawing feeling that you're not doing what's best for you. It's perfectly normal to question law school when you're having a bad day, or when you're behind on your outlines (or you were just humiliated in class). But if you have frequent and persistent misgivings, take them seriously. Again, the best course is to discuss your hesitations about law school with a career counselor—either in or outside of your law school. Start exploring why you're constantly questioning your choice of law, and then think about what you would need to be happy in any job or career. Next, start talking to law school dropouts, lawyers and non-lawyers to see whether you would truly prefer doing a legal or non-legal job. You should also consider taking a semester off to work in a legal or non-legal setting that interests you. Whatever you do, don't just make a decision based on the experience you're having as a law student—decide whether you should continue to pursue a JD based on whether there are legal jobs you'd actually want to do.

> **"M**y law school loans were as large as I thought they would be. What I didn't take into account was my salary coming out of law school. Those first few years were desperate financially."
>
> —Jonathan, tax attorney at a consulting firm

Mental Accounting

☑ **G** **My family is paying for law school, so I may as well get a free graduate degree.**

If you checked this statement, you may have fallen victim to the next Choice Challenge—**Mental Accounting.** You might want to have your parents read this section, too.

Mental accounting is the tendency to treat money differently depending on where we get it (salary vs. gift, for example), how we spend it (education vs. vacation), and how much we're spending (people will make a greater effort to save $25 on a $50 purchase vs. saving $25 on a $500 purchase). The basic idea is that we make financial decisions inconsistently because of our differing views of the money involved. That's why we tend to purchase more—and pay more for what we purchase—when we use credit cards. We treat—or *mentally account*—for the plastic money as somehow being less valuable than hard cash.

In the context of this book, *mental accounting* goes to the question of who is paying for you to attend law school. If your parents or grandparents are paying most or all of the tuition, ask yourself whether you would to stay if you were footing the bill. If the answer is "no," that itself might be a sign you're not interested in becoming a lawyer, in which case staying in law school is a mistake that would not only waste your family's money but complicate your future. If being a lawyer isn't the best fit for you, your time and their money would be better spent another way.

☑ **H** **I like being a student, and I enjoy the academic qualities of law school.**

☑ **I** **The skills I'm learning, and the JD I'll get, may be beneficial even if I don't practice law.**

If you checked either of these statements, your sentiments have validity but you still need to do some more research. If you enjoy the academic environment of law school, you might enjoy taking steps to becoming a judicial law clerk, a law school professor (adjunct professor), or other legal jobs outside the law school universe. Indeed, if you find other settings where your JD would be useful, it will reassure you that you'll enjoy the job as much as you're enjoying school. Similarly, looking for enjoyable legal, law-related and non-legal jobs that would let you draw on your legal training will help you feel better about staying in school. Some people we interviewed felt the training and degree benefitted them even if they didn't practice; others thought it was a waste. That's why you should investigate several law-related (non-practicing roles within the legal profession) and non-legal careers and identify jobs you'd enjoy, then assess if a JD will help enough to warrant the investment. Only you can determine if the investment of time and money will benefit you in a non-legal career.

☑ E I've started speaking with lawyers in various practice areas to see what jobs I would prefer over others.

☑ B I'm speaking with people in various non-legal careers so that I can compare them with legal jobs and see which I prefer.

Not surprisingly, these are the smartest two statements you could have checked in Decision Assessment II. If you're taking these steps, you're on the right track to making a decision that's right for you. That's because speaking with attorneys and non-attorneys is an effective way to see what type of jobs will be a good fit. If you're finding a number of legal jobs that sound interesting and enjoyable, perhaps remaining in law school is the right course. You can deal with any unpleasant aspects of law school and look forward to legal work you'll enjoy. If non-legal jobs are beginning to sound like a better fit, you should think seriously about taking a semester off (or a year; or leave entirely) to get some hands-on experience in another field. Okay, let's turn to the final Decision Assessment in this chapter.

We'll score your responses at the end of the chapter. For now, let's review the statements you did or did not check.

DECISION ASSESSMENT 3

✓ *Check every statement that reflects your thinking about law school.*

❑ **A** I don't know what I would do if I left law school.

❑ **B** I'm exploring getting legal work experience to see what jobs I would like.

❑ **C** I'm doing well in school, so I may have a lot of options for my JD.

❑ **D** I find some of my classes interesting.

❑ **E** Maybe I should stay. I've gotten good grades, and that must mean something.

❑ **F** What I'm really looking forward to are the upper-level courses, clinics, and externships.

❑ **G** It can't hurt to stay in law school. I can figure out what to do after I complete my degree.

❑ **H** I'm exploring non-legal work to see if I would prefer that environment instead.

Decision Paralysis

☑ **A** I don't know what I would do if I left law school.

☑ **C** It can't hurt to stay in law school. I can figure out what to do after I complete my degree.

If you checked either or both of these statements, you're likely facing a Choice Challenge called **Decision Paralysis.**

Decision paralysis refers to the tendency to avoid making a decision when we feel overwhelmed with choices. This particular mental trap occurs when law students choose to remain in law school largely because they haven't figured out what else they might do. But staying put just because the variety of alternatives seems overwhelming is a poor way to decide. Still, it happens frequently. First- and second-year law students don't know how to identify and explore more appealing options for themselves, so they invoke what we'll call the Plan B defense—as in, "I can't stand law school, but I can't leave without a Plan B."

What's the solution? Take small, achievable steps to explore your legal and non-legal job options, thus making it easier for you to compare. Here are some suggestions:

Schedule an appointment with a career counselor (at your law school or in private practice).

Line up one informational interview with a lawyer and one with a non-lawyer.

Spend a day volunteering in a legal and a non-legal organization.

Spend a day shadowing one lawyer and one non-lawyer on the job.

Taking one step, any step, forward tends to motivate people to do more. Do as much as you're comfortable with, and then pull back and consider whether it makes sense to take a semester or a year off from law school to explore in depth some legal and non-legal alternatives. By the way, if you wind up taking time off or leaving law school, the next thing you do doesn't have to be your dream job; it just has to be a stepping-stone that's better than law school. One law school drop-out we know took this approach. Stephanie left law school halfway through her first semester without a specific idea of what she would do, but with a clear plan of attack—to talk to a ton of different people about their work, and to take an interim job while she continued to explore different careers. One of her informational interviews led her to what she thought would be a transition job. Instead, she stayed *nine years*, winning multiple promotions and getting extensive training in skills she never imagined she'd develop. Her employer even paid for her graduate degree in another field.

Sometimes a leap of faith can help your career by leaps and bounds.

The Endowment Effect

☑ C   I'm doing well in school, so I may have a lot of options for my JD.

☑ E   Maybe I should stay. I've gotten good grades, and that must mean something.

If you checked either of these statements, you may be falling for the **Endowment Effect.** To see how it can influence decisions, consider this hypothetical.

> *Situation A*—You win a ticket to a Bruce Springsteen concert. You can't wait to attend until a stranger offers you a fistful of cash for the ticket. What is the smallest amount for which you would sell?
>
> *Situation B*—In this scenario, you are the stranger. How much would you be willing to pay for the concert ticket?

Most of us would want at least twice as much to *sell* the ticket as we would to *buy* it. (That is, we would not pay more than $100 for the ticket, but we would not sell it for less than $200.) This is an example of the *endowment effect*—the tendency to place a higher value on things we already have, relative to the value we would place on them if they belonged to someone else. The problem with over-valuing what we have is that it makes decisions to change far more difficult, and we may fail to pursue options that are more in our interest.

In the case of law school, the *endowment effect* occurs among students who may be miserable but who get high grades or make law review anyway. Because law school is so competitive, and a high GPA is so coveted, the unhappy law student feels guilty about not taking advantage of his or her stellar transcript. Of course, some of these students will wind up eventually liking law, but others will kick themselves for not leaving sooner. If you overvalue what you have—good law school grades or a spot on law review—you risk ignoring your opportunity costs, and failing to properly value what you could have...a more satisfying career. In short, the *endowment effect* makes it hard to be objective about what's best for you.

If law isn't the right career path, your grades (or ability to get legal jobs) are totally irrelevant. You're smart, you got into law school—don't be so impressed by your own results. Instead of focusing on what you have in hand, you need to honestly assess whether there are *any* legal jobs you'd actually like. Then explore whether there are non-legal jobs that interest you more. In this way, you can make a decision based on whether there are any legal jobs you'd enjoy and not on your ability to get them. Think of it this way—if you can succeed at something you don't like, imagine what you could achieve by pursuing something you love.

☑ **D**　**I find *some* of my classes interesting.**

☑ **F**　**What I'm really looking forward to are the upper-level courses, clinics, and externships.**

If you checked either of these statements, it's a good sign that continuing your legal career is appropriate. If your current or future classes interest you, consider what it is about them that's so appealing. The subject matter? The classroom discussion? Once you've given that some thought, then start investigating jobs that incorporate those elements. So, for instance, if you love your Property Law class, start speaking with attorneys who work in real estate, land use, or other related areas (your career services office can help you find them). Similarly, if you're looking forward to clinics, externships and other lawyering skills courses, consider: what is it about those classes that interest you? Client counseling? The fast pace of a criminal law setting? Brief-writing? Working with a judge? While it's good to look forward to those classes, don't wait until they roll around to resolve the question of whether law is the right path for you. Use your school's CSO to help you find real legal jobs that incorporate the aspects of classes and clinics that appeal to you. That way, you can make a connection to what your law school experience is preparing you for.

> The best way to determine if law is right career path for you is to get real-world experience before you ever get in law school.

☑ **B**　**I'm exploring getting legal work experience to see what jobs I would like.**

☑ **H**　**I'm exploring non-legal work to see if I would prefer that environment instead.**

The best way to determine if law is the right path for you is to get hands-on experience in the real world. So if you checked these statements, you're taking a sound approach to your law school decision. Real-world work experience that lets you compare legal and non-legal jobs will give you the best possible decision-making information. You'll be more confident of your decision to stick with, or leave, law school if you assess your interest level in various legal jobs. If some sound appealing, use your CSO to help you find part-time work experience (paid or unpaid) in a legal setting. If you strongly suspect that you might be happier in a non-legal job, start looking to work (paid or unpaid) in a non-legal position. If you're worried about having time, then volunteering once a week (or even a few hours) is better than nothing. The point is to get engaged in doing legal or non-legal work to see what's a better fit.

Although law school doesn't last forever, paying off student loans often stretches into what feels like an eternity. So the most important questions to consider when you're deciding whether or not to remain in law school are these: Is there a job I'm excited about that requires a JD, and is it worth the time and money I still have to invest? Or, will a JD greatly assist me in landing and performing a law-related or non-legal job that I want? If the answer to either is "no", it's far better to pull the plug on your law school career now and pursue a path that's more fulfilling (or at least less stressful). Let's recap how you can make it happen:

> *Re-read your law school admissions essay*—Revisit your reasons for attending law school in the first place, and what you wanted to accomplish with your law degree. If the essay was more about getting you into school than finding a career for which you felt a calling, you still need to figure out if a JD will help you achieve any goals you now have.
>
> *Self-assessment*—Begin with our self-assessment process, and consider reading (okay, skimming) one or more books on career satisfaction (we list some in the Tool Kit, starting on page 214). Also, make an appointment with your Career Services Office or a private career counselor.
>
> *Research*—Do a little research to see if there are any legal jobs that would be a good match for your favorite skills and fields of interest. Read Lisa Abrams' The Official Guide to Legal Specialties, or Kimm Walton's America's Greatest Places to Work With a Law Degree. Checkout web sites like www. Vault.com and www.Wetfeet.com (and read our own chapters 7 and 8) for overviews of various legal practice areas.
>
> *Visit your Career Services Office*—Meet with one of your law school's career counselors to discuss your interests and possible legal jobs that would be a good match.
>
> *Seek out lawyers and nonlawyers*—Speak with lawyers and nonlawyers in a variety of work settings to see whose jobs sound remotely interesting to you. Also, start attending local bar association functions, and ask your law school's

Adding it Up: Should You Really Stay in Law School?

Okay, it's time to score your three Decision Assessments. Go back to the Decision Assessments, and add up your scores at the bottom of each.

Decision Assessment 1 (page 115)

Statements—A, C, E, G & I (1 point each) _____

Statement—F (5 pts) _____

Statement—H (3 pts) _____

Statement—B (10 pts) _____

Statement—D (7 pts) _____

Subtotal _____

Decision Assessment 2 (page 123)

Statements—A, C, D, G (1 point each) _____

Statements—F & I (3 pts) _____

Statement—H (3 pts) _____

Statement—B (7 pts) _____

Statement—E (10 pts) _____

Subtotal _____

Decision Assessment 3 (page 129)

Statements—A, C, G (1 point each) _____

Statement—E (3 pts) _____

Statements—D & F (5 pts) _____

Statements—B & H (10 pts) _____

Subtotal _____

Total points _____

While not a perfect predictor, your score will provide a broad sense as to the merits of continuing on with your legal education.

So, if you scored…

0 to 25 points—Consider leaving law school or, at the very least, consider taking a semester or a year off to reassess whether a legal career is right for you. (Most law schools make this process enormously easy.) Think about the reasons that led you to law school in the first place and start investigating legal and non-legal job options that might lead to a better educational or career fit.

26 to 64 points—This is a gray area. If you're in your first semester, consider taking second semester off to work in a legal or non-legal job, and to speak with a wide variety of attorneys and non-attorneys about their work. If you're already in your second semester, use the summer to speak with a variety of attorneys and non-attorneys, and to get some work experience in a legal and non-legal environment. If summer break isn't enough time to help you make a thoughtful decision, consider taking the fall semester or the following year off to continue working and exploring legal and non-legal options. Then make your final decision about returning to law school based on whether there are legal jobs that you'd be excited to do, or if there are non-legal paths that sound more interesting. If you ultimately decide to pursue law school, read the next chapter to assist you with future job decisions.

65 to 100 points—Chances are good that you belong in law school. What you're feeling is the normal pangs of anxiety and stress that accompany a legal education. That said, you're reading this book because you have doubts, so be sure to take the three steps that are necessary to making an informed decision—identify what you really need in a job; speak with attorneys and non-attorneys about their work to see what appeals to you; and get work experience in legal and non-legal settings so you can compare the two. If you ultimately decide to pursue law school, be sure to read the next chapter to assist you with the job-related decisions that you'll encounter down the road.

career counselors to help connect you with alumni in various practice areas.

Get some work experience—Work, or at least spend some time, in a legal or nonlegal setting to see if there are legal jobs you'd enjoy. Again, ask your law school's CSO for assistance with lining up a part-time job or internship with a legal organization that interests you, and read the essay (Shadowing) that begins on page 221.

Practically Speaking

If you're reading this during the school year, you're probably wondering when you're going to have time to do all that we suggest. It depends on your situation and your level of misery or uncertainty (and because both of the authors of this book attended law school, we have a good idea about your level of both). If, after tackling some or all of the foregoing suggestions, and it becomes clear that you don't want to be a lawyer, we suggest you leave law school sooner than later—if only because it increases your chances of getting back some of your tuition. (Gary left in the middle of his second semester—the day after he had any shot at getting his tuition back.) If, however, you're *less* certain about leaving law school, then we suggest you put off your decision until finals are over to avoid additional stress. That way, if you do eventually take a semester—or a year—off and later decide to return, you won't have to repeat a semester.

Of course, some students will want to tackle the steps we've outlined here while they're still in law school. For them, it's important to be organized and efficient, to carve out time each week for exploring legal and non-legal alternatives. It calls for greater discipline, though, because the very pressures and anxieties that caused you to pick up this book will work against you when you're trying to make time for something other than Torts or Contracts. Moreover, a

The Devil's Advocate Says...

Prepare a soft landing—If the idea of quitting law school unnerves you—or makes you feel irresponsible—line up a short-term job or internship, or a certification program, to jump into when you leave. One law student we know quit in the middle of his second semester, and he immediately enrolled in a course to get a real estate license. He actually never sold a single piece of property, but having something to do made it easier to stop doing something else—law school.

phenomenon called the **the planning fallacy** might impede your progress, unless you plan for it. *The planning fallacy* simply refers to people's tendency to underestimate how long it will take to complete a given task. We bring this up to point out that in planning for anything, especially making time for something other than law school studies, you had better plan realistically. Setting reasonable goals for yourself will increase your likelihood of achieving them. However you manage your time, if you choose to stay in law school, the final chapter of this section will help you make better job-related decisions as your progress in your legal career.

The Decision Makers

"**W**hen I was considering leaving law school, my biggest difficulty was the pressure I felt from friends, family and fellow students. They could not understand why I'd give up on something just when I was getting over the hardest part (the first year).

"I didn't go to anyone about this decision before I made it. Once I did commit to leaving, I felt empowered and was willing to face whatever difficulties as a result of my decision. Since leaving, I've worked my way up Director of Technology at an Internet security software company. My career in high-technology has been very rewarding and I wouldn't change a thing. It's what I expected my law career to be but never felt that spark or excitement.

"From the day you announce your decision (to leave law school), and for years after, people will ask you why you did it, and whether you're happy with your decision and whether you would consider going back. These are questions you must answer for yourself first and be really comfortable with before you can face the rest of the world."—**Rob**

"**W**hen law school began, I quickly realized I had signed on to three years of hard work, financial setbacks and personal sacrifices without being able to answer the question, CWhat for?'

"From Day One, I had little confidence that when law school was over—when I finally Carrived'—that I would find myself where I actually wanted to be. Thankfully, the first year of law school was unpleasant enough and expensive enough that it made me question whether it was worth continuing.

"Once I accepted the idea that I didn't have to continue, I had many conversations with friends and family about leaving, each time trying to get someone to give me The Answer. My parents let me know they were extremely supportive of any decision I made, and would be hesitant to lead me one way or the other. My brother, who had recently finished law school himself, and who was a pretty miserable attorney, listened sympathetically. He said I was the only person who could decide what was right for me. I even spoke with the Dean of Student Affairs, who tried to convince me that I should give it more time (by that time, I had been at school for less than two months).

"The more opinions I sought, though, the more confused I became. After a while, I couldn't stand talking or thinking about it anymore, and finally decided to leave. What helped was knowing that the decision wasn't permanent. I reminded myself that if I ever thought I was mistaken, I could always go back. Admittedly, I was concerned how it would sound when I told people I left law school. Would they think I was someone who couldn't handle the work, or someone who lacked perseverance? Actually, the overwhelming response was, CGood for you '

"I realize now that it takes more courage to go off course than to stay on it."—**Sherrie**

(Continued on facing page)

"The greatest obstacle I had to leaving law school was grappling with one question—*What else would I do?* I didn't have a Plan B. I did decide to leave, though, and it created a void in my life that was extremely uncomfortable for someone like me who had never deviated an inch from the path of least resistance. I mean, the idea of starting over with a blank sheet was truly frightening, but at the same time exciting and energizing if you know what I mean. I know I'll never be one of those people who gets a thrill from exploring the unknown. But now I understand that there's nothing wrong with experiencing periods of flux in your life every now and then.

"Leaving school was *absolutely* the right decision for me. And once I made the decision, a huge burden was lifted, and I felt like I had taken control of the direction of my life again."—**Andrea**

"I dropped out of law school after my first year to get a Masters Degree in psychology/counseling. I was unhappy in law school, and didn't believe I'd have the opportunity to advocate for the disenfranchised through the legal profession. Since leaving, I've worked as a floral designer, a health coordinator for a Native American tribe, a director of two nonprofits and, most recently, as a grant writer. I've loved all of those jobs. As a floral designer, I got to be creative and work with my hands. As a nonprofit director, I learned valuable management skills that benefitted the elderly and disabled. And working for the tribe gave me a chance to work one-on-one for a population that needed resources and education.

"Now, as a grant writer, I'm able to use the writing skills that law school instilled in me. I left law school to find a more direct path for advocating for the disenfranchised. I'm glad I did."—**Nicole**

"I had four reasons for attending law school—career advancement, increased earning potential, more education, and increased opportunities. You'll notice my list didn't include any desire to actually be an attorney. That's why I left midway through my first year of law school, when I realized I was not getting the hard skills I wanted and that I was likely to graduate making less money than when I came in. The dean and others tried talking me out of my decision, but ultimately those discussions helped solidify my choice. I don't regret it.

"Since leaving, I have become the most senior member of an international IT professional association. It's very fulfilling work, and being successful has helped me feel I made the right decision."—**Adam**

"About a month into my first semester of law school, I was already weighing the decision to leave. And things didn't get any better. The deeper I got into the work, the less I liked it. I liked the idea of law school, but not the experience itself. By the time I actually told people about my decision to leave, I had already spent plenty of time thinking about it. I really grappled with the decision. These days, I work as an assistant health editor for a magazine. I love it. I feel challenged, and I love the creative environment. Should you leave law school? I don't know. My advice is to trust your instincts. It's a cliche but it's true."—**Genene**

"In choosing my first job (after law school), I did what everyone else did. I was such a lemming. Finding work was mindless, expensive and utterly rote. I wish now that I had taken a few deep breaths and thought hard about what kind of work I really wanted to do, which was to work for a legal newspaper, or a regular newspaper on the legal beat, or work at a nonprofit. Anything but go to work for a fat law firm. But what happened? Not only did I go to a fat law firm, but the basis of my decision was almost entirely about the money. It took me five years of being miserable practicing law to realize that, as grateful as I was for my law degree, I really didn't want to be a lawyer. It's important to think for yourself. But I seem to have turned off my brain when it came to my career."—**Whitney**

Chapter 11

So, You've Decided *to* Stick it Out

"I was never so intimidated in an academic setting
as I was in law school. But I graduated and have
been in practice five years now. I'm glad I persevered
because my legal education enriched my view of the
world and empowered me on behalf of my clients
and in support of worthy causes."

—Samantha, public interest lawer

$\mathcal{B}$y now, it must be apparent that the need for sharp decision-making doesn't end just because you've chosen to remain in law school and to pursue your legal career. Nor should it come as a surprise that many of the Choice Challenges we've already covered will appear again and again during your legal education. There's hope, though: by learning to navigate some of these mental traps, you can make choices that will lead to legal jobs you'll like. But you still have to keep your mind open to alternative ways of thinking. Consider the conversation one Career Services counselor had with a law student who was trying to decide between two summer law firm jobs. The conversation went something like this:

CSO—So, what differences did you notice between the firms?

Student—Well, the West Coast offices were all pale wood; very art deco, you know? Very 1970's. The East Coast office was all, like, dark wood. Mahogany, you know?

CSO—Did you notice a difference between the office cultures, and the attorneys themselves? Did you talk about the training, the mentoring, the assignments for summer associates. And did you talk about the feedback you could expect on those assignments?

Student—Well, no. But I really liked everyone I met. I talked politics for an hour with one attorney.

CSO—Good, but maybe next time you should talk about the work they do.

Variations on conversations like this occur in law schools every day, in part due to the Choice Challenges that influence law students' choice of legal jobs and career paths. These obstacles affect decisions ranging from how to approach a job search to what kind of jobs to pursue (*should I go to a small firm versus a large firm . . . should I work in the public or private sector . . . how do I go about finding a job, anyway?*). As we've said, the way to overcome Choice Challenges is to ask and answer the right questions. Unfortunately, when many law students begin thinking about their job search, they tend to focus on the wrong issues. They'll ask, "What are my options?" or "What's out there?" The problem is that before you can effectively look for a job you need to ask yourself what you want in one. So, the right questions one must consider when beginning a job search are:

What **skills** do I most enjoy using?
What **subjects** interest me the most?
What would my preferred work **environment** be like?
What are my **career priorities**?

Once you clarify what you need in a job, you can begin to explore different options that provide what you want "out there." You explore them by reading about various career paths in books or online, by speaking with different lawyers about their work, and by working in different legal jobs to see how they align with your preferences. We'll explain how to do all of these things at the end of this chapter, but keep these general ideas in mind as we discuss how to avoid letting common Choice Challenges impact your job decisions, and how to adopt a better approach to them.

Revisiting the Choice Challenges

Remember the **herd mentality**? It's what happens when we let the actions of others influence our decisions.

Because we learn at an early age that it is desirable to conform, we become more apt to make decisions based on what other people are doing. The *herd mentality* may explain why half of this country's law students are in law school to begin with—because "everybody else" decided they should go. And, once you're there, the *herd mentality* continues to exert a major force. Indeed, law students commonly complain that law school feels eerily like high school in that students become highly attuned to what "everyone else" is doing. The *herd mentality* plays a major role in other ways, too.

When second-year students see their classmates dressed in conservative suits and interviewing with large law firms through the On-Campus Interview (OCI) program, the 2L's feel as though they should fall in line. The problem is, jobs at large law firms aren't the best fit for many (if not most) law students. But students often report they participated in OCI primarily because "everyone else" did. Although it is tempting to try to wrap up your job-search in the Fall, the wiser strategy is to continue searching until you find the right job for you. Of course, if the right job is an OCI employer, great. For some, a law large firm is their ideal employer chiefly because it enables them to repay their loans more quickly; others truly enjoy the work and the environment, and can deal with the hours. But if a job in Big Law is not right for you, be patient and take the time and energy to find a job you'll enjoy. As difficult as it might be to tell friends and family that you don't yet have summer (or post-graduate) plans, it's better than winding up five to six figures in debt and stuck in a job you can't stand.

If a job in Big Law is not right for you, be patient and take the time and energy to find a job you'll enjoy.

One lawyer we know resisted going to a law firm right after law school because she knew it wasn't right for her. Instead, she persisted with her search until she found a job in a corporation's legal department. "I love my job," said Kathy. "I'm probably one of the only people from my graduating class who can say that. I have a lot of responsibility, I work directly with my clients, and I'm expected to work when there is work and to be driven by business need, not billable hours. Even if I sometimes work long hours," she added, "I know exactly why and who I'm helping, rather than being expected to stay late because someone said I should. I feel like I work in a team environment and that my colleagues care about the job they are doing."

The *herd mentality* can also compel law students to pursue the same types of jobs that everyone else does. When some students hear about classmates gunning for judicial clerkships, or jobs in intellectual property or international law, they often feel as though they should, too. Why? Because if you don't know what you want to do with your JD, it seems easier to follow the lead of your peers. And it is easier…in the short run. But by following the herd, you may be overlooking opportunities that would be a better fit for you.

Consider what happened to Nancy and Molly:

Nancy suffered through her first year of law school. But then she got a nice surprise—a $5,000 inheritance from her great-grandfather's estate. With that money, Nancy decided to leave law school and do something more personally rewarding. She founded Dress for Success, a nonprofit organization that provides career development and professional clothing to low-income women transitioning back into the workforce. After two years, though, Nancy returned to law school because she felt it could help her run her organization more effectively. She carefully selected her courses, taking trademark and not-for-profit law, and convinced her law school to award her credit for taking business school classes. Nancy continued to run Dress for Success after her graduation, and the organization she founded now serves more than 45,000 women a year in nearly 100 cities.

After three years of law school, **Molly** was convinced that she didn't want to practice law. So she pursued an internship with National Public Radio's Washington, D.C. bureau, and helped NPR Legal Affairs reporter Nina Totenberg cover President Clinton's impeachment hearings. The excitement and intensity of that experience sparked Molly's interest in journalism. She's been working ever since as a journalist and radio producer for an NPR affiliate.

The Devil's Advocate Says…

Don't follow the herd—Even if it looks like "everyone" is planning to practice law after graduation, seekout and talk to JDs who did the opposite—who followed the road less traveled. You'll find many nonpracticing graduates who have accomplished extraordinary things, and who had fun along the way. Brad Meltzer became a best-selling author of thrillers like The Tenth Justice (which he wrote in law school). Rich Buery founded iMentor, a mentoring program for disadvantaged youth. Dan Pink worked as a White House speechwriter and wrote the national bestseller—Free Agent Nation. Stacey Stern co-created Findlaw.com, the popular legal website. Then there's Tim Russert, host of NBC's "Meet the Press," and author Studs Terkel, neither of whom practiced law a day in their lives.

The lesson is this: Follow your gut instead of your classmates. It isn't easy to resist the *herd mentality*, but your school's career counselors are there to help you translate your personal skills, interests and values into the right kind of work. A counselor can also help you arrange informational interviews with attorneys who themselves didn't follow the law school herd, and who pursued careers they enjoyed. Meeting happy lawyers can inspire you to follow your heart instead of the herd. Conversely, it can help to speak with unhappy lawyers who did follow the herd… right into jobs they disliked. Hearing from attorneys about how important it is to pick a job that's the right match can make a convincing case.

Beware the Information Cascade

Ever find yourself on the receiving end of constant news or information about a hot stock, a fabulous restaurant, or a must have wireless laptop, and you felt compelled to make a purchase? Of course, you have. We all have. That's the power of an **Information Cascade**. It's a subtle psychological trap that occurs when our decisions come under the influence of a constant stream of information. If, for example, an *information cascade* comes in the form of media accounts about a bad economy, a law student might get too discouraged to begin looking for a job, or simply give up and study abroad instead. The problem with delaying your job search is this: starting early is almost as important as starting wisely. Here's how to avoid the trap:

Keep data in perspective—Just because you hear from other law students how difficult their job search is going, don't lose focus. You must still conduct your own search, so you might as well be smart about it. Regardless of the state of the job market, do some self-assessment, conduct plenty of informational interviews, and make sure to get some hands-on work experience. You need to enhance your resume, not your tan, and if you don't find some work—paid or volunteer—prospective employers might question your work ethic and commitment to law.

Focus on helpful information—Find out which practice areas are still relatively strong and see if any of them interest you. People still sue each other, even in a weak economy, so there will still be litigation jobs. And people still get arrested, so there will still be criminal prosecution and defense jobs. Read legal newspapers, the business sections of local and national newspapers, and consult your career services office to keep informed of practice areas with the most potential.

Seek out hopeful news—Talk to other lawyers who landed jobs during the last recessions (in the 1980s and 90s), and learn from their success stories. Ask your CSO to help you find such lawyers, as well as law students who landed summer jobs during tough times.

Ignoring the Base Rate

In their search for work, law students are especially vulnerable to this next Choice Challenge—**Ignoring the Base Rate**. It refers to our tendency to overlook or disregard important odds and statistics when making decisions. Here are six important examples, and we encourage you to read each one:

The odds of succeeding with OCI—You *ignore the base rate* if you look to your school's OCI program as your only means of looking for work. Statistically speaking, most of you won't get your jobs that way. According to the National Association for Law Placement, a base rate of only about 25% of students find jobs through OCI. Most law students find jobs the old-fashioned way—networking, informational interviewing, working part-time, or volunteering. It's true that at Yale, Harvard, Stanford, and other top-tier schools, a higher percentage of law students get jobs through OCI, but most students don't attend those schools, and those Ivy League grads aren't any happier at big firms.

The odds of working in large firms—You ignore the base rate if you center your job search on large firms, and overlook the fact that most law school grads (and lawyers, for that matter) do not work in huge firms. The majority of new grads work in small and mid-sized firms. So, if you seek jobs largely with large firms, you're probably not playing the job-search odds in your favor (unless you're in the top of your class). Since the chances are higher that you'll wind up in a small to mid-size firm, it's wise to look for jobs with them. But it usually takes awhile before students realize this. They flock into their CSO asking, "Are there any more law firms coming to interview here?" Wrong question. They should be asking, "What are the most effective strategies I can use to find a job I'll like?" As always, your CSO is a great resource, as are two helpful books—Kimm Walton's *Guerilla Tactics for Getting the Legal Job of Your Dreams*, and Donna Gerson's *Choosing Small, Choosing Smart*.

The statistics of job-search techniques—You *ignore the base rate* if you put too much faith in mass-mailed resumes or online job listings. Here again, law students often seek the wrong advice from their CSO. The question to ask is not how many resumes you should mail out or which web sites you should surf for job announcements. The issue is the job-search base rate—which is that roughly 75% of jobs—are never listed. That's because most people get jobs through personal contacts—employers hire people they know or people who are referred to them. Even if a job is listed, employers prefer hiring someone they know or who has been referred, rather than sifting through dozens or hundreds of resumes from people they don't know. To improve your odds of getting hired, use the most effective job-search methods—networking, personal contacts, working part-time, volunteering, and shadowing current practitioners. By the way, for every 100 resumes you send out, you will probably generate only two job interviews.

> Although nearly half of incoming law students prefer to do public-interest work, only about 4% go into public-interest law directly after graduation.

That's job *interviews* ... not offers. That's why it's smarter to contact lawyers who do work that interests you, to conduct informational interviews with them, get work experience to build your resume, and to meet people in the legal community. Yes, we know, all this requires more time than running to the mailbox with a stack of resumes, but it's a more effective use of your time.

The odds against practicing public interest law—You *ignore the base rate* if you disregard the numbers—the amount of debt you carry, the amount you'll have to repay for years after graduation, and the amount you would earn in public-interest law. Students who ignore this simple arithmetic usually abandon their public-interest aspirations and take private-sector jobs. Although nearly half of incoming law students profess an interest in public-interest work, only about 4% of all law school graduates go into public-interest law directly after graduation (25% when you include government jobs and judicial clerkships). This is not intended to discourage you, but to alert you to the importance of exploring ways to make a public-interest job feasible. Take advantage of your

CSO's resources and speak with attorneys about the steps they used to make public interest work for them. And see the public-interest law resources in the Tool Kit beginning on page 214.

The odds of competition—You *ignore the base rate* when you ignore the level of competition for certain types of legal positions. Law students often make a tactical blunder by only applying for the most competitive jobs, and overlooking less competitive but equally valuable opportunities. If you only apply to a handful of competitive jobs in international, sports and entertainment law and government (such as the U.S. Department of Justice Honors Program), you overlook less-competitive positions where you could build valuable experience and move to another position later. To broaden your thinking, tap your law school's career counselors and alumni for ideas.

The odds against finding work in competitive markets—You *ignore the base rate* when you limit your job search to a narrow and competitive geographic region (such as the East or West coasts). Some students decide they simply must live in, say, New York City or San Francisco, and won't accept a substitute. But when you're looking for a job in a competitive market, staying geographically flexible might mean the difference between finding work or not. Being open to looking for positions in other cities can dramatically increase your chances of landing a job you'll enjoy. For example, students who insist they must work in San Francisco overlook the fact that the LA legal market is seven times larger than the Bay Area. That's why it's important to consider taking an interesting job in a city that's not your first choice. After all, you don't have to stay there forever. Sticking around long enough to acquire some valuable experience can help you become more marketable to legal employers in your preferred city. One law student who realized this was Jason, who was a recent law school grad determined to pursue public interest law. After failing to find work in San Francisco, he expanded his search and landed a job in Alaska with the American Civil Liberties Union. Not only is he getting great experience, he's having an adventure. You never know how you might broaden your life, and your legal experiences, until you broaden your horizons.

It's easy to *ignore the base rate* if you're not aware that you're ignoring anything to begin with. So pay attention to the facts, the odds, and the statistics related to your particular situation. Figure out what your loans will amount to, and estimate what salary you can realistically expect to earn when you graduate. (See the worksheet on page 58.) If you're interested in highly competitive positions (public-interest fellowships, judicial clerkships, large law firms and the like), find out the percentage of applicants who wind up in those positions (and what it takes to land them), so you can decide if it's even worth competing. And always have a Plan B in case your dream job doesn't work out. How? By looking for less-competitive positions that might offer similar opportunities.

Getting Unstuck

In Part I, we described the ways that anchoring, might have affected your decision to attend law school. Likewise, anchoring affects the law student experience as well. To refresh your memory, **Anchoring** refers to the tendency to let your decisions be unduly influenced by meaningless numbers, facts, or ideas that should have no bearing on your choices. Perhaps the most common example among law students regards salaries—unrealistically high salaries, that is. When you hear that a classmate is making six figures at a large law firm (the kind of firm where only 22% of private practitioners work), a salary like that tends to stick in your head and makes it hard not to measure all other salaries against it. That's when *anchoring* becomes a problem; when it leads students to feel they are entitled to one of those rare, overly-inflated salaries, and to perceive any lower salary as beneath them. Two things result from this: (1) students fail to go after lower-paying jobs early enough; and (2) when students land jobs with salaries below their "anchor," they are needlessly disappointed.

How does one get *un-anchored*? By getting a reality check.

According to NALP, the median for starting salaries in all legal jobs nationwide these days is $60,000. And most starting salaries in public interest, government and small firm jobs tend to be considerably lower than this median, especially in certain geographic areas. Therefore, contrary to popular belief, most law school graduates aren't pulling down fat six-figure salaries. A more realistic figure to focus on is the starting salary in the geographic area and practice setting that interests you—private (small, mid-size or large firm), government or public interest. (NALP; can supply you with the median stats, but it's even better to ask your law school's career services office for a range of graduates' starting salaries in different practice settings and geographic regions.) If you make more money than you expected, you'll be pleasantly surprised. But do be realistic.

Law students also *anchor* themselves to money when they seek out higher-paying jobs without asking critical questions. It really pays to look beyond a paycheck when you're evaluating different employers. So, be sure to ask the right questions to properly compare job offers. Ask questions like:

Is there a difference in the number of hours you'll work?

What are the billable hour requirements?

Are there differences in the job responsibilities and workplace cultures?

What are the people like? Do they socialize? Are newcomers on their own?

What are the opportunities for professional development, training and mentoring?

Is there a commitment to pro bono work?

In other words, think about what you need to be happy in a job, and look for employers who have what you're looking for. We hear from attorneys all the time who tell us that failing to ask these questions put them in jobs that made their law careers needlessly harsh. People like Joe, who works at a large firm. "I wish I had known the difference between working until 7 p.m. and working until 9 at night," he told us. "When I was interviewing for jobs, working an extra 10 hours a week at one firm versus another didn't seem like a big deal. But (I realize now) it's the difference between a sustainable job and one that's all-consuming."

When they're not anchoring to money, students focus too much on their grades. Because the law school environment tends to be highly grade-obsessed, students fixate on marks and class ranking as they approach their job search. They'll race into their CSO, waving their transcripts, and ask: "Given my grades, what are my job options?" They're terrified that their first-semester or first-year grades will dictate the rest of their career and limit their choices. The problem with fixating on grades (aside from the neurotic angst it can bring) is that you can become too discouraged to begin a job search and too fearful to contact employers, or even to speak with attorneys. Although it's hard to believe this when you're in law school, your grades needn't limit you.

Many happy, successful lawyers had low grades in school, even lower than yours. Really. (By the way, did you know that 50% of all attorneys were in the bottom half of their class? They got jobs and so will you.) Even if your grades initially keep you out of a job you want—say, at a large firm—you can get in the door later. Happens all the time. It's called a lateral move. True, large firm employers are themselves more obsessed with grades, but most other employers will take a more holistic look at your resume and experience. The way to get over your grades and get a job you'll enjoy is to talk to attorneys and target your potential employers carefully. Meeting enough people who had grades like yours and have cool jobs—okay, enjoyable jobs—should put your mind at ease. After all, if your grades are like their grades, they can't hold them against you.

Decision Paralysis

Yet another common Choice Challenge that plagues law students is **Decision Paralysis**, the tendency to defer decisions or overly simplify them because we're faced with too many options. Law students suffering from *decision paralysis* are more likely to put off beginning their job search because they're overwhelmed by the prospect of figuring out what they want to do with their JD. Students who entered law school with no prior work experience and with very little knowledge about the legal profession are most susceptible to this "paralysis by indecision" because they're most likely to be clueless about where to begin. We see it all the time. They stroll into the CSO, take one look at the shelves of job-related books and binders, and suffer a panic attack. Seeing all those job-search resources makes them realize all their options—too many options—and they don't know how to decide, let alone how to investigate them. Consequently, they return to their CSO late in the semester, or early in the summer and admit, "I haven't started my job search yet because I don't know what I want to do."

There's an old saying in golf—100% of all putts that don't reach the hole never go in. Translation: if you don't start looking for a job, you'll never get one. Procrastinating also means you'll miss out on opportunities and deadlines for jobs you'd really like to have. And if you never clearly define what you really want in a job, you won't get the job you want. As with most other things in life that we tend to put off—dentist appointments, a trip to the DMV, marriage—the longer we hesitate, the longer we'll wait. The good news is that overcoming *decision paralysis* is easy once you break things down into small, manageable, tasks. If you're interested in multiple career paths, explore one practice area at a time. As a starting point, your career services counselors can help you answer some useful questions. Such as:

Do you want to be a litigator or a trial lawyer or a transactional attorney?

Do you want to work for a private law firm? If so, what size?

Do you want to work for the government? If so, at what level?

Do you want to work for a corporation? Any particular industry?

Do you want to work for a public-interest organization? Any special cause?

Do you want to work in a law-related position, such as human resources, public policy, government affairs or alternative dispute resolution?

If you don't know the answer to any of these questions, don't despair. Once you identify a few niches to explore, you need to speak with attorneys who work in them. For starters, ask your law school CSO to help connect you to alumni (See Tool Kit page 214 for more ways to meet attorneys). As you begin to learn more about different fields of practice, you'll begin to narrow the field. And, again, if all this still sounds overwhelming, just commit to doing one thing each

The Devil's Advocate Says...

Don't get paralyzed—Some of you are worried that whatever summer or post-graduate job you get will lock you into one career path forever (e.g, "if I work for the DA's office, I'll be boxed into criminal law "). As a result, you take jobs just because you think they will "keep your options open." Bad move. Your first summer or post-graduate job won't be your only job—just one in a series of stepping stones in a long career. If you're like a lot of lawyers, you'll change practice areas and settings, maybe even leave law altogether. People who have enjoyed satisfying law careers simply chose each of their jobs based on what sounded like the most fun.

day (or week) towards landing a job. And have faith you will figure out what you want to do and a way to do it.

Rules of Thumb

Earlier, we pointed out how prospective law school applicants rely on a Choice Challenge called **Rules of Thumb**, the tendency to use mental shortcuts to simplify decision-making. Unfortunately, some otherwise bright law students also rely on *rules of thumb* when deciding whether to pursue (or not pursue) certain career paths. Here's how it works: a law student hears that "large firms offer better training," or, "small firms make you work less hours than large firms", or "legal work at small firms is not as sophisticated as at a large firm," or "government jobs are too bureaucratic." Then, on the basis of these often misleading *rules of thumb*, the student makes his or her career decision. Here are a few other perilous *rules of thumb*...

> I like to talk, so litigation will be a good fit for me.
> Transactional jobs are boring, paper-pushing desk jobs.
> I'll avoid paper-intensive work if I go into a courtroom practice.
> I love travel and speak French (Spanish, German), so it makes sense for me to go into international law.
> I'll start in the private sector since I can easily get into public-interest law later.
> If I move to LA, there will be plenty of opportunities in entertainment law.
> Solo practice would be a nice, easy option for me if I don't find a job.
> It makes no different who I represent as long as I'm getting good work and learning.

As law students discover, *rules of thumb* are often flat-out wrong.

You can work just as hard in a small firm as in a bigger one.

There are interesting and satisfying government jobs that are less bureaucratic than private-sector ones.

The training at some mega-firms is often far less instructive than the training at smaller shops (and some public-interest minded students who opted for "good training" at large corporate firms wound up getting trained in things like securities or bankruptcy law, which didn't exactly help when they wanted to jump into public interest work.)

That's the big problem with *rules of thumb*: they distract students from asking the right questions about what they want in their ideal job. So, don't rule out one type of job just because you heard something negative about it, and don't get your heart set on another just because you heard something positive. Investigate and evaluate.

Overconfidence

One final Choice Challenge that plagues law students is **Overconfidence**, which refers to a tendency to overestimate one's abilities, skills or knowledge. *Overconfidence* can affect a law student job search in many ways. For example, many law students are convinced they know what career path to pursue even though they've had zero exposure to it. Those who just "know" they would be good litigators, or just "know" they would do well at transactional work, most likely base those statements purely on *overconfidence*, not work experience. We know one woman who was so certain she would thrive as a criminal lawyer that she sold her small business to go to law school. After two and a half years of various *crim-law* internships, she realized she wasn't suited for this specialty and had to start her job search from scratch. That's the problem with committing yourself to an area without getting experience in multiple specialties: you may discover it's not what you expected, and you might miss the chance to try something else. Playing catch-up is possible but stressful. And you could have used your time in law school to build your resume, rather than having to learn through trial and error.

There are numerous other ways that overconfidence can affect the legal job search. Students with high grade-point averages often just assume that all they have to do is show up to the interview to get the job. Sounds silly, right? But career counselors often counsel otherwise outstanding students who didn't grasp the basics of what we call "humble interviewing." So, just in case you're one of them, here they are:

Never assume the job is yours by virtue of grades alone.
Always take interview prep seriously by doing a mock interview.
Always dress appropriately for that firm's culture.
Always research the employer—find out, for example, about some of its clients. (You can learn this from the firm's web site and by speaking to students who summered at the firm and alumni who work there).
Always bring a list of intelligent questions to ask.
Always send a thank-you note immediately after your interview.

See the Tool Kit for more resources about law-related job interviews. Additionally, check in your law school's CSO for interview preparation resources and ask the counselors there for pointers. They'll have plenty.

Finally, and perhaps most importantly, *overconfidence* leads many law students to make faulty assumptions regarding what they want, and can withstand, in a job—particularly regarding the ability to bill seven or eight hours a day, which often means working 10 to 12 hours daily. "I assumed that I could do a job I disliked and remain psychologically intact because I was hard-working and smart and because so many others did it," said Laura, a lawyer-turned-legal newspaper reporter. "I was wrong. It was impossible." The way to avoid overconfidence—aside from being honest about how little you know—is similar to the strategies we've offered for many of the other Choice Challenges. They are:

Ask and answer some basic self-assessment questions.
Speak with a variety of attorneys about their work.
Get experience working in a variety of legal settings.

At the risk of sounding like a broken record, these steps do take more time and energy than relying on some of the shortcuts you've been using, but they will greatly increase your odds of finding a job that's right for you. As one law school career counselor observed: "If students put as much energy into their job search as they put into one course outline, they would radically change the course of their career."

Step 1–Self-Assessment

You can't look for a job—effectively, anyway—unless you know what you really want and need in a job. At a minimum, here are the four basic self-assessment questions you need to address:

What **skills** do you most enjoy using?
What **subjects** interest you the most?
How does your preferred **work environment look**?
What are your **career priorities**?

One by one, we'll walk you through these questions and help you create a list of the *skills* you most enjoy using, the *subjects* you most enjoy thinking about, the things you want in a *work environment*, and what are your *priorities* when it comes to work. After you've made some comprehensive lists, you'll pick your five favorite in each category. That will give you an outline to help you find the types of jobs you'd enjoy, and you can use that criteria to look for legal (and, possibly, non-legal) jobs that have what you're looking for. So, once you've completed your chart, keep it within reach. Okay, let's take them one at a time.

What Skills Do You Most Enjoy Using? By skills we mean the day-to-day activities that you do on the job—the way you spend your day at work. You know what lawyering skills are: writing (briefs and other legal documents), researching (legal issues), interviewing (clients, witnesses, experts), advising (clients and

---

Skills Preference Exercise #1

This chart is the first in a series of self-assessments intended to help identify your preferred skills. Take a few moments to recall specific work or volunteer experiences, and circle the skills you most enjoy using. Feel free to add any not listed here.

General writing	General analysis
Counseling	Problem-solving
Researching	Mediating
Editing	Advising
Planning	Lecturing
Recruiting	Managing projects
Coordinating	Investigating
Legal Writing	Legal analysis
Negotiating	Programming
Interviewing	Persuading
Organizing	Selling
Managing people	Budgeting
Teaching	Designing
Lobbying	Training
Brainstorming	Motivating
	Strategizing
_____	
_____	_____
	_____

colleagues) and negotiating with others (opposing counsel). But you might not be aware of the extent to which different types of attorneys utilize different skills. For example, one important *skills* question to ask is whether you prefer to spend more time working alone or in the company of others. If you're a people person, you may be miserable in a job where you're regularly working alone all day. If you're not a people person, a job that requires constant interaction with others could be a real drag. If you're clerking for a judge or working as a new associate at a large law firm, your job is likely to involve more legal research and writing and less interaction with other people (like clients). On the other hand, if you're a district attorney or a public defender, you're likely to spend more time dealing with people and less time consumed with legal research and analysis. The point is, there are many varieties to a lawyer's work. It's important to identify legal jobs that emphasize the skills *you* enjoy using.

Skills Preference Exercise #2

Draft two short paragraphs identifying your *most-preferred* and *least-preferred* skills, and the circumstances in which you used them. One law student wrote the following:

"One of my favorite experiences was organizing a non-profit fund-raiser. I coordinated the entertainment, invited guest speakers, sent out invitations, recruited and managed a team of volunteers, solicited local businesses for donations, publicized the event and served as master of ceremonies. The skills I most enjoyed were public speaking (as emcee), promoting and marketing (publicizing the event) and brainstorming (conceptualizing and planning the event). I enjoyed using these skills because I love interacting with people, performing to a crowd and filling a room for a cause I believe in.

"One of my least-favorite experiences was researching and writing a legal memo about a civil procedure issues. I had to research case law, read cases and analyze the relevant legal issues, and write a memorandum presenting and analyzing the legal issues. The skills I least enjoyed using were legal research (researching cases that presented a similar legal issue), reading legal cases (for case law on the same issue), and analyzing a civil procedure issue (to see how different courts have handled a similar legal issue). I didn't enjoy this project or the skills I used because it meant working alone in a library and thinking about subjects that didn't interest me."

Skills Preference Exercise #3

Imagine you could have any job in the world without regard to education or training. Now, draft a series of responses to this question: "I would be absolutely thrilled if I could get paid to _____". List as many jobs or occupations as you like and describe the skills most likely required for each (refer to the list in Exercise #1 if you need help).

Skills I Most Enjoy Using

Of all the skills you identified in the previous three exercises, list the five you do really well and would potentially want to use on the job.

1. _____
2. _____
3. _____
4. _____
5. _____

When identifying your favorite skills, be as specific as possible. For example, if you listed *writing,* consider what it is you like to write—legal memoranda, poetry, research papers, fiction, non-fiction? If you listed *working with people,* think about how you most enjoy working with others. Do you like interviewing people? Counseling people? Negotiating with people? Collaborating with others? And while you're at it, think about whether you'd enjoy using your favorite skills in a legal or non-legal job. Note: To those of you who may be thinking, *I've never worked before, so I feel like I don't have any skills,* stop a moment—and think about the *inherent* skills you use in college course-work, extracurricular activities, volunteer experiences and hobbies.

What Subjects Genuinely Interest You? By this we mean, what subjects interest you intellectually and would you enjoy thinking about on the job every day? For example, in the legal profession...

Tax lawyers spend their day studying tax regulations and client financial information.

Divorce lawyers think about divorce laws, marital property and client issues.

Corporate lawyers immerse themselves in contracts, mergers and acquisitions, and the legalities of assorted business matters.

Litigators think about the specific legal issues in dispute, as well as pre-trial procedural matters like deadlines, court filings, witnesses, settlement negotiations and trial preparation.

It's easy to see why it's so important to consider what subjects you enjoy thinking about when you're deciding which jobs to pursue. Because if you're bored by what you have to think about at work, the profession itself will probably come up short. Sadly, many current practitioners find this out too late. So before you commit yourself to any field, ask yourself what you enjoy thinking, reading and talking about. Having trouble thinking of areas yourself? Just go to a bookstore and walk around. What subjects sound interesting? Or look through an online course catalogue from a large university and note what departments, majors and courses interest you. Dare to dream. What if you prefer thinking about multiple subjects? Some people worry they have no direction if they're not interested in one subject only. That's fine—maybe you'll be happier doing general civil litigation or in-house corporate legal work, where you're constantly thinking about multiple subjects.

In any event, when generating a list of favorite subjects, this is the time to be brutally honest. Don't list what you think you're supposed to be interested in. (Don't write "regulatory issues" if you're infinitely more interested in wine.)

Subjects of Greatest Interest

Of all the subjects you identified, list the five of greatest personal interest in order of their importance:

1. _____

2. _____

3. _____

4. _____

5. _____

Note: It's helpful to jot down any details that might help define your area of interest. For example if you're interested in the environment, is it about clean water, air quality, or saving endangered manatees? If you're interested in business, is it in entrepreneurship, commercial finance, banking? If you're interested in property, is it in land use, or real estate? You get the idea.

What Do You Want in a Work Environment? By work environment, we mean the type of work setting you would most enjoy—the type of coworkers, the physical surroundings, the office culture, the hours, the dress code, the level of formality, the bureaucracy, the commute, etc. In short, the overall environment in which you'd feel most comfortable. Our appreciation of work environments differs from one person to the next. Some prefer formal environments; others find them stifling. Some love fast-paced offices; others a laid-back atmosphere. Some thrive on 60-plus hour work-weeks; others hate working longer than 40. Some people like formal attire; others prefer Friday-casual every day.

As you speak with various lawyers (and non-lawyers) about their work, you'll discover that different practice settings have different work environments. In fact, it's fair to say that the differences in workplace culture between, say, a large corporate law firm and a public-interest organization are like the cultural differences between New York City and Salt Lake City. Work environments vary among law-related and non-legal jobs as well. Just compare the difference between a large insurance company and a small ad agency. Or a large tech company and a nonprofit arts organization. Unfortunately, many lawyers learn, too late, that work environment can be just as crucial as the work.

So, what if you're not sure what kind of work environment you're best suited for? It's yet another reason for getting work experience that allows you to sample different settings. At the very least, you should *shadow* people in different types of legal and non-legal offices. That is, spend a day (at least a few hours) with them in a large corporate environment, a small firm, a nonprofit organization, a government agency or any other type of organization that sounds interesting. Compare workplaces that are formal versus casual; workplaces where 12-to-14-hour days are typical versus the traditional eight-and-go-home; workplaces that feel high-pressured and caffeinated versus relaxed and laid-back; workplaces that have plush set-ups and lots of support staff versus sparse surroundings and fewer resources. An investment of no more than a few days will give you an eye-opening sense of the most satisfying work environment for you.

The lowdown on billable hours. In law, the work-environment issue cited most frequently as impactful by lawyers is billable hours. We cannot overstate the surprise that most new lawyers feel when confronted with the pressure to produce 1,500, 1,800, even 2,200 annual billable hours (hours your firm can bill to the client). So, what's the big deal about billable hours?

Billable hours are the way private law firms make money—by billing clients for each hour an attorney works on their legal matters.

Many firms require attorneys to track their time in six-minute increments. Imagine this—you must stop every six minutes to record what you've done, or wait until the end of the day and try to remember. Of course, not every minute you spend at work is billable. Yes, doing legal research, taking a deposition, or having a phone conversation on a client's behalf, is billable. But there are all sorts of personal activities that have nothing to do with clients. So, it means that while you may spend 10 to 12 hours at work each day, perhaps only six to eight of them are billable.

Many firms have billable-hours requirements in which associates are expected to bill a certain number each year. This varies, often depending on the firm's size. Currently, the largest firms require new associates to bill a minimum of 1,900 to 2,200 hours per year, while mid-size firms require around 1,600–1,900 per year. If the number of hours you spend at work are an issue for you, it's important to ask about a firm's billable requirement before you commit to working there. Many firms list their billable requirements in the *Directory of Legal Employers*, published by the National Association for Law Placement (www. nalpdirectory.com). Better yet, ask new associates how many hours they're required to bill and—just as important—how many hours they must put in to hit that quota. For example, if they're required to bill 2,100 hours a year (not uncommon), but must actually work a total of 2,900 hours per year, a little arithmetic will tell something about their work day (e.g., if you divide 2,900 by 365, it translates to an eight-hour work day—*if* you worked 365 days a year). So, is one's work environment important? Most definitely.

The exercises on the facing page should help define what kind of setting is appropriate for you.

What Are Your Career Priorities? By priorities, we mean what is truly important to you when it comes to a job?

Is it a huge salary, even at the expense of having a life outside of work?

Is it a strictly 9-to-5 job with no weekend work?

Work Environment Exercise #2

Identify three previous jobs—paid or volunteer—and specify some of the qualities you liked or disliked about those work environments. Be specific.

This is an important exercise, and if you wish to make the most of it, draft a short paragraph describing what appealed to you (or not) about one particular work place. One law student wrote: "In one of my favorite jobs, I liked the 9-to-5 work day, the friendly colleagues, the casual dress code, the ability to work independently, the laid-back environment, and the short commute. In one of my least-favorite jobs, I disliked the harried pace, the formal dress code, and the intensity of some coworkers. However, I loved the plush office setting."

Job: _____   Job: _____

1. _____   1. _____

2. _____   2. _____

3. _____   3. _____

4. _____   4. _____

5. _____   5. _____

Job: _____

1. _____

2. _____

3. _____

4. _____

5. _____

My Preferred Work Environment

By now, you should have a pretty good sense about what sort of work environment appeals to you. Rank those five criteria below:

1. _____

2. _____

3. _____

4. _____

5. _____

Many people don't realize the importance of having a job that's in line with their priorities until they're in one that isn't. Being in a job that doesn't mesh with your priorities can be tolerable for some people and intolerable for others. For example, if it's important that your work is personally meaningful, you may be unhappy with a job that doesn't provide a sense of purpose. Or if you're representing clients that raise ethical conflicts, you may not be comfortable advocating on their behalf. Think carefully about what will motivate you to get up in the morning.

Career Priorities Assessment

Circle the priorities with the greatest appeal. Feel free to add others not listed here.

Helping people	Making a lot of money
Traveling	Having fun
Having a life outside of work	Being innovative
Job security	Having power
Meeting new people	Being entrepreneurial
_____	_____
_____	_____

Now it's time to list your top five priorities in the box below.

Career Priorities

Identify five career priorities from this list (or add your own criteria), and draft a paragraph (or a few sentences) for each that provides additional detail and why it's important to you:

1. Priority: _____
2. Priority: _____
3. Priority: _____
4. Priority: _____
5. Priority: _____

Work Assessment Exercise

In this important final exercise, you're invited to go online—to sites such as www.JDPost.com, www.AttorneyJobs.com, and www.PSLawNet.org—and create a list of every job that sounds remotely interesting regardless of salary or qualifications. (If you're more interested in law-related or non-legal jobs, skim the Help Wanted section of a major newspaper and check out web sites like www.Monster.com and www.HotJobs.com). For each position, identify what appeals to you as regards your own preferences for skills, subjects, work environment and priorities. Here's an example:

Job that appeals to me—Plaintiff-side employment lawyer
Skills that appeal to me—Client counseling/interaction
Subjects—Employment law and civil rights
Work environment—Public interest-minded colleagues; small office; casual attire
Priorities—Helping others, challenging work, professional growth

Self-Assessment Grid

This grid brings together the results of the previous four exercises regarding skills, subjects of interest, preferred work environment, and career priorities. So now it's time to transfer the results of those exercises to the grid.

Skills

1

2

3

4

5

Subjects

1

2

3

4

5

Work Environment

1

2

3

4

5

Priorities

1

2

3

4

5

For some of you, this opportunity at self-assessment will be the first time your work preferences have been grouped together. For others, self-assessment will only raise more questions. For example, "Why am I having trouble identifying my skills… why are my priorities so hard to define… why don't I know myself better… what am I going to do with my life?" This is natural, and there is no cause for panic. Still, if you filled in most, if not, all of the Grid, we recommend that you make an appointment with a law school career counselor, and bring the Grid along. Or make an appointment with a private career counselor. (See the Tool Kit page 222 for tips on finding a career counselor or, for a regional roster of consultants who specialize in working with lawyers, check out www. DecisionBooks.com and click on Law Career Experts).

Of course, we'd like to assure you that this self-assessment process is a self-contained, one-stop formula for career happiness, and for knowing which legal jobs are right for you. We'd like to offer that assurance but we can't. Still, what you have done here is to put in capsule form the single most important elements you need for job satisfaction. The next step is to use the information to explore various legal and non-legal jobs to see which ones offer a better fit. Hopefully, by using what you learned here, you will have a better idea of whether legal or non-legal jobs will meet your needs.

Step 2—Informational Interviews

Once you have your list—rip it out of the book if you have to—see your law school's career services counselor to discuss what types of legal jobs might offer what you're looking for. If you want additional assistance consider hiring a career counselor in private practice. Once you have identified what you want in a job, you can begin looking around in the real world to find one that meets your criteria. The strategy for that is to speak with a variety of attorneys about their work. This process is called *informational interviewing*.

They're informational only, of course, because all you want is information about a person's job or field—you're not scrounging for a job (not yet anyway).

Basically, an informational interview simply means talking to people to learn about a particular career field before you decide whether you would want to pursue it. And, while it sounds obvious to advise you to speak with lawyers in selective practice areas before you conclude where you want to work, many law students don't. And they live to regret it. Informational interviews can also help generate more creative ideas of things you might do with your law degree. Too many people don't look broadly enough at different career paths. Think about your passions (food, travel, sports, politics), and speak with people who are working in legal (and possibly non-legal) jobs in those areas. For example, if you love wine, seek out lawyers who represent vineyards, and non-attorneys who manage wineries, or handle public relations for them, or work in other non-legal capacities. Informational interviews can also help you create professional contacts that can be invaluable in landing your ideal job. The more people you speak with, and who know what you're interested in, the more likely someone will help lead you to a job. Meeting people with jobs that truly excite you could very well lead to future jobs or internships. That's how most people get their jobs, by the way. Not through the traditional job-listings and the standard interviewing processes. Now that we've explained why informational interviewing is so important, let's put it to work:

An informational interview simply means talking to people to learn about a particular career field before you decide whether you would want to pursue it.

Using your Self-Assessment Grid as a guide, create a list of types of lawyers with whom you wish to speak. The key to successful informational interviews is to talk with people who have jobs you might enjoy. That's why we had you do those annoying boxes earlier in the chapter. The answers you listed for your favorite skills, interests, work environment and priorities will help you identify lawyers whose work meets your preferences. So take another look at your grid and brainstorm a list of legal jobs that have your preferred criteria. For example:

Skills

If you listed negotiating, talk to mediators and litigators.

If you listed legal research and writing, talk to judicial law clerks and junior associates at law firms.

If you listed client counseling, talk to lawyers who work directly with clients (such as legal-services or estate planning).

If you listed drafting contracts or other legal documents, talk to transactional lawyers who work in private firms or corporate legal departments.

Subjects

If you listed business, talk to lawyers who work in corporate legal departments (in-house counsel) and corporate lawyers in law firms.

If you listed politics or policy, talk to lawyers at policy or public-interest oriented nonprofit organizations, or in legislative bodies or government agencies.

If you listed criminal justice, talk to lawyers who work for government offices such as the district attorney or public defender, or in private practice.

Work Environment

If you'd prefer a casual or non-bureaucratic environment talk to lawyers in public interest organizations, or in small firms (fewer than 25 lawyers), or in small companies (fewer than 100 employees).

If you'd like an intense, formal, deadline-driven environment, speak with lawyers in large law firms and in large corporations.

If you prefer creative environments, talk to lawyers who work in creative organizations dealing with entertainment, technology or the arts.

If you like entrepreneurial environments, talk to small companies and small law firms, and any type of not-for-profit organization.

Priorities

If you listed big salary, talk to mid-sized firms (25 to 75 lawyers) and large firms (more than 75 lawyers), and large corporations (more than 1000 employees).

If you listed a 9-to-5 schedule, seek out government agencies or public-interest organizations.If you listed autonomy, talk to solo practitioners or to lawyers in small firms or in small companies.

These are generalizations, so you'll want to investigate specific organizations to see if they meet your needs. Once you've made a list of general types of

The Devil's Advocate Says...

Go straight to the horse's mouth—Why do so many law students take career advice from people who have never practiced law (peers, parents, professors)? Beats the hell out of us, but we can say with confidence that if you want to make better job decisions, speak with those who are actually working at jobs you think that you want. If you don't know any lawyers, seek out some alums through your law school's Career Services Office, and get real-world insights about various practice areas and settings. Go straight to the horse's mouth. It makes all the difference in finding the right job for you.

attorneys, you need to generate a list of actual people who are in legal jobs that sound interesting. If you're thinking this step will require some time and effort, you're right. But don't let that stop you. Informational interviews are one of the smartest ways to use your time right now. We've outlined some additional steps in the Tool Kit (page 221).

Step 3–Get to Work

Finally, once you've had some informational interviews, try to line up a job or internship so you can get hands-on experience. If you discovered organizations that looked interesting during the course of your informational interviews, start there. If you didn't, use the same steps you used to line up informational interviews: use your Self Assessment Grid, ask your law school's CSO to recommend specific organizations, and do some Internet-based research to find local organizations where you might work.

Even the busiest of law students have options for getting legal work experience. Work part-time, or volunteer a few days or a few hours a week. Try to get credit for real-world experience by doing clinics or externships. If you're short on time, arrange to shadow someone at work. (See page 221 for the mechanics and benefits of *shadowing*.) Whatever manner you choose, the reward for working in different legal settings is that it will help you compare them to see which is a better fit. If you think you're interested in saving the environment, you'll know for sure if you spend some time working for the staff attorney of the Sierra Club, or a government lawyer at the Environmental Protection Agency. It's equally important to check out the difference between working in the private and public sector to see which is the better fit. If you're interested in, say, working on employment issues, you can get a taste in a private law firm (plaintiff or defense side), a corporation, a government agency or a public-interest organization. The key is seeing which work environment is right for you. And, yes, doing all of these steps requires more time and energy than merely applying to the same jobs as your friends. But we can assure you that it be well worth the effort, ensuring a much greater chance that when you actually become a lawyer, you'll be glad of it.

Of course, there is a chance that, after speaking with a variety of attorneys and getting some legal work experience, you may have even more questions about the wisdom of practicing law. If that's the case, the next section of this book will help you address the decision of whether or not to practice.

The Devil's Advocate Says...

Do something—Law students tell us they don't have time to explore different legal jobs. So, most often they do nothing at all. But doing even one thing a day toward your career search—even spending an hour a week—is better than blowing it off entirely. If you devote as much time to career exploration as you do on one course outline, you would make infinitely better job decisions.

Confess—One reason that leaving law school is so difficult is admitting—to yourself and to others—you may have made a mistake. Would you rather admit it now to family and friends—or later, to a shrink or career counselor? Many lawyers tell us they wish they'd had the nerve to admit their mistake much earlier, and certainly long before they launched their law career.

Do the math—If you're thinking about leaving law school, focus on what you'd save now (e.g., time and tuition), rather than on what you've already spent. You can beat the sunk cost fallacy if you really understand what's at stake. Some students rationalize staying in law school because "it's only two more years. But that's just not true. If you factor in the bar exam and a few years of practicing, you will have sunk much more time and money into the law just because you didn't want to see that one semester (or year) go to waste. So when you're thinking about leaving, calculate what's really at stake.

Prepare a soft landing—If the idea of quitting law school unnerves you—or makes you feel irresponsible—line up a short-term job or internship, or a certification program, to jump into when you leave. One law student we know quit in the middle of his second semester, and immediately enrolled in a course to get a real estate license. He never actually sold a single piece of property, but having something to do made it easier to stop doing something else—law school.

Choose carefully—Believe it or not, summer jobs can affect the enthusiasm with which you approach your legal career. Choose badly and you might conclude you're headed into the wrong profession. We know a 1L who did nothing other than legal research and writing projects at her summer job. She never got to speak to a single client, and, by the start of her second year, her appetite for law was wavering. Fortunately, in her next summer job she provided legal services to indigent clients, and she loved the experience. By the start of her third year, he enthusiasm for law had been reignited. Don't let one bad job turn you off to law; make an effort to find a job that turns you on.

Don't follow the herd—Even if it looks like "everyone" is planning to practice law after graduation, seek out and talk to JDs who did the opposite—who pursued the road less traveled. You'll find many nonpracticing graduates who have accomplished extraordinary things, and had fun along the way. Brad Meltzer became a best-selling author of thrillers like The Tenth Justice (which he wrote in law school). Rich Buery founded iMentor, a mentoring program for disadvantaged youth. Dan Pink worked as a White House speechwriter and wrote the national bestseller—Free Agent Nation. Stacey Stern co-created Findlaw.com, the popular legal website. Then there's Tim Russert, host of NBC's "Meet the Press," and author Studs Terkel, neither of whom practiced law a day in their lives.

Ignore the gloom-and-doomers—Don't obsess over rumors of a weak job markets or reports that "no one is hiring." There has never been a time when new people weren't being hired somewhere. Even firms in the middle of down-sizing will have needs that can only be filled by new talent. Sometimes these jobs go to the best students, and sometimes they go to students who ignored the conventional wisdom, and who sought out those positions anyway.

Reach out and touch someone—Surveys show that you are more likely to find work by initiating contact with prospective employers, or mining leads from family, friends, professors, law school and undergrad alumni, former employers, and other law students. Some of you will get jobs by being in the right place at the right time; others will meet future employers at weddings or in yoga class. One lawyer we know got her first two post-law school jobs by running into friends at a restaurant and, later, sitting next to a CEO at a luncheon. So, reach out and touch someone. Tell everyone you know—and meet—what you want. You might get lucky.

Don't be a clerkship snob—Too many of you who are interested in judicial clerkships will apply only to the 1,200 trial and appellate judges at the federal level. Big mistake. Doing so, you ignore the 29,000 or so state and local judges whose hiring criteria is often far more flexible than those of federal judges.

Investigate, investigate—Lawyers who admit to having chosen their job largely based on the salary tell us they wish they had asked a lot more questions—about the projects they would be given, the clients they would represent, how work was assigned to associates, the opportunities for training and mentoring, the people they would work for and with, the office culture, the billable-hour demands, and the overall workload. Besides salary, these are the other big issues you need to focus on before accepting a job.

Don't get paralyzed—Some of you are worried that whatever summer or post-graduate job you get will lock you into one career path forever (e.g, "if I work for the DA's office, I'll be boxed into criminal law"). As a result, you take jobs just because you think they will "keep your options open." Bad move. Your first summer or post-graduate job won't be your only job—just one in a series of stepping stones in a long career. If you're like a lot of lawyers, you'll change practice areas and settings, maybe even leave law altogether. People who have enjoyed satisfying law careers simply chose each of their jobs based on what sounded like the most fun.

Go straight to the horse's mouth—Why do so many law students take career advice from people who have never practiced law (peers, parents, professors)? Beats the hell out of us, but we can say with confidence that if you want to make better job decisions, speak with those who are actually working at jobs you think that you want. If you don't know any lawyers, seek out some alums through your law school's Career Services Office, and get real-world insights about various practice areas and settings. Go straight to the horse's mouth. It makes all the difference in finding the right job for you.

Volunteering pays—It's impossible to overstate the importance of getting real-life legal and non-legal experience. Of course, a salaried job or internship is ideal, but, failing that, you can always volunteer for firms, nonprofits, or government agencies. Even if it's for a couple hours a week—and even if it has little to do with lawyering—it's worth the effort. Sometimes government rules prevent firms from letting people work for free. But if you offer, several things might happen—they might say yes; they might even offer you a paid position. If you do volunteer, you might prove yourself so valuable that your boss will start paying you. Finally, you'll get useful insight into that job and that firm.

PART IV

Should You Really Practice Law?

From Here *to* "Attornity"

*I*f you're just joining us here, you're either a practicing lawyer who has begun to seriously question what more satisfying ways there are to make a living, or you're a law student who is wondering whether you're on the right career path at all.

Considering the investment you (lawyer or law student) have already made, the question of whether to practice law will demand the most careful evaluation and decision-making you can muster. That's the purpose of this section. And we'll do our best to help you make smarter decisions by isolating some of the reasons behind your job dissatisfaction and career confusion, and to introduce you to ways you might find a more satisfying job inside, outside or related to the law. Although deciding whether or not to leave your job (or profession) can be complicated, it's never too late to start making better career decisions. Just remember as you revisit your past career moves here, try not to beat yourself up (*if only I hadn't gone to law school…if only I hadn't accepted this job…*). Beating yourself up for past decisions won't help make better decisions in the future. Rather than obsessing over what's no longer in your control (the past), focus on what you can control (the present).

Do you feel stuck right now? Maybe it's because you're unsure whether you're in the wrong job or the wrong profession. Maybe you're clear that law isn't the right path for you, but you're worried about how to get out and the ramifications if you do. Or, maybe you're content with your work right now, but are looking ahead, and wondering how you can transition into something even more satisfying down the road. Or, as one attorney succinctly asked, "Am I going to die a lawyer?"

One factor that complicates the end of any job or career is a group of decision-making pitfalls we like to call **Choice Challenges.** These are the psychological traps that impair our judgment and influence us in ways that are not in our best interest. In their own way, each of these Choice Challenges presents a psychological minefield made all the more treacherous because they operate at a near-unconscious level. The aim of the section is to make you more conscious of them, and to learn how to navigate the minefield as you make decisions about the future of your legal career.

> Choice Challenges are the psychological traps that impair our judgment and influence us in ways that are not in our best interest.

In Parts II and III of this book (which we invite to read or skim if you haven't already), we presented 12 different Choice Challenges. In this section, we'll explore six of them and explain how they might be impacting your career decisions, how to overcome them, and how to make better choices. First, here's a brief definition of each:

Anchoring—When we attach ourselves to a fixed position regardless of evidence to the contrary.

Confirmation Bias—When we shut out information that contradicts our initial preferences.

Decision Paralysis—When we avoid making decisions because we're overwhelmed by choice.

Endowment Effect—When we place a higher value on things we already have than if they belonged to someone else.

Herd Mentality—When our actions and decisions are weighted by those around us.

Ignoring the Base Rate—When we ignore the odds (the base rate) in a given situation.

Information Cascade—When our actions or decisions are influenced by repeated exposure to a barrage of information.

Mental Accounting—When we treat money differently depending on where we get it and what we want to do with it.

Overconfidence—When we overestimate our skills, abilities or knowledge.

Regret Aversion—When our decisions are based on the fear of feeling bad in the future.

Rules of Thumb—When we adopt intellectual shortcuts to make choices less complicated.

Status Quo Bias—When we resist change and prefer to stay with what's familiar

In parts I and II we discuss how these Choice Challenges may have led you to law school and into your post-graduation jobs. In the following pages, we'll summarize that discussion and address how these Choice Challenges may be contributing to your current career dilemma. Whether you also skim parts II and III or just read the following recap, you'll gain helpful insights into how you've made career decisions in the past. That's because you're more likely to make better decisions once you understand how you have been making them. So let's review what you might have been thinking when you chose to pursue law, or particular legal jobs.

The Urge to Herd. If you're like many lawyers or would-be lawyers, you chose a legal life under the sway of the **Herd Mentality**. It's a powerful Choice Challenge that refers to the tendency to let your decisions be unduly influenced by the actions of people around you. It explains why trends and fads take hold: because people often adopt the habits and activities of those around them. When it comes to career decisions, the urge to herd can become even more powerful. People often decide to go to law school because they see many of their peers taking the LSAT and busily filling out law school applications. The problem with following the herd to law school is that just because it was a good path for some, it may not have been the best for you. If you relied on the herd for guidance, you might have skipped researching what law school was really like, or what legal practice actually involved. Or, once in law school, you may have followed the herd and pursued the same types of legal jobs as everyone else. That could be one reason you're dissatisfied with your current job, and are questioning whether law is really the right course. This may sound obvious, but it bears our stating it clearly: Most people who succumb to peer pressure and the *herd mentality* don't realize the extent to which they are in sway of these forces.

A Port in the Storm. If you were influenced by the *herd mentality*, you may also have been swayed by a related Choice Challenge called the **Information Cascade**. It refers to the way our decisions can be impacted by the barrage from the news, advertising and PR media. So, for example, if you were constantly exposed to news of a weak job market as you were deciding the direction of your career, you may have been more inclined to seek refuge in law school. The problem with letting the *information cascade* drive that decision is that enrolling in law school to escape the job market is an insufficient reason to be there. Because if law isn't the right career for you in general, you won't enjoy being a lawyer in a good or bad economy. Also, if there's a bad overall job market, the legal job market can be tough, too. So if the news of a bad job market figured heavily into your pursuit of a JD, and you didn't explore what lawyers actually do before you went to law school, it's understandable that you might be questioning the wisdom of your decision.

Ready, Aim... Aim... Aim. Speaking of decisions, if you're like many lawyers, a Choice Challenge called **Decision Paralysis** may also have influenced you to pursue a JD. When faced with too many options, we're often paralyzed from making any choice at all. A mundane example of *decision paralysis* occurs when we stroll the breakfast cereal aisle of a supermarket. Try it sometime, and see how difficult it can be to choose from so many options. In the same way, some students come to law school because they didn't know what to choose among all the professional and educational options open to them, so they enrolled in law school to "keep their options open." If that's the case, you may have entered law school knowing little about the legal profession, and you may now wonder if there were better paths for you. *Decision paralysis* also occurs when unhappy law students choose to remain enrolled because they don't know what to do if they drop out. Disliking law school is par for the course, but staying because it's too difficult to find an alternative is a poor way to make a career choice. Likewise, you may have been struck with *decision paralysis* during your post-grad job search, and been too overwhelmed to research and thoughtfully evaluate your options. If that's the case, you adopted an *I-just-want-a-job-any-job* mantra, and accepted the first offer that came along.

Whom Do You Believe? Another Choice Challenge that may have cemented your decision to attend law school is the **Confirmation Bias**. It refers to our tendency to seek information and advice that supports our original preferences. For example, if you asked only happily practicing lawyers about law school, you might not have gotten all the information necessary to make the best decision. Furthermore, you may have never set foot in a legal setting or talk to any unhappy lawyers or law students; in fact, you may not have spoken with anyone who might challenge your reasoning just because you didn't want to stray from your plan.

As you can guess, the *confirmation bias* may have led you to overlook some important perspectives. After all, if you had listened, someone could have pointed out holes in your reasoning, or encouraged you to sit in on law school classes, or to work in a legal environment, or even to speak with lawyers who left the law before you had made a final decision. The *confirmation bias* may have also come into play if you questioned your decision to remain in law school but then decided to stay because you were assured "it gets better after first year." If you only sought advice from happy lawyers, law students, professors or parents, they might have encouraged you to stay because they have positive associations with law school and the legal profession. Likewise, the *confirmation bias* may have contributed to your post-grad job decisions if you solicited most of your advice from your peers, parents or professors.

Conversely, when choosing to stay in law school you may have also been swayed by the **Disconfirmation Bias**. It's the tendency to ignore or discount information or opinions that *conflict* with what we want to believe. It helps explain how some law students can brush aside their concerns about the law even though they suspect that it isn't the best career path for them. Anxious about leaving law school and worried about what to do next, these students ignore the their lack of interest in legal studies and their lack of enthusiasm about a future in law. Instead, they rationalize why staying in law school is the right decision. Likewise, a working lawyers might ignore his or her gut feelings and allow the *disconfirmation bias* to keep them in a job that isn't right for them.

A Failure to Evaluate. Another common Choice Challenge that sends people to law school—or to push them into the wrong job—is a reliance on **Rules of Thumb.** These "rules" are the mental shortcuts we all use to simplify our decisions. For example, many students flock to law school not because they know what being a lawyer involves, but because they are persuaded by such mental shortcuts as, "you can do anything with a law degree" … "a law degree opens doors" … or, "law school teaches you how to think." The problem is that too many students fail to evaluate the validity of these *rules of thumb* to their particular situation. Nor is the problem confined to law students and new grads. If you're a working attorney, you may be betting your employment prospects on your own *rules of thumb*, such as, "large firms offer better training" … "it's impossible to afford a public interest legal job" … or, "I like to argue, so I'll like litigation." Without adequate evaluation, you may discover that these rules have no basis in reality for you.

Digging In. People who went to law school largely because they "always knew they'd be a lawyer" may have fallen prey to **Anchoring**. It's the Choice Challenge that refers to the way we allow our decisions to be influenced by ideas or notions that should have no bearing on them. For example, many students decide at an early age to be lawyers, and they nurture this dream into young adulthood. But when the time comes to choose a career path as a mature adult, this pre-adolescent fantasy isn't subjected to enough scrutiny and the individual has little or no idea what it's like to be a lawyer or whether they would enjoy it. Likewise, *anchoring* may also have something to do with your continuing to work in a legal setting that you dislike because of having attached—*anchored*—yourself to the notion that you must do something "prestigious" in law like work in a big firm. One of the dangers of *anchoring* is that it can lead you to overlook other jobs or career paths that would be a better fit.

> One of the dangers of anchoring is that it can lead to overlooking other jobs or career paths that would be a better fit for you.

Details, Details. Perhaps you were drawn to law with a specific idea of how you wanted to use your law degree—say, as a public interest lawyer, a sports agent, or a large-firm attorney. It's great to have a goal, but along the way you may have fallen prey to another Choice Challenge called **Ignoring the Base Rate**. It refers to a tendency to pay little or no attention to important odds and statistics relative to a particular situation. For example, if you entered law school thinking you wanted to be a public-interest lawyer, you may have ignored the fact that only 4% of recent law school grads wind up in public-interest jobs (25% when you count government jobs and judicial clerkships). Or if you came to law school thinking you wanted to be a sports agent, you might have ignored the fact that there are practically more licensed sports agents than professional athletes to represent. Or, if you were drawn to law by visions of pulling down a six-figure starting salary, you also may not have paid attention to the fact that roughly 12% of law school grads manage to snag those competitive, high-paying jobs (and many don't remain more than two or three years in them). By *ignoring the base right*, a lot of lawyers find themselves in jobs they dislike and never imagined doing.

Head Trip. There's also a good chance you were drawn to law school because you were confident that you wanted to pursue a specific area of legal practice, or that you'd figure out what you wanted to do with your JD during school. While confidence is admirable, you may have been suffering from a Choice Challenge called **Overconfidence**, which refers to the tendency to overestimate one's skills, ability or knowledge. Now that you're in practice, you may have realized that you overestimated how much you knew about the specific legal job you thought you wanted to do (or your ability to figure out what you wanted by the time you graduated from law school).

Staying the Course. Some or all of the Choice Challenges we've already covered may have been instrumental in how you decided to become a lawyer and how you continue to chose your jobs. But there are still other mental blind spots.

One of them is called the **Sunk Cost Fallacy.** It describes the tendency to make *future* decisions in order to justify *past* ones. So even if unhappy students want to bail out of law school after they've survived first semester and first year, many resist because they fear "wasting" all the money and energy they've already expended. Likewise, lawyers hate to "give up" on their investment in school and their career no matter how miserable they are because of it.

Disenchanted lawyers and law students also tell us they are staying the course because they're worried they may ultimately regret the decision to abandon ship. This sentiment reflects a Choice Challenge called **Regret Aversion.** The occurs when you base your choice to remain in law on the fear of feeling bad in the future, rather than on a clear and present desire to be a lawyer. *Regret aversion*, by the way, is connected to yet another Choice Challenge called the **Status Quo Bias.** This describes our inclination to resist change and to stick with what's familiar. Here's how it works:

A random selection of students were asked to pretend they had received an inheritance, and to choose from among four investments—Treasury bills, municipal bonds, a risky biotech, or a solid Blue Chip firm. Not surprisingly, the students chose the investment option that matched their willingness for risk—most of them were split between the two middle-of-the-road choices (bonds and the Blue Chip stock), and the rest were divided between the least- and most-risky investment (Treasury bills and the biotech). Actually, the researchers didn't care how the students invested the money; they just wanted to see how a randomly selected group of people would invest. Once they had a statistical baseline, the researchers divided the students into four groups and asked them to pretend they had inherited shares of stock, and to invest the money on their own. Half the students decided to *keep their money in the very risky biotech firm*. What's curious about that is that in the first scenario only a third as many said they would be comfortable with that amount of risk. What the study reveals is that when faced with a choice, half of us would choose to do nothing at all. We prefer the *status quo*.

Our propensity to stick with what we've got explains why unhappy lawyers choose to stick it out in jobs they dislike. Lawyers stricken with the *status quo bias* often suspect they don't belong in their job but stay anyway because leaving seems like it will require too much time, energy and risk. Being a lawyer in general or being in your particular job feels familiar (even if it feels lousy), and facing the unknown seems infinitely scarier by comparison. In other words, the devil you know often feels safer than the one you don't.

Do any of these Choice Challenges sound familiar?

If you recognize yourself as having fallen for any (or many) of the Choice Challenges described above, don't despair. It's understandable that you may be questioning what to do with your degree (and your life). We'll devote the rest of this section to walking you through a process for deciding whether or not to remain in legal practice and what to do whether you stay in or leave law.

"**I** absolutely hated my post-law school experience at a very large firm. I had worked in an even larger firm as a paralegal so I wasn't surprised by the firm's atmosphere. What was a shock, though, was the deadly dull work that I couldn't understand, the pressure to work around the clock, and how completely out of my element I felt every second of the day. I thought about leaving right away, but it took close to a year before I did anything about it. In the end, it was an easy decision because I was so incredibly miserable. I'd wake up nauseous every morning, wondering how I would get through the day. It finally clicked when two friends took me out to lunch on my birthday, and I was little more than a zombie obsessing about the unfinished work on my desk. Like I said, I didn't quit right away. It took a couple of months until I found work as an editor at a book publishing company. As I see it now, there were only two *pros* for staying in law—pleasing my father and making a ton of money—and the cons were too numerous: Never in my entire life had I felt so unhappy and so incompetent. When I arrived at the publishing house, I was incredibly happy, and I felt as *right* about that industry as I felt *wrong* in the law."—**Patty**

"**A**fter law school, I worked at a big law firm. It was sort of what I expected—crazy hours and a tremendous pressure to work billable hours, and a mania to record every spare moment of my day.

"But on a more personal level, I simply did not care about the causes I represented. And, even if I enjoyed drafting legal documents, I didn't have a personal connection to my clients.

"To compensate, I did a lot of volunteer work (in family practice and children's advocacy). But even then, I realized I just didn't enjoy the paperwork and day-to-day practice well enough to practice law the rest of my life. Of course, the main obstacles to leaving were financial and the writing-off of all the years I spent becoming a lawyer and then actually practicing.

"Surprisingly, everyone I met was supportive of my decision to leave law... even the partners of my firm. Before I did, though, I explored alternatives within law, consulted with career counselors, read books about career change, took tests, wrote in a journal. I did my best to make sure that whatever I did next I really wanted to do. I continued to a lot of volunteer work, and I made sure I spoke with a lot of people to help me determine if I was making the right decision."—**Susan**

"**W**hen I graduated from law school and went to a large national firm, the practice barely resembled my preconception. I wish now I had better understood the billable hour), and how the business model of law would affect my life. But it wasn't until I had already practiced law for 18 years, and was my firm's managing partner, that I finally began to seriously question whether I was in the right business.

"At first, I was just tired of the acrimony in the litigation practice. The more I analyzed what I was doing, the more I began to question the whole legal profession as a way of life. I saw people 20 years my senior still working just as hard as me. Of course, the biggest challenges to leaving law were 1) finding another career path; and 2) facing the fact that I probably wouldn't find anything that paid as well as practicing law. Anyway, I started by reading magazines, mostly about entrepreneurship and the new economy. This convinced me that there were other ways to make a living. I then began talking to anyone who would talk to me about what they did in their job, and I also worked with career counselors. Together, they enabled me to successfully transition into the business world."—**Rick**

"**W**hat I've learned is that money isn't everything... that I shouldn't listen to people whose ideas of success aren't the same as mine... and that if you dread getting out of bed in the morning, and can't wait to leave at the end of the day, you need to change jobs.

"I finally decided to leave the practice of law because I wasn't happy. I realized that, since we work most of our waking hours, it's better to find something to do that you love. I'm very satisfied now. Aside from marriage, leaving my law practice was the best decision I ever made."
—Jeremy

"I was a corporate litigator. Or maybe I should say 'unhappy corporate litigator.'

"On the one hand, there was all that tedious paper work, and, on the other, I had a practice where the depositions and court appearances were increasingly adversarial because huge punitive damage awards were at stake. So, I was either bored or dissatisfied.

"One day, I realized I just didn't want to spend the rest of my life honing my fighting skills! But what options did I have? Transactional law would be too boring; trial work too stressful. And if I left the law, I'd have to take a salary cut and start at the bottom again. But I knew one thing above all—I wanted to work for myself and I wanted flexible hours.

"To help choose my next direction, I took a class about career alternatives for lawyers, and I did a lot of research into ways I could leverage my legal skills. Ultimately, I decided to get into public relations. The same skills I developed as a lawyer—writing, interpersonal skills, analytical thinking, problem solving—I'm now able to transfer into business."—Jennifer

"After six years of practicing plaintiffs' employment law, the work just stopped being fulfilling. But it was hard to give up the prestige of being a lawyer. My career was at a stage where I was recognized and complimented by seasoned attorneys... even by federal judges. And then there was the 'suiting up' for oral argument in an imposing courtroom, or the drama of a day-long mediation. All of it had become a big part of who I was. Also, although most people say they hate attorneys, they seem to hold them in a certain esteem. Letting go of all that was hard, but I knew I had to do it.

"I finally asked myself if I wanted to be practicing law in 5 or 10 years. The answer was *no*, and that's when I started making plans to leave."—Greg

"After years of doing corporate law at a firm, I reached a crossroads. I didn't want to become a partner, and I knew I didn't want to go in-house or to a different firm. So, rather than quit, I arranged to take a leave of absence. Mostly, I wanted to travel and just experience life and be able to pick up my dry cleaning—all the things you can't do when you're working 60-80 hours a week.

"Going on sabbatical was the best thing I ever did. I got some perspective on life and work. I realized my job wasn't as horrible as I thought, and, if I had to go back, I could. I also discovered that I have skills, talents, and interests that are very far from being a lawyer—including photography and film.

"For me, it was important to take time to tap into my creative side. Now that I'm at the end of my sabbatical and starting a job search, I'm looking for balance. I may work a reduced schedule as a lawyer and continue to explore my creative interests, like taking film courses at night. I'm also looking at doing something in the legal field where I use different skills, like assuming a management role in a law firm. What makes this easier is the realization that I don't have to make an entire career change. It was very daunting when I thought in terms of redefining myself and my career completely.

"Taking a leave of absence was like taking baby steps. I would encourage anyone who's uneasy about career change to do it incrementally."—Seth

Chapter 13

The **Decision Assessments**

"Here's how I've learned to make decisions: I just ask myself, 'What will I regret not doing when I'm 70?'"

— Doug, general counsel for an arts organization

*T*he first step to figuring out whether to leave your firm, leave your job, or leave law entirely, is to pinpoint the source(s) of your dissatisfaction. It's no easy task. Many of us blame our unhappiness on job- or career-related issues; others blame external factors. How can you find out which is accurate? The following series of Decision Assessments should help you decide whether to continue practicing law or to leave and pursue another career path. By going through this process carefully, you should emerge with a better sense about your work life so you don't make any precipitious moves.

Answer every Decision Assessment statement as honestly as possible. The more candid your responses, the more you'll be able to improve the way you're approaching your decisions. Let's get started by examining some scenarios that lawyers commonly encounter when they contemplate leaving law.

D ECISION ASSESSMENT 1

✓ *Check every statement that reflects your thinking.*

- ❏ **A** I'm not happy in my practice, but I can't see myself as anything but a lawyer.
- ❏ **B** I've already begun assessing what's wrong with, or missing from, my current job.
- ❏ **C** I'm taking steps to explore legal and non-legal work that might be a better fit for me.
- ❏ **D** I've invested so much in my law career that I just can't throw it all away now.
- ❏ **E** There are aspects of legal practice that I do enjoy.
- ❏ **F** The hardest thing about leaving law is that my family, my friends and my colleagues all know me as a lawyer.
- ❏ **G** One good thing about my job is that I like the subject matter of my practice area.
- ❏ **H** I'm not sure I want to leave law, so I'm looking into ways I can modify my job so that it's more enjoyable.
- ❏ **I** I can't stop practicing now, otherwise it'll look like I couldn't hack it.

In the pages that follow, we'll examine each statement for its potential to contribute (or not) to smart decision-making. We'll score your responses at the end of the chapter. For now, let's review the statements you did or did not check, and tell you what they say about your decision-making process:

The Sunk Cost Fallacy

☑ **D   I've invested so much in my law career that I just can't throw it all away now.**

If you checked this statement, you may be a victim of the **Sunk Cost Fallacy.**

This refers to the way we make decisions in the present to justify decisions made in the past. In other words, we let previous investments of time, money, effort, or emotion dictate how we approach choices in the future. And while this may be perfectly appropriate in some decisions—say, marriage—it doesn't make good sense in others. For example, when you decide to finish a bad book simply because you're halfway through it, you're only wasting even more time simply to justify the time you've already spent reading. The same applies to bad movies— we refuse to walk out because of the time we've already spent watching.

By this same reasoning, you may be reluctant to leave the law…even though your career feels draining and unfulfilling. You think to yourself, "Well, I've already sunk all this time, money and effort into my legal education and legal practice, it would be a tragedy to throw it all away now."

You've fallen for the "sunk cost fallacy" when walking away from your law practice seems worse than staying unhappily employed.

That's why you feel trapped—walking away from your investment seems worse than staying unhappily employed. Wall Street investors face a similar dilemma every day. But the money they pay for shares of a can't-miss IPO is irrelevant once the check has been written. All that should matter is what the stock is worth to them in the present moment. So, what's your career "stock" worth right now?

We're not suggesting you disregard the considerable investment you made in law. What we are saying is that your investment has already been made, and that it shouldn't overly influence your decision about the future. Sometimes, the book, the movie (the career) doesn't get any better. The truth is, whatever resources you have invested in becoming a lawyer, you won't get any of them back no matter what career choices you make from now on. If you're not fully comfortable with the idea of leaving law entirely, it may be time to explore legal, law-related and non-legal jobs to see what appeals to you. For example:

Janet, an attorney who left a boutique law firm for a political consulting outfit, did just that. "I looked at a ton of different legal jobs," she said, "until I finally realized that none of them really excited me. But when I expanded my search to *non-legal* jobs, I quickly found one that felt right."

If you are not ready to jump ship yet, consider taking smaller steps.

Elissa was miserable in her firm, but was hesitant to leave law altogether. So, she decided to become in-house counsel for a trade association, a position which turned out to be less stressful but not terribly interesting. That job helped persuade Elissa to try making a career out of her favorite hobby— pottery. She opened her own studio, grew it into a thriving business, and then—drawing on her legal background—began providing consulting services to new studios. Like Elissa, some lawyers are able to overcome the *sunk cost fallacy* by putting their legal background to work in a new guise.

However you do it, the point is to find a job that excites you and pursue it with as much doggedness as you pursued your legal career. Doing that can help divert your attention from what you've sunk.

Anchoring

☑ A   I'm not happy in my practice, but I can't see myself as anything but a lawyer.

☑ F   The hardest thing about leaving law is that my family, my friends and my colleagues all know me as a lawyer.

☑ I   I can't stop practicing now, otherwise it'll look like I couldn't hack it.

If you checked one or more of these statements, your decision-making process may be adversely affected by a Choice Challenge called **Anchoring**. It refers to a tendency to allow certain ideas or data to unduly influence our choices. For example, when unhappy lawyers consider leaving their practice, a number of *anchors*, or notions, quickly attach themselves—notions of professional identity, and the prestige and money associated with the job. The problem with *anchoring* to money, prestige, or professional identity, is that these alone usually don't manifest happiness. Studies show over and over that people who like what they do—who have what we think of as professional fulfillment— usually have a greater sense of happiness and well-being than those who focus on the perks associated with the job.

Regress—If you have a hard time seeing yourself as anything other than a lawyer, think about the dreams you had before law school. A few lawyers we know decided not pursue their entrepreneurial dreams because of family considerations. When they finally got too dissatisfied with law, they left and proceeded to thrive in business. What were your dreams way back when? Thinking about what you wanted to be when you grew up really can help uncover clues about what you need from your work now.

The expectations and judgments of spouses, parents, friends, and colleagues are yet another kind of *anchor*. In our experience, lawyers inevitably worry about what "everyone" will think of them if they leave the law. As if somehow their decision signifies a personal failing. This notion, this *anchor*, is often so oppressive that some lawyers find it more productive to keep their families out of the loop while they can make career decisions on their own. Some even wait until they actually land their next job before saying anything to their family.

If you're not getting the listening and objective support you need from the people closest to you, then seek out a career counselor (see the Tool Kit for pointers on finding one or, for a list of law-related counselors, go to www. DecisionBooks.com and click on Law Career Experts), or talk to

> **I**f you're not getting the listening and objective support you need from the people closest to you, then seek out a career counselor.

some former practitioners who found success in areas outside law. Speaking with them, and realizing that your legal background can help you break into enjoyable new jobs and careers, will help you let go of your anchors. The number of ex-lawyers who find success in other fields is legion. Most are not well-known, but some are. They include actor/former U.S. Senator Fred Thompson; CNN commentator/former judge Catherine Crier, British actor John Cleese, singer Julio Iglesias, former EPA Administrator Carol Browner, writer/producer David E. Kelley (*The Practice, Ally McBeal*), and Southwest Airlines founder Herb Kelleher. Most of them leveraged their legal backgrounds to help them in new fields; all of them succeeded in their new careers because they pursued what they enjoyed. Once again, people are more successful at things they like doing. So if you leave law for something that excites you, you're far more likely to thrive.

☑ **E** **There are aspects of legal practice that I do enjoy.**

☑ **G** **One good thing about my job is that I like the subject matter of my practice area.**

If some aspects of legal practice still have appeal, or you're still interested in your practice area, maybe leaving law isn't the best choice at this time.

To figure out your best career move, it often helps to assess what you like and dislike about your current job. Then look for ways to modify your current job enough to make you want to remain in it, or begin looking for a new job that has the aspects of practice you enjoy without the negatives of your current position. You might also explore whether there are law-related or non-legal jobs that still offer the things about your practice that you do enjoy.

Here are a few examples:

If you like the subject matter of your practice area, consider applying your expertise in a different practice setting. If, say, you're a patent attorney in a large firm, you might be happier in a smaller boutique patent-law firm. If you're an employment lawyer in a firm, you might explore bringing your expertise to a corporation, a government agency (like the Equal Employment Opportunity Commission) or a public interest organization. Or, if you enjoy client counseling but are tired of a legal environment, consider applying your counseling skills in a different context (as a consultant or financial advisor). The point is, if there are things you like about your job, explore ways to incorporate them in a new context. That's what Jeanette did. "I chose my first law firm job without giving it a lot of thought," she said. "So, when I was looking to leave my firm, I was determined to make a more informed decision the next time around. I figured out that what I liked most about my big firm job was doing tax work for nonprofits. So I looked for lawyers who did that as their full-time job. I found them in boutique firms, in the tax practice group of larger firms, and in hospitals and nonprofits. I had informational interviews with all of them, which was incredibly interesting. And through that process, I got a job offer (legislative aide to a locally elected official) and I was very happy in my new position."

One way to find lawyers in different fields is to join a professional association. Many cities have a women's bar association, a minority bar association, a young lawyers group, and even groups for lawyers in career transition. Joining any of these organizations can help you brainstorm ways to find greater satisfaction in your present job, or how to find a new job. The groups can facilitate professional contacts that just might lead you to your next position.

☑ **B** I've already begun assessing what's wrong with, or missing from, my current job.

☑ **H** I'm not sure I want to leave law, so I'm looking into ways I can modify my job so that it's more enjoyable.

If you checked either of these statements, they represent the right steps to learning what you want from your work and what needs changing. Carefully assessing what you like and dislike about the way you spend time at work, the people with whom you spend it, the subjects you think about, and the quality of the work environment, will all help determine whether anything can be done to make you happier in your present job. It's also useful to take a step back and think about what drew you to law in the first place. Perhaps you entered law school with meaningful goals, but ended up in a job that doesn't relate to them. Then think about whether you can reduce your work hours or switch practice groups. If not, then begin looking for other jobs (legal, law-related and non-legal). At the end of this section, we'll walk you through the process of assessing what's working and not working in your job.

☑ **B** I've already started exploring legal and non-legal jobs that might be a better fit for me.

If you checked this statement, you're on the way to finding a career path that's right for you. Taking the time to explore fields inside, outside, and related to the law will give you greater clarity about the jobs you ought to pursue. In fact, sometimes investigating one career path can lead you to another one you never considered. Above all, researching new jobs will help prevent you from getting

---

DECISION ASSESSMENT 2

✓ *Check every statement that reflects your thinking.*

☐ **A** I'd like to change careers, but I wouldn't know what to do if I did leave legal practice.

☐ **B** I can't give up the salary I make as a lawyer.

☐ **C** I've started talking to other lawyers about other legal jobs I might enjoy.

☐ **D** As much as I dislike my job, making a switch feels risky in this economy.

☐ **E** I still enjoy having the potential to affect social change through the legal process.

☐ **F** I've started looking outside the law to see if there's work there I might prefer.

☐ **G** Right now, I value the security my job provides.

stuck when you start *anchoring* your identity as a lawyer, or succumbing to the *sunk cost fallacy*. We'll offer plenty of career-exploration tips at the end of this section.

We'll score your responses at the end of the chapter. For now, let's review the statements you did or did not check, and tell you what they say about your decision-making process:

Decision Paralysis

☑ **A** **I'd like to change careers, but I wouldn't know what to do if I did leave legal practice.**

If you're confused about leaving law, you may have been tripped up by **Decision Paralysis**. This Choice Challenge is triggered when we're overwhelmed by our options and can't choose. In our work, we often see this among lawyers who are eager to leave law, but who are not certain what law-related or non-legal options exist, how to find them, or which would offer the greatest satisfaction. So they stay stuck. But *decision paralysis* is no reason to remain in a job that makes you unhappy. You need a systematic approach to identifying, exploring and evaluating legal, law-related and non-legal jobs. Here are some ideas to keep it manageable:

> Seek out non-practicing lawyers and talk to them about how the new direction they found after leaving the law.
> Use vacation days to volunteer in a different work setting.
> Shadow someone whose job sounds appealing to you.
> Read Deborah Arron's *What Can You Do With A Law Degree?* (5th ed., 2004). Work through the section on self-assessment, and then consult the book's appendices for hundreds of legal and nonlegal jobs into which other lawyers successfully transitioned.

Even the busiest of lawyers tell us that once they reached a certain level of misery, they made time to do at least one thing per day towards finding another job or career. Taking just one step a day can help you maintain your momentum.

Please note: In counseling unhappy lawyers, we often see a tendency towards perfectionism... a desire to find The Perfect Job. If you're truly unhappy in your current position, your next job needn't be perfect... just better than the one you have now. It may be more realistic to land a new job that doesn't have worst aspects of your present job (hours, projects, a micromanaging boss, etc.) and to continue to lay the groundwork for your next position. Without that groundwork, you could end up like one associate we know who said, "I've had the same terrible job in two different buildings." Remember, a career is a series of stepping-stones; it may take several incremental steps (a number of jobs) to reach your dream job. One lawyer who learned this lesson was Jane, a small-firm litigator who spent two years researching dozens of careers while growing increasingly unhappy at her job. Finally, Jane decided to get into the real estate profession, one option that seemed relatively appealing. "When I let go of thinking my next job had to be my dream job," she says, "I was able to stop researching and take action. I'm in a better place now because I enjoy real estate more than litigation."

The Information Cascade

☑ **D   As much as I dislike my job, making a switch feels risky in this economy.**

Another reason that unhappy lawyers might not initiate a career change or job search is a Choice Challenge called the **Information Cascade**. It's a term reserved for the avalanche—or, the *cascade*—of electronic news, data and opinions with which we're bombarded. Much of this news is as irrelevant as it is hard to ignore, but it can—and does—affect the way you might perceive the probability of a successful job search. In short, you may become so discouraged by consistently bleak information that you put off taking important steps to change your career. But just because the economy is soft doesn't mean you can't research alternative careers, or speak with non-practicing lawyers or non-lawyers who have jobs that interest you. Even if employers aren't hiring right now, the contacts you make may pay off eventually. Think about it: if you get to know people who work in places

> If you're truly unhappy in your current position, your next job needn't be perfect...just better than the one you have now.

The *Devil's Advocate Says*...

Ignore the Wall Street Journal—Don't let a soft economy prevent you from activating your job search. Even a recession presents opportunities for employment. For example, we know one unemployed Silicon Valley lawyer who co-founded a group called "Recession Camp," a social and networking group for Bay Area job seekers. He made valuable professional contacts through that venture and eventually landed an in-house counsel job.

where you'd like to work, you'll have a tremendous advantage when that organization eventually hires anew. And, if you're truly dissatisfied in your present job, taking any action towards finding a new job can help you endure your current situation. "One thing that made it easier to quit my job in a bad economy was to stop reading the news, especially the business news," says Steve, a former attorney who now works for a litigation consulting company. "Once I stopped hearing about layoffs and business failures, I was more productive and less stressed."

☑ **B   I can't give up the salary I make as a lawyer.**
☑ **C   Right now, I value the security my job provides.**

Money and stability are powerful reasons to hesitate leaving your legal practice. But if you're unhappy in your job, and there's no way to modify it, you should at least start exploring alternatives to see where the grass might be greener ... and the salary reasonably comparable. Some lawyers we know switched to corporate or government practices; others made lateral moves to different types of firms. All still earned relatively similar salaries. Still others found work that paid less but was so satisfying that they felt the cut in pay was worth it. And a large group of lawyers found a happy medium: jobs that didn't pay as much as their former jobs, but not as little as their dream job. In the case of Maura, an unhappy lawyer, she left a large firm for a job as in-house counsel at a university. "When I was 25," she says, "I could have pursued my ideal job (legislative director for a nonprofit), but it wasn't financially feasible. I had just become a parent and a homeowner. But I'm satisfied with the way things turned out. I have a job I enjoy well enough, and I've come to terms with my choices."

If the jobs that attract you the most pay the least, don't automatically reject them. Your starting salary won't be your salary forever. We know some lawyers who left law to join public relations firms, government agencies, or nonprofits, and ended up earning a lot more after just a few years. For example, there's Ted, who left a large firm after six miserable months, and took a massive pay cut to work on Capitol Hill. After a few enjoyable years on the Hill, he joined a trade association as a vice president, and got a tremendous pay increase. Here's something else to keep in mind—many former lawyers tell us that when they were in more stressful, higher-paying jobs, they spent more money on leisure pursuits and material possessions to compensate for their misery at work. Once they landed more enjoyable jobs, they spent less and managed perfectly well on a reduced salary.

One way to judge the merits of psychic income against real income is to speak with lawyers who switched to lower-paying jobs and ask how they managed the financial implications. Above all, keep in mind that you do have options. Staying in law versus leaving law is not a stark choice between feast or famine.

That's also important to remember if job security is keeping you from making a change, or at least exploring the possibility. You can remain at your present job until you find a new one that you like more. And while no job is 100 percent secure, some organizations are more solid than others. So look for jobs that play to your strengths and interests within a framework that will meet your need for stability. While job security is never guaranteed, you can surely find a new job that's equally as stable as your old one.

☑ **E I still enjoy having the potential to affect social change through the legal process.**

Checking this statement suggests that remaining in practice may be appropriate. Still, if you're reading this book, it would be a good idea to think about what's working and not working for you. Perhaps you're burned out or need a vacation or a sabbatical. Maybe your biggest gripes (hours, workload) can be modified so that you can be even more effective.

Another option is to modify your practice so that it's more fulfilling and less frustrating. A growing number of lawyers are doing just that, through a movement that's called "progressive law" (also known as "renaissance law" or "transformational law"). Essentially, the goal of this movement is to enable lawyers to use more creative, and less adversarial, ways to resolve conflicts. These lawyers emphasize alternatives to litigation (like mediation) and use planning and counseling to prevent legal problems from arising in the first place. This growing trend has allowed lawyers who might have otherwise left law to enjoy a satisfying practice that's more in line with their values. If you're interested in learning more about the progressive law movement, we list a few groups in the Tool Kit (on page 233) that can help.

If none of the above options work for you, it's time to start looking elsewhere for where you can contribute to social change. Think about what you need in order to feel as though you're contributing to change, then speak with lawyers (and non-lawyers) who have jobs that look fulfilling. Remember, there are many avenues to social change without practicing law, so don't limit your conversations to lawyers.

☑ **C I've started talking to other lawyers about other legal jobs I might enjoy.**

☑ **F I've started looking outside the law to see if there's work there I might prefer.**

If you're talking to people about what their jobs involve, you're taking one of the most effective steps to figuring out what type of job you'd like next. You may discover that there are appealing legal jobs you never knew existed, or you may find law-related or non-legal jobs that interest you more. Throughout this book, we continually emphasize the benefits of speaking with current and former lawyers (and nonlawyers) about their careers. You're far more likely to make better career decisions if you get practical information and emotional support from others. This worked wonders for Lance, who hit a wall after 10 years as a litigator. The best thing he did to address his self-described "mid-career crisis" was to speak with a wide array of lawyers about his options. The conversations sparked his interest in transactional and licensing work, so he launched a new round of meetings, coffees, and lunches with transactional lawyers to learn more about it and how to make the transition. His contacts advised him to attend CLEs, to write articles for local bar publications, to join professional associations where he would meet transactional lawyers, and to continue networking. In time, one of Lance's informational interviews led to a job in a corporation's legal department.

We'll score your responses at the end of the chapter. For now, let's review

DECISION ASSESSMENT 3

✓ *Check every statement that reflects your thinking.*

- ❏ **A** I don't really enjoy my work, but I'd be crazy to give up such a good job.
- ❏ **B** As a way to explore different legal jobs, I've started volunteering and participating in a variety of CLE's.
- ❏ **C** I've worked hard to establish myself in my legal career.
- ❏ **D** I'm exploring law *and* non-law jobs by volunteering, taking classes and seeking out people in different fields.
- ❏ **E** I'm afraid that if I left the law I would regret it later.
- ❏ **F** I'm so busy right now, I just don't have the time to explore other jobs.
- ❏ **G** I still enjoy the professional respect that comes with being a lawyer.
- ❏ **H** What I like about the law is its intellectual dimension—the legal analysis and strategic thinking.
- ❏ **I** What's the point of leaving my job? I may not like the next one any better.
- ❏ **J** I'm concerned that if I try to leave law, non-legal employers may not hire me.

the statements you did or did not check, and tell you what they say about your decision-making process:

The Endowment Effect

☑ **A** **I don't really enjoy my work, but I'd be crazy to give up such a good job.**

If you checked this statement, you may be letting a Choice Challenge called **The Endowment Effect** sway your decision. Here's how it applies to career decisions: Research shows that we tend to value (e.g., endow) our own job more highly than if someone else had the same job. Thus, unhappy lawyers are able to advise other unhappy lawyers to chuck their jobs or careers much more easily than they would tell themselves. So, suppose you dislike your colleagues, your projects, your long hours, and all the weekends you spend in the office. If a friend listed these same problems, you would probably advise him or her to start looking for a new job. But, according to *the endowment effect*, if these same negative characteristics describe *your* job, you're less likely to see the downside and more likely to overemphasize the good. The way to override *the endowment effect* is to thoroughly evaluate your current job. List its positive and negative aspects with ruthless objectivity, and pretend the job belongs to a friend (and not you). Now what is your advice—stay or go? If you honestly recommend that your "friend" should start looking for another position, then you know what needs to be done. For many lawyers, this so-called Misery Index is a great motivator—because once you cross a certain threshold of unhappiness, and start exploring more appealing alternatives, it becomes easier to not overvalue (*endow*) your present job and pursue a new one.

> The Misery Index is a great motivator to change. Once you cross a certain threshold of unhappiness, it's a lot easier to not overvalue your present job and to pursue a new one.

Regret Aversion

☑ **E** **I'm afraid that if I left the law I would regret it later.**
☑ **I** **What's the point of leaving my job? I may not like the next one any better.**
☑ **J** **I'm concerned that if I try to leave law, non-legal employers may not hire me.**

If you checked any of these statements, you may be succumbing to **Regret Aversion**, the Choice Challenge that plays into our fear of making any decision for fear we might live to regret it. Indeed, leaving the law might prove to be a mistake for many reasons. But without ESP, you can't know the future until you begin to explore some alternatives in the present. Alas, many unhappy lawyers who worry that they won't like any other jobs usually haven't even assessed what they'd enjoy in a new job, or explored other options in depth. Getting more information—especially that which comes from self-assessment and informational interviews—will help demonstrate how many alternatives there are to your present situation. So, the way to overcome *regret aversion* is to identify compelling jobs that sound like a better match for you, and to speak with—and shadow—the people doing them. The more you can find some specific jobs you're reasonably sure you'd enjoy, the less you'll worry that you'll regret leaving law for them. If you begin exploring and don't like anything you see at first, don't be discouraged. A job-search or career change requires patience, endurance, resolve—and some courage—and can often seem like a career of its own. At the very least, doing a little occupational reconnaissance should distract you from your current job misery.

Incidentally, a good deal of research has been done on the subject of regret. What it reveals is that people most often regret *actions* in the short term, and regret *inactions* in the long term. So, if you ask someone what they regret over the past year, they most likely will tell you about actions they did take. If you ask what they regret over the past 10 or 20 years, they will tell you about actions they *didn't* take. In our experience, lawyers who leave the law to pursue other opportunities usually have no regrets. Even if they left law and later returned to it, they reaped the benefits from having tried. Which brings us to another observation: we know many lawyers who left their law practice and successfully returned to it later on. They say they were glad to have tried something different, and that getting back into the profession wasn't as difficult as they had imagined. Why? Because they maintained their bar memberships, remained in contact with attorneys, attended bar association events and CLE's, wrote articles for legal trade publications or bar journals, took a few cases on the side or did pro bono work. In this country, some people reinvent their careers an average of 12 times during their lifetime. So, go ahead and try something new. If it doesn't work, you can always come back into the embrace of law.

As for the fear that no legal employer will hire you, you can put that to rest. Tens of thousands of attorneys leave the profession each year, and many of them successfully find nonlegal positions. If you're still skeptical, seek out lawyers who left the law and found satisfaction in nonlegal settings. If they made the sort of career change you're contemplating, they can provide motivation and practical strategies for your own transition. Specifically, they can instruct you on how to market yourself to nonlegal employers by emphasizing your "transferable skills" (e.g., writing, research, analytical thinking, problem-solving), and they can recommend classes, volunteer work and associations to help you learn about a particular field and make contacts in it.

☑ **C I've worked hard to establish myself in my legal career.**

This is a perfectly reasonable issue to consider when mulling a career change. After all, the knowledge, experience, contacts and skill sets we acquire as we go through our career are, in the end, our most valuable assets. But people often forget how fungible—that is, how easily transferable—are their knowledge, experience, contacts, and skills. If you've developed expertise in a particular area of law, but are still ready for a change, you can explore numerous options that would still allow you to capitalize on your experience. You could bring your knowledge to a different employment setting (switching from law firm to government), or play a different role (switching from attorney to a leadership position such as a corporate officer or executive director of a nonprofit). Our point is that your hard work and expertise in law won't go to waste; there are myriad ways to apply what you've learned, and to leverage who you know in an interesting and challenging new job. That's what career counselors do best: help you discover how to do this.

☑ **F I'm so busy right now, I just don't have the time to explore other jobs.**

Your concern about fitting a job search into an already busy schedule is perfectly understandable—and easily dismissed. The trick is to break a job search into small, manageable pieces, and work the steps into your schedule in a way that's doable for you. Some lawyers spend one or two evenings a week, or a few hours over the weekend, reading books and surfing web sites devoted to alternative careers. (See the Tool Kit for suggestions.) Others use their lunch hours, sick days or vacation days to conduct informational interviews, or to shadow others on the job, or to attend conferences in other fields and (eventually) interview for new jobs. Still others opt to work part-time, or to take a career sabbatical. But even the busiest of lawyers made time to take one step a day, once they committed to becoming proactive. We'll give you more ideas for streamlining your job search at the end of this section so you can choose which seem most feasible for you.

☑ **G I still enjoy the professional respect that comes with being a lawyer.**

☑ **H What I like about the law is its intellectual dimension—the legal analysis and strategic thinking.**

If you checked either of these statements, they are common sentiments that may signal you're not ready to leave the law. However, if you're unhappy in your current job, or merely interested in exploring alternatives, don't let these reasons keep you stuck in your practice. Leaving the law doesn't mean you can't have the same level of professional respect in a new role. You might leverage your JD into a high-level position in another field. And if you excel at what you do, you'll command respect from your colleagues; having a JD after your name isn't the only way. Besides, even if you stop practicing, you don't have to relinquish your identity as an attorney. You can always write "Esq." after your name, stay involved with the legal community or take pro bono cases, and people will know you're a lawyer. Likewise, there are other careers besides law that offer intellectual challenge, although it's hard to remember that if you've only been immersed in practice. So, in addition to looking for a more appealing legal job, you might also look for law-related jobs, like litigation consulting.

☑ **B   As a way to explore different legal jobs, I've started volunteering and participating in a variety of CLE's.**

☑ **D   I'm exploring law and non-law jobs by volunteering, taking classes and seeking out people in different fields.**

You'll earn big points here by getting some hands-on experience as part of your search for a new job or career. It's not that we necessarily want you to change careers; instead, we're hoping that by getting some hands-on experience you discover what it is that really satisfies you. You might discover that the grass really is greener, and decide that law in general or your job in particular is more suited for you than you thought. But you will only know this if you seriously investigate other options. And, of course, we also like these answers because the kinds of activities we're recommending are often the ones that lead to meaningful and satisfying career transitions. Many lawyers we know found their jobs by volunteering on political campaigns or for nonprofit organizations, for example. While taking a class may not tell you exactly what it's like to do a job, at least it will help you see if you're interested in the subject matter.

We hope this exploration has sparked significant rethinking and action. We'd like to think that you now have a pretty good idea already if you're a candidate for a job or career change. But some people, especially lawyers, like to make their cases air-tight. Toward that end—and now that we've analyzed some common issues and obstacles you've been facing—it's time to add up your Decision Assessment scores and see how you fared.

Adding it Up: Should You Really Continue Practicing Law?

Okay, it's time to score your three Decision Assessments. Go back to the Decision Assessments, and add up your scores at the bottom of each.

Decision Assessment 1 (page 180)
Statements—A, F, I (1 point each)
Statements—D & H (3 pts)   _____
Statements—B, E, G (5 pts)   _____
Statement—C (7 pts)   _____

                          Subtotal   _____

Decision Assessment 2 (page 185)
Statement—A (1 point each)   _____
Statements—B & D (3 pts)   _____
Statements—E & G (5 pts)   _____
Statements—C & F (7 pts)   _____

                          Subtotal   _____

Decision Assessment 3 (page 190)
Statements—A, E, F, I, J (1 point each) _____
Statement—C (3 pts)   _____
Statements—G & H (5 pts)   _____
Statements—B & D (10 pts)   _____

                          Subtotal   _____

                          Total points   _____

There are 100 possible points. While not a perfect predictor, this number will provide you with a broad sense as to the merits of continuing on with your legal career.

So, if you scored...

0 to 25 points—Consider a job or career change and start taking steps to explore leaving the law. You need to think about what's missing from your current job and what you really want in a future one. Speak with lawyers and non-lawyers who are doing work that sounds interesting, and get some exposure to both legal and non-legal settings so you can make an informed decision about whether you would be happier in another legal job, or a law-related or non-legal one. If you feel completely clueless about what you might do, start some serious self-assessment, either on your own or with the help of a career counselor.

26 to 60 points—This a gray area, which means you have good reason to be confused. You have some valid reasons for staying, so there's no rush to make a change today. But your reasons may not be sufficient. That's why it's important to explore legal, law-related and non-legal jobs to see if something sparks greater interest. Speak with the attorneys and non-attorneys who are doing work that appeals to you, and that leverages your favorite skills and interests.

61 to 100 points—Chances are good that you belong in the law and in your current position (or something like it). In any event, you seem to be taking the necessary steps to know for sure. That said, you're reading this book because you have doubts, so a little self-examination wouldn't hurt. Start by trying to identify what you really need in a job, either with a basic self-assessment or by making an appointment with a career counselor. If someone is profoundly unhappy in his or her job, a career counselor is like an ER doc whose services are needed. But for someone who's less than satisfied with his or her job, a career counselor is more like a personal trainer or nutritionist. No one ever regrets hearing from either.

Chapter 14

Next Steps

"It took working as a lawyer to force me to finally
look inside and figure out what I wanted to do
with my life. Until then, I was coasting and taking
cues from others. I literally had to start over, asking questions I should've asked years before—
'What am I meant to do? What am I suited for?
What kind of work would make me happy?'"

— Doug, lawyer-turned-legal staffing vice president

If you walk away from your job with too little thought or preparation, you risk winding up—as one lawyer said—"with the same terrible job in two different buildings." We've met too many lawyers who could acknowledge their unhappiness, but made one switch after another without pausing to examine the roots of their dissatisfaction. That's why the process we describe here—e.g., self-assessment, informational interviewing, and the application of hands-on experience—will help you identify a new job…either legal, law-related or non-legal…that is right for you. This same process will also help you market yourself to prospective employers and reassure them that you aren't just running from the law—that is, you've thought carefully about your future career direction and have done your due diligence in checking it out. Trust us when we tell you that this plan is far more enjoyable than you might imagine. And be assured that you can make time to orchestrate a job or career change. Here's a recap of options for making it happen:

Remain in your full-time job while carving out a little time each day to investigate new jobs.
Work part-time while you explore new careers part-time.
Take a sabbatical from your job to explore new options.
Leave your job and embark on a full-time job search.

We suspect many of you will be like Ellen, a busy litigator with a stressful practice who can't afford to leave her job without having another one lined up. The strategy she adopted was to take one action a day towards finding a new job.

"I'll have an informational interview during a lunch hour or on a sick day," she says, "And I'll spend a few evenings working with a career counselor to help me set goals. The most fun thing I did was use a few vacation days to attend an art law conference. I met a ton of people and made great contacts. I even feel better about being in my current job because I'm taking steps to leave it and pursue something more in line with my interests."

Next Steps: Self-Assessment

As you've heard many times here, self-assessment is the key to learning what is—and what is not—working for you on the job and what you want in a future job. And that's important because you may discover that you're not ready to leave law, and that there is a legal job that's right for you. Some lawyers who decided to bail out of the legal profession entirely based on one bad job experience, and without any self-assessment, later realized there were legal jobs they would have enjoyed.

Grab a legal pad—or open a new file on your computer. You've got some self-assessment to do.

So, grab a legal pad—or open a new file on your computer. Here are some basic self-assessment questions to get going:

What do you like and dislike about the projects you work on?

To what degree do you like or dislike using the skills you apply on the job?

How do you feel about the degree of interaction you have with others?

Which of the subjects you deal with at work are of interest, and which are not?

To what degree do you like or dislike your office culture and work environment?

Who are your favorite and least-favorite colleagues? Describe why.

How satisfied are you with your work-life balance?

How do you feel about the opportunities at your office for training, mentoring or professional development?

To what degree do you find your work meaningful and satisfying?

Describe what other types of work have greater appeal?

You'll find more detailed self-assessment exercises for lawyers and law students available as downloadable PDF files if you go to www.DecisionBooks. com and click on Career Boot Camp. And we list plenty of other career development books in the Tool Kit, starting on page 228.

Once you've identified what works and what doesn't, look for ways to modify your current position and role so that you would want to stay. For example, can you work with a different group of people...trim your hours or work part time...transfer to a different practice area? If these solutions don't provide a remedy, it's time to go deeper. This is the point where many lawyers get off track. They ask questions like, *What else can lawyers do?* or, *What else is out there?* These are the wrong questions. If you're serious about finding work that satisfies and makes the most of your skills, interests, and values, use these next four questions as a starting point:

What Skills Do I Most Enjoy Using? Having spoken with many unhappy lawyers, we have a pretty good idea about the varied nature of their complaints. They go something like this:

> *I spend too much time working alone.*
> *I hate legal research and writing.*
> *My job is too adversarial.*
> *There's too much admin.*
> *I hate document reviews.*

Sound familiar? They speak to a particular issue: lawyering skills, and the day-to-day activities required of attorneys. Turns out, many lawyers make the same complaints. That's both understandable and problematic. Think of it this way: you can be a fine journalist even if you don't like fact-checking. It's an important part of the job, but it's not especially fun. But disliking the skill of fact-checking doesn't mean you shouldn't be a reporter. On the other hand, if a reporter doesn't like writing, or interviewing people, he or she has a problem. That's the fundamental nature of the job. Similarly, a lot of lawyers like the intellectual aspects of what they do, but not the chores required. Plenty of lawyers echoed the sentiments of John, a former litigator who is now chief operating officer of a biotech company: "I learned that just because you have a great aptitude for something doesn't mean you'll enjoy it."

What Subjects Genuinely Interest Me? Here's a novel thought: some people actually work in careers in which the basic subject matter is of enormous personal interest. Now, some people are wildly interested in contracts or civil procedure or the nuances of the tax code. But if you've come this far, it's likely that there are other topics more likely to float your boat. So ask yourself this question: what

Skills Preference Exercise #1

This chart is the first in a series of self-assessments intended to help identify your preferred skills. Take a few moments to recall specific work or volunteer experiences, and circle the most enjoyable skills. Feel free to add any skills not listed here..

Advising	Drafting
Analyzing	Editing
Auditing	Legal writing
Brainstorming	Interviewing
Budgeting	Investigating
Coaching	Leading
Coordinating	Lecturing
Counseling	Lobbying
Counseling	Mediating
Designing	
_____	_____
_____	_____
	Public speaking
Managing people	Publicizing
Managing projects	Recruiting
Negotiating	Reporting
Organizing	Researching
Planning	Selling
Presenting	Teaching
Persuading	Training
Programming	Writing
Problem-solving	_____
_____	_____
_____	

topics would you most enjoy thinking about on the job every day? You see, some lawyers are unhappy because they're simply uninterested in the topics they have to read, write and think about at work. So, think about previous jobs, classes, volunteer experiences and avocations. Go to a bookstore and walk around: what topics draw you in? The happiest lawyers we know met are those who incorporated their personal interests (art, politics, sports, civil rights, wine, technology, health) into their legal career. In fact, it was a few ex-lawyers with an interest in food who started the California Pizza Kitchen restaurants and the successful Zagat restaurant guides.

In any event, the important thing in this exercise is to be honest. Don't list what you think you're supposed to be interested in. Don't write "regulatory issues" if you're infinitely more interested in soccer— like one lawyer we know who works for the U.S. Soccer Federation. We're looking for what you would do if you could. In fact, a helpful way to think about this is to present yourself with this proposition: If money and education were no barriers and I could have any job I wanted, I'd be a _____, _____, _____.

Feel free to list as many jobs as you want, limiting yourself only by your physical or intellectual capabilities (my co-author would like to be the starting quarterback for the Arizona Cardinals but he doesn't have the arm for it). On the other hand, if your dream job is to be President of the United States, write that down. You might not be good at it, and you might not have the requisite political background, but there's no reason you couldn't have the job.

Some people actually work in careers in which the basic subject matter is of enormous personal interest. What topics interest you?

In fact, if you list a dream job that might be equally difficult to attain, ask yourself "What exactly is it about my dream job that appeals to me?" For example, does being President of the United States appeal to me because I like thinking about policy issues? Because I like power? Because I like holding a leadership position? Being in a high-profile job? Because I want to serve my country? Next, list those attributes and think about other jobs with those similar attributes, just in case you never make it to the Oval Office. Enlist others to help you brainstorm.

Still having trouble coming up with subjects? Try this exercise: think about other careers you might have considered before choosing law school. Go back as far as you want. The point of this question is to help you forget that you're a lawyer, so you can start with a blank slate and think freely about what interests you.

What Do I Want in a Work Environment? It's hard to know what aspect of lawyering is most responsible for lawyer dissatisfaction. But the actual work environment is right up there—the stress and excessive hours are draining, no one mentors you, everyone at work is unhappy, your job's family-friendly policies aren't very friendly, everyone at the office is so uptight, and the billable hours are shaking the foundations of your marriage. If you've been in a job where the work environment wasn't to your liking, then you have an acute understanding of

Subjects of Greatest Interest

Of all the subjects you identified, list the five of greatest personal interest in order of their importance:

1. _____
2. _____
3. _____
4. _____
5. _____

the incredible importance that physical setting and emotional vibe play in job satisfaction. This includes the type of people you work with, your physical surroundings, the firm culture, the number of hours you work, your commute, the dress code and the level of formality and bureaucracy.

So, take a few moments to consider the characteristics of your ideal workplace:

Is it fast-paced or laid-back?

Formal or casual?

Part of a big organization or an entrepreneurial firm?

Do people work in groups or alone?

Do they work long hours or a standard work week?

Is there a lot of training and mentoring or an abundance of autonomy?

Don't limit yourself to the kind of office you think is appropriate for adults, but rather the kind of environment in which you'd enjoy spending eight to 10 hours a day, five days a week, 48 to 50 weeks a year. One lawyer who took this advice to heart left his law practice to run a summer camp in Wisconsin so he could spend his workday in his favorite place in the world. It can be helpful to recall what you've liked and disliked about previous work environments, no matter how far back. If all you discover in this exercise is that your happiest work moments came when you were mowing lawns as a teenager, well, you've learned something.

Work Environment

Circle the aspects of a work environment that appeal to you.

Large organization	Short commute	People work in groups
Small organization	Access to public transportation	People work individually
Fast-paced	Traditional 40-hour work week	Colleagues socialize
Laid-back	Work week of 50+ hours	Colleagues not especially sociable
Casual	No-frills environment	Emphasis on training and mentoring
Formal	Plush environment with many resources	Emphasis on autonomy and independence
Clearly defined rules		
Flexible		

Work Environment Exercise

Identify three previous jobs, specifying some of the qualities you liked or disliked about those work environments:

This is an important exercise, and if you wish to make the most of it, draft a short paragraph describing what appealed to you (or not) about one particular work place. One lawyer wrote: "In one of my favorite jobs, I liked the 9-to-5 work day, the friendly colleagues, the casual dress code, the ability to work independently, the laid-back environment, and the short commute. In one of my least-favorite jobs, I disliked the harried pace, the formal dress code, and the intensity of some coworkers. However, I loved the plush office setting."

Job: _____

1. _____
2. _____
3. _____
4. _____
5. _____

Job: _____

1. _____
2. _____
3. _____
4. _____
5. _____

Job: _____

1. _____
2. _____
3. _____
4. _____
5. _____

My Preferred Work Environment

By now, you should have a pretty good sense about what sort of work environment appeals to you. Rank those five criteria below:

1. _____
2. _____
3. _____
4. _____
5. _____

What Are My Career Priorities? Many people don't realize the importance of aligning their job with their personal priorities until their job and personal priorities are badly out of synch. By priorities, we simply mean the things that are important to you: emotionally, ethically, practically. Your greatest priority can be to fix the world or to have more time on the 14th green. There's no judgment here. What's important to you is... what's important? And while being in a job that conflicts with one's priorities is tolerable for some, it's disconcerting for others, and incredibly painful for many more. Small wonder that some of the most common lawyer complaints range from "I don't derive a sense of meaning from my work" to "I represent clients who make me feel unethical" to "I have no life outside of work." Each of these, in their own way, is about an unmet priority. Here are some exercises to get you started.

Career Priorities

Circle the priorities with the greatest appeal. Feel free to add others not listed here.

Career advancement	Making a difference in the world
Family-friendly policies	Meaningful work
Professional growth	People with whom you enjoy working
Entrepreneurial work	Work/life balance
Ethically compatible	_____
High salary	_____
Leadership opportunities	_____

Priorities Exercise

Identify five career priorities from this list (or add your own criteria), and draft a paragraph (or a few sentences) for each that provides additional detail and why it's important to you:

1. Priority: _____
2. Priority: _____
3. Priority: _____
4. Priority: _____
5. Priority: _____

Here's one more exercise to make this discovery process even more helpful. Put this book down for a bit and devote some time to reviewing job listings in the classified-ad section of a major newspaper and on web sites such as JDPost.com, Attorneyjobs.com, PSLawNet.org, Monster.com, and HotJobs. com. As you scroll down through these sources, keep track of every job listing that sounds attractive to you, regardless of salary or your qualifications. In other words, don't rule out any job just because the salary is low or because you're totally unqualified for the position—the point is to pay attention to what sounds appealing to you. For each job, what does the position offer in terms of skills, subjects, work environment and priorities that appeal to you? Compare what you're written in this exercise with how you filled in the four boxes in the preceding pages. You'll get two things out of this exercise. First, you'll see how well you know yourself in theory versus real-world opportunities. Second, you'll have refined your Self-Assessment Grid further. Which reminds us—it's time to fill that in. In a page or two you'll see what you can do with them.

A word of advice about self-assessment questions: For some people, these kinds of exercises raise more questions than they answer, such as: Why don't I know myself better? Why can't I answer these basic questions? What am I going to do with my life? Why are priorities so hard to define? Why am I having trouble identifying my skills? This is perfectly natural, and no reason to panic or beat yourself up. That said, some people find it enormously useful to get help from a professional career counselor, which is neither as expensive nor time-consuming as you might think. You can always start by availing yourself of your law school's career services office, which frequently extends counseling services to alumni. Or you can see a career counselor in private practice (see page 222 or the Tool Kit to help you find one, or go online to www.DecisionBooks.com and click on Law Career Experts for a national roster of counselors who work with attorneys).

One additional note about your Self-Assessment Grid. While it can certainly help lead you to a new job or career, you can also use it to identify new pursuits outside of work. When Adam, an immigration attorney, was introduced to self-assessment, he was reminded of his love of circus. It didn't mean he had to chuck his legal career for a shot at Cirque du Soleil; instead, he was able to scratch an old itch by signing up for an after-work trapeze class. Other lawyers we know still practice by day, but pursue their passions—writing, music, acting, sculpting, comedy—at night. If you are seeking to change jobs or careers, you might combine your personal interests with a legal career (like the former musician who became in-house counsel for a record label).

Self-Assessment Grid

As you can see, we've given you the building blocks to construct a Self-Assessment Grid. This grid brings together the results of the previous four exercises regarding skills, subjects of interest, preferred work environment, and career priorities. So, in addition to filling in your career priorities, fill in the other three boxes based on your answers to the skills, subject and work environment exercises you completed earlier in this chapter.

Skills

1

2

3

4

5

Subjects

1

2

3

4

5

Work Environment

1

2

3

4

5

Priorities

1

2

3

4

5

The Devil's Advocate Says...

Loosen your legal limits—A lot of unhappy lawyers stay that way because they don't want to "waste" their degree. Fine, we won't argue that point with you here. What we will argue against is a strict definition of the phrase "legal career." You don't have to be a practicing lawyer to use your law degree. Legal recruiters, bar-association executives, labor negotiators, law school librarians, legal career counselors and government administrators are just a small handful of the many ways in which you can put your legal background to use.

Next Steps: Informational Interviews

For some of you, this opportunity at self-assessment may be the first time your work preferences will have been collected together. For others, self-assessment will only raise more questions—*Why am I having trouble identifying my skills… why are my priorities so hard to define… why don't I know myself better… what am I going to do with my life?* This is natural, and no cause for panic. Still, if you took the time to fill in the Self-Assessment Grid, that is more than sufficient to begin work with a private career counselor. (See page 222 for tips on finding career counselors, or go to www.DecisionBooks.com and click on Law Career Experts.

In an ideal situation, you would get to sample different jobs to help shed light on the work and working environment that best suits you. Of course, that's not realistic. That's why informational interviews are so helpful. You get to interview people who work in all sorts of legal, law-related or non-legal jobs as a way of intelligence gathering about potential careers for you. It sounds simplistic, but remains one of the most effective—yet underutilized—ways to explore potential career paths. Informational interviewing is underutilized because most people are afraid to ask others how they do what they do, and if they like the work. That's a shame, because the process is easier than you think, and it can have tremendous payoff. After all, a single conversation may make a connection to a new job or reveal career strategies you didn't know before.

> **"I** identified 10 people in fields in which I had an interest, and had each of them recommend two more people with whom to speak. By the time I finished all the informational interviews, I not only had a lot of information… I had a network.**"**
>
> —Randy, management consultant and former law firm partner

Here's another benefit of informational interviews: they can motivate even the most risk-averse lawyers to overcome hesitations about changing jobs or careers by providing tips for getting hired in new fields. Tim, a former litigator, discovered through informational interviews that he was interested in becoming a financial advisor. In meetings with financial pros, he learned how to tailor his resume, prepare for interviews, and learn about the financial services industry. Another former lawyer we know successfully transitioned from law firm, to bank, to auction house, to technology company, and *back* to a law firm (this time as marketing director), by skillfully utilizing informational interviews to orchestrate every career change. By now, you're probably thinking, *This sounds like a lot of time and effort.* You're right. But spending, say, a month conducting informational interviews with people in different jobs in and around the legal universe is certainly easier and less time-consuming than getting stuck in a series of jobs you dislike.

Of course, we'd like to offer assurance that informational interviews, and the other elements of our career-building process, offer a guaranteed formula for career happiness. We'd like to offer that assurance but we can't. But if you have completed your Self-Assessment Grid, at least you have a capsule form of some of the most important elements you need for job satisfaction. Hopefully, we've sold you on these ideas. So, start making your calls. If you're still a little perplexed about where to start, revisit your Self-Assessment Grid. The key to useful informational interviews is to focus on speaking with people who have jobs you might potentially enjoy. That's why the answers you listed for your favorite skills, interests, work environment and priorities will help you identify lawyers whose work meets your preferences. What do we mean? We mean this:

Skills. If you listed writing, talk to journalists, obviously, but also public relations professionals, marketing executives, and technical writers.

If you listed teaching, seek out HR professionals (who do a lot of teaching) or seminar management companies.

If you listed organizing, seek out people who work in the travel business, or in logistical services for almost any major corporation.

Subjects. If you posted sports, talk to sports teams, obviously, but also sports media outlets and publications, or people who work for makers or marketers of athletic clothing and equipment.

If you listed music, talk to people who work in the record industry, of course, but also speak with those who work in government cultural affairs offices or in philanthropic or concert promotion.

Environment. If you'd prefer a casual, non-bureaucratic or entrepreneurial environment, talk to small companies (fewer than 100), of course, but also non-core business units of large corporations, where the culture is often significantly less "corporate" than those of the parent company).

If you prefer creative environments, think beyond traditional career paths (publishing, music, the arts) and explore customer service outsource firms, management consultants, advertising and public relations.

Priorities. If you listed being innovative, talk to people who work in fast-changing industries, like healthcare, transportation and technology—whatever your skills and preferred subjects, you'll have to innovate constantly.

If you listed fun, talk to people who have fun at their jobs. Sounds simple, but sometimes a seemingly boring industry can be made enjoyable by a specific corporate culture, manager or boss.

If you need help brainstorming more ideas, enlist your friends or a career counselor and check out the resources in the Tool Kit.

Next Steps: Hands-on Experience

Of course, once you've identified the type of industries or companies or environments you'd like to explore, you actually have to start exploring. That means once you've had some informational interviews, the next step is to narrow the field to a handful of careers that interest you and find ways to get real-world exposure to them. Easier said than done, especially for those of you who have full-time jobs or family obligations. But there are various ways to experience what a particular job or field is like. Here they are, listed from most to least time-consuming:

Volunteer—Spend a few evenings or weekends, as your schedule permits, assisting with a project in an organization that interests you.

Shadow someone—Shadowing (see Tool Kit, page x) simply means following someone around on the job to observe what they do, read and think about all day. Ideally, you can shadow someone for a couple of days. Even one day—or just a few hours—is better than nothing.

Serve on a board—If you want to understand an organization, nonprofit or otherwise, serving on its board of directors—or on a board-sanctioned committee comprised of outsiders—is one of the smartest ways to achieve that goal. You'll likely meet interesting people who could help you make valuable contacts.

Take a class—No matter what the subject, you can almost always can find evening or weekend classes offered by community colleges, for-profit educators like The Learning Annex or continuing-education arms of local universities.

Attend conferences—Sounds a little geeky but it's actually an under-utilized strategy for breaking into an industry. These gatherings may only last a day or two, but you'll get a sense of what the people in the business are like along with overviews of topics relating to that particular industry. You'll also get a chance to meet people and make contacts that are sure to be valuable as you pursue this path.

Get on-the-job experience at your present job—Some lawyers find clever ways to develop new skills at their job that they later took on the road to another. One became involved with her firm's recruiting and later became a legal recruiter. Another government attorney wound up dealing with the media on a regular basis, enjoyed it, and started her own public relations firm, with government agencies as clients. So think about any new experience or expertise you could develop in the comfort of your own job.

In Conclusion

> **"A** few weeks into my new job, I new I was in the right place when I woke up one morning and thought, 'I'm healed.'"
>
> —Kim, managing partner of a legal recruiting firm and former lawyer at a mid-sized firm

We recognize the scope and magnitude of what we're dealing with here. Making career changes once you're a lawyer can be infinitely more difficult because there's more at stake: money, professional identity and security, to name a few. And lawyers are trained to demand facts, evidence and logical answers. But when it comes to career decisions, your instincts, energy and intuition are important guides. Once you learn to make decisions based on your true preferences—and on real information about the career alternatives available to you—we're confident that you'll be more satisfied and more confident about the path you ultimately choose. So that, hopefully, this will be the last career book you'll ever need to buy.

Final Thoughts

Hopefully, by now we've accomplished what we set out to do with this book: transport you to a new level of consciousness, one where you are more aware of your decision-making issues and are better prepared to solve them. That is, as you make career choices, now and in the future, you'll be able to sidestep at least some of the more common psychological traps that have plagued so many aspiring and practicing lawyers alike:

Allowing others to unduly influence your decisions

Relying on decision-making shortcuts to make your choices simpler

Overlooking or ignoring the right information and failing to ask the right questions

Giving too much weight to ideas or facts that have little relevance to your decision

Thinking you know more than you do about the choice at hand

Ignoring your instincts and information that conflicts with your preferences

Allowing fear of change or regret to prevent you from making the best choice for you

Letting your actions in the past unduly influence your decisions about the future

If you recognize yourself falling prey to any (or all) of these habits, you've taken Step 1 to making better decisions. Step 2 is making the effort to overcome them. We found that lawyers with deeply satisfying careers were willing to do the work they needed to achieve those careers. They thought carefully about what they really wanted in a job or career. They thoroughly researched a variety of fields by speaking with people in them and getting hands-on exposure to the nature of the work. They pursued opportunities they were truly excited about and didn't waste time on ones they weren't. They trusted themselves and their instincts—and didn't remain in a situation that didn't feel right to them. Above all, they were tenacious and believed in their ability to find a career they loved at the end of their search.

We trust the stories and strategies we've shared over these many pages will inspire you to make the effort needed to find the best career for you. And we hope you find the journey itself both satisfying and rewarding.

Take a break—If you're considering changing careers and a little voice says, "nothing seems appealing" or, "what if I won't like anything else better?" you might just need a vacation, not a career make-over. Don't wait until you're burned out with your current job to make a career change; you may not get very far.

Flip a coin—For a book based on behavioral science, we would be remiss not to mention that a simple coin flip can be a powerful decision-making tool. It's just another way to deal with conflicting options. For example, you assign one choice (say, leaving the law) to heads, and the other option (staying in law) to tails. Then, before you send the coin spinning, you promise to abide by the outcome. This is where it gets interesting: Research suggests that most people have an unstated preference; they're just afraid of the consequences associated with the less-desirable outcome. So, if you flip a coin and the less-desirable outcome comes up, you will feel an immediate pang of regret or displeasure that will tell you—magically—how you really feel about your options. See for yourself.

Just do something—Don't agonize about what to do with your life while neglecting to do something...anything. Pick one thing and get started. Volunteer, take a class, visit a museum, pursue a hobby. Lawyers often tell us they've lost touch with who they are because they're consumed with job responsibilities. So reconnect. It doesn't have to be career-oriented, just something you enjoy. Maybe it will lead to a new career, maybe not. Once you reconnect with activities you enjoy, you'll approach your career crisis with more energy and resolve.

Take back your life—While growing up, what were the messages you heard about work and careers? Did your parents value money, prestige, and stability above all else? Are those really your values? Some lawyers have told us they decided to leave the law for more creative pursuits when they understood how their parents had dissuaded from going into an "impractical"career. Once you separate your family's career goals from your own, you can begin taking back your life.

Cut your losses—People often don't abandon even miserable jobs because they remind themselves how much they've already "put into it"—time, money, effort, emotional investment. Before you make the same mistake (the sunk cost fallacy), remember that you won't get those miserable years back by hanging in there and being miserable for even longer.

Imagine the worst—If you're worried about the consequences of remaking your career, ask yourself this question—"What's the worst that could happen?" Your worst-case scenario may not be that dire. If you leave your job and don't like your new one, you'll find another in time; if you want to return to law, they can't keep you out. In our experience, people view career change as nuclear explosions. In retrospect, they're more like a series of firecrackers.

Regress—If you have a hard time seeing yourself as anything other than a lawyer, think about the dreams you had before law school. A few lawyers we know shied away from their dream of entrepreneurial pursuits because of family considerations. When they finally got too dissatisfied with law, they left and proceeded to thrive in business. What were your dreams way back when? Thinking about what you wanted to be when you grew up can help you uncover clues about what you need from your work now.

Don't be a snob—Some lawyers believe non-legal jobs are beneath them, or they're conflicted about doing work that doesn't make use of their hard-won legal skills. Don't be a snob. Finding work that you're genuinely excited about—that feels intuitive to you—will allow you to approach opportunities with an open mind. Many former lawyers achieve career nirvana by pursuing things they love. Warren Brown, a former government lawyer, started Cake Love, a Washington, D.C.-based bakery. And Paul Mecurio left his gig as a Wall Street lawyer for standup comedy gigs, and wound up writing jokes for Jay Leno and Comedy Central's The Daily Show.

Ignore the Wall Street Journal—Don't let a soft economy prevent you from activating your job search. Even a recession presents opportunities for employment. For example, we know one unemployed Silicon Valley lawyer who co-founded a group called "Recession Camp," a social and networking group for Bay Area job seekers. He made valuable professional contacts through that venture and eventually landed an in-house counsel job.

Change is here to stay—Did you know that Americans change jobs or careers an average of 12 times during our working lives? Switching tracks isn't as risky, or uncommon as you may think.

Loosen your legal limits—A lot of unhappy lawyers stay that way because they don't want to "waste" their degree. Fine, we won't argue that point with you here. What we will argue against is a strict definition of the phrase "legal career." You don't have to be a practicing lawyer to use your law degree. Legal recruiters, bar-association executives, labor negotiators, law-school librarians, legal career counselors and government administrators are just a small handful of the many ways in which you can put your legal background to use.

A Guide to Informational Interviews

Informational interviewing is simply seeking out and talking to people in various professions with one goal in mind: mining their experience, knowledge, and insight, to help you sort through your career issues. It's true that a job or a useful referral might come from an especially fruitful informational interview. But what's really important is to benefit from others who have gone where you have never gone before. So, whether you're a prospective law student, current law student or practicing lawyer, informational interviews are among the simplest—but the most useful—tool for making informed career decisions:

If you're a prospective law student wondering whether legal studies are right for you, then seeking out attorneys and non-attorneys is absolutely essential to deciding whether to pursue the law or something else. We wouldn't offer such obvious advice if not for the fact that too many students enter law school without speaking to any lawyers or non-lawyers to determine which career path to take. If you find out what attorneys do, and identify several different legal jobs you think you would enjoy, you will enter law school with valuable career direction and a game plan for pursuing jobs that interest you.

If you're a law student who is questioning whether your educational decision was the wrong one (or what to do with your JD), it is equally vital to speak with lawyers in different practice areas and settings to help you figure out which to pursue. Too many law students decide to pursue or not pursue certain legal jobs without ever having talked with the attorneys who do them. And if you think you don't want to practice law in a conventional firm or government setting, then speaking with lawyers in law-related or non-legal jobs is all the more critical to finding alternatives. Speaking with non-lawyers and law school dropouts can also help you decide whether it makes sense for you to continue pursuing a JD.

And, if you're already a practicing lawyer and less than thrilled with your job (or simply curious about exploring other paths), speaking with other kinds of practicing lawyers will help you determine if there's another branch of the law that's more suitable to your temperament and interests (and give you valuable tips on how to land such a position). If you're thinking about giving up legal practice entirely, seeking out lawyers who left the law and successfully established themselves in new careers can help bolster your confidence to initiate a similar move. (In the meantime, read Deborah Arron's *Running From the Law: Why Good Lawyers Are Getting Out of the Legal Profession*; 2004).

Informational interviews can also help generate ideas for a wider range of legal and non-legal job options to explore and make valuable contacts that could lead you to your ideal job. After all, the more people you speak with, and who know what you're interested in doing, the more likely it is someone will connect you to a future job. If you're thinking that informational interviews sound like they will take some time, you're right. But don't let that stop you. They are one of the smartest ways to use your time. Spending, say, two or three weeks conducting informational interviews with people about myriad jobs is clearly a better course than committing to a career decision without direction.

Presuming we've sold you on the importance of informational interviews, we'll walk you through the process:

Create a list of people to contact. Once you've identified the type of industries, companies, or environments you want to explore, begin assembling a list of contacts—real live people whose jobs sound interesting. This requires a three-step process. The first step is easy: Start with who you know. Do any friends, family members, coworkers, former employers, or professors know lawyers or non-lawyers with interesting jobs? Are you involved with any social, athletic, extracurricular or religious organization whose members have jobs that interest you? How about your doctor, dentist or hairdresser? Seriously, these folks spend their days interacting with a people in a wide variety of professions and are likely to know someone you might like to meet.

After you've exhausted everyone you know, the second step is to get connected to people you don't know. It's not that hard, really: Whether you're an undergraduate or a law student, seek out your school's career service or alumni office to connect you with alumni in legal and non-legal fields. And if you're already established in law, turn to your school's alumni-relations and career services offices to connect you with other alumni for the purposes of informational interviews. To find a career development organization near you, ask your undergrad or law-school career counselors for referrals, or call a career counselor in your area (or go to DecisionBooks.com and click on Law Career Experts for a national roster of career counselors who work with lawyers and law students). If you're seeing a career counselor in private practice, see if he or she will connect you with people for informational interviews and coach you through the process. The third step sounds the most daunting, but it's really not: Pick some organizations that sound interesting and contact people who work there.

For example:

If you wish to speak with lawyers, call your local bar association to get a list of bar association leaders and a calendar of events. If you're interested in, say, intellectual property law, see if there's a local IP organization and ask the group's leader for an informational interview. Or call any law firms, corporations, government agencies or public-interest organizations that interest you. If you're looking to speak with non-lawyers, you can contact any organization that sounds potentially interesting to work for. For example, if you're intrigued with the media, call a local news station. If you're interested in advertising, call an ad agency. Try contacting the HR director or the internship coordinator, for starters. If that doesn't work, look at a staff directory (often on the organization's web site) and contact anyone who has an interesting-sounding job.

If you don't know which organizations are in your area, there's the Web (see jobhuntersbible.com, for example, and click on "Research"), and there are two great library resources—the National Trade and Professional Associations Directory, and the Encyclopedia of Associations, a directory of associations and professional societies including business and trade associations, and legal, government, educational and cultural organizations.

Note: Ask everyone you speak with for the name of at least one other person in that field you can contact. That way, you'll automatically expand your list of contacts with every contact.

Contact the people on your list. Once you've created a target list of people, you actually have to speak with them. (Informational interviews only work if you actually conduct them.) It's one thing to have target lists, and another to actually get in touch with the people on them. This is usually the stage when people procrastinate, because they're hesitant about contacting strangers. So, if you're as anxious as most of us at the prospect of contacting people you've never met, here are a few thoughts to keep in mind.

You're not asking people for a job. You're simply asking for information— about their work, their advice on breaking into that field and referrals to other people you could contact to learn more. Most people are willing to have informational interviews because they tend to enjoy talking about themselves and dispensing advice (especially lawyers). Former lawyers are generally eager to help because they've walked in your shoes.

It's easier and more fun to contact people with interesting careers. In other words, when you hear of people you're interested in meeting, you'll be more motivated than you feel right now to contact them. We know this from years of experience.

Informational interviewing gets easier with practice. When my co-author was just getting started in journalism, he found the process of calling strangers and asking questions incredibly awkward. Soon, the act became second nature simply because he'd done it so many times before. Loads of psychological research tells us that almost any activity becomes less extraordinary or difficult with repetition.

You might not imagine that to be the case now, but we promise that if you commit to lining up at least six informational interviews, the seventh will be a piece of cake. The best way to feel more confident is to keep at it and contact people in any way you're comfortable with. Send a letter or e-mail or leave a short voice-mail. You can also ask friends or family members to contact folks on your behalf, with follow-up by you. If you're still not comfortable, get help. Ask your law school's CSO to help arrange informational interviews with fellow alumni, and to coach you through the process. Ask friends or colleagues or see a career counselor. Some requests for informational interviews will get turned down. Don't get discouraged. These individuals may get a lot of requests for informational interviews and have to decline some in the interest of time. If you persist, you will get enough people to say yes, and the odds are even better if you come through a referral.

Once you've set up an informational interview, preparing for it is the easy part. Here are 14 great questions to get you started:

What does a typical day or week in your job look like?
What types of activities does your job involve?
How much do you work on your own? With others?
What skills do you use in your job?
What work-related topics do you think about on the job?
What do you like/dislike about your work?
What is the work environment like (hours, atmosphere, people contact, etc)?
In what way do you find the work interesting? Fulfilling?
What did you find most surprising about your job and this field?
What do you wish you had known about this job before you started?
What is the compensation range for this field and position?
What opportunities for advancement are there in this field?
Do you see yourself remaining in this job or organization? Why or why not?
If you had to do things over, would you choose the same career path?
What type of person would/would not be a good fit for this job?

What abilities and characteristics are needed to get hired and to succeed in this field?

What kinds of experience should I get to enter this job/field?

Who else in this field should I talk to? May I use your name when I contact them?

Where else should I go for more information about this field?

Note: Members of special-interest groups (women, minorities, gay/lesbians, and people with disabilities, etc.) should also use informational interview to ask questions specific to their group . . . to learn what special challenges you may face, and what success strategies you might use for dealing with the challenges. If you need helping finding attorneys in one special-interest group or another, call your local bar association. Follow it up with a call to the special-interest group, and ask who would be willing to meet you for a brief informational interview. During that interview, it would be helpful to take notes. It's not rude; that's why you're there.

Overall, be sure to compare the jobs you discuss in your informational interviews with what you listed on your Self-Assessment Grid because your skills, interests, preferred working environment and priorities may be vastly different from someone else's. In other words, just because one person likes his or her job, it doesn't mean that you'd like doing it. For example, if an attorney tells you she enjoys spending most of her day doing legal research and writing, ask yourself if you'd be just excited about spending your day that way. As Richard Bolles cautions in *What Color is Your Parachute?*, "One person's best career is another person's poison."

After you've completed a round of informational interviews, compare your notes from each, and consider the following questions:

Which jobs seem to utilize my favorite skills?

How do they match?

Whose projects and daily activities looked most appealing?

Who worked in organizations that most closely matched my preferred work environment?

What was the appeal?

Who had jobs that are compatible with my priorities?

What was the match?

Keep In Touch. After you've completed an informational interview, be sure to send a thank-you note, and make a point of staying in touch with anyone you met who is doing work that appealed to you. Later, you might follow up with them about working or volunteering in their organization, or to ask them about other similar organizations where you might work. Or you might just send them an interesting article that you read and thought they'd find useful. If you ultimately decide to pursue law, let them know you're attending law school—you never know how they might be able to help you in a future legal job search. In short, people like and respect follow-up. You never know how you might be of service to them someday.

Once you're comfortable with informational interviews with lawyers, repeat the process with non-lawyers. Why? You already know why—if you're a prospective law student, it's vital to see if there are non-legal jobs that are a better match before you sink time and money into becoming an attorney. Talking to non-lawyers will help you conquer specific Choice Challenges, too. For example, it will help prevent you from relying on such *rules of thumb* as, "I'll make a lot of money in law", by showing you that there are other careers where you can also make a good living, and that many JDs may not make as much as you think. Similarly, if you're a law student or attorney considering alternatives to legal practice, informational interviews will help you discover if there are law-related or non-legal careers that you would also enjoy

Lining up and conducting informational interviews with non-attorneys simply requires you to repeat the same steps you did with attorneys. Start by looking at your Self-Assessment Grid, beginning with your list of skills.

> If you listed writing and interviewing people, for example, you might talk to journalists,
> investigators and market researchers.
> If you listed negotiating, talk to business development managers, political staffers and lobbyists.

Next, look at your list of subjects.

> For instance, if you listed environmental issues, talk to people at non-profits and government agencies.
> If you listed international issues, seek out people in the Peace Corps, think tanks, government agencies and non-profits.

Examine your work environment preferences, too.

> If you listed, say, a creative work environment, talk to someone at an advertising agency, cultural organization or public relations firm.
>
> If you listed a formal work environment, talk to someone at a corporation or government agency or a foundation.

Finally, look at your list of priorities.

> If work-life balance is a high priority, talk to people in government agencies, non-profits, academia or anywhere else where people seem to have a life outside of work.
>
> If you listed making a lot of money, talk to people in investment banking, business or real estate.
>
> If you listed public service, talk to people in non-profits, government agencies and foundations.

Once you've completed informational interviews, you can take comfort having mastered a technique that will serve you throughout your career.

The Art of Shadowing

"Shadowing" simply means observing someone (a lawyer or non-lawyer) on the job for a day (or a few hours) to observe what they do and how they do it. It's a great way to see what a particular job involves so you can see if you might enjoy doing similar work.

As a college senior, my co-author had a chance to shadow a member of the bar before she enrolled in law school. It was part of her school's "Shadow Program," which invited students to follow professionals for a week. Deborah made an appointment to shadow a real estate lawyer... but at the last minute she cancelled the appointment to go on vacation with her boyfriend. She persuaded herself that since she eventually planned to be a lawyer, there was no point in shadowing one. Big mistake! Deborah says that had she seen what one lawyer did at work every day, she might not have been so quick to go to law school.

You can shadow a lawyer for all or part of a day; the important part is to get a clear idea of what they're reading, writing, thinking about and doing on the job. It's also important to get a realistic picture of what a typical day is like, so don't just follow a litigator on the rare day they're going to court. See what they do back in the office. We're not suggesting that you sit and watch someone answer emails or make phone calls all day long. Try to sit in on a meeting, read some of the documents they read, observe a client intake, or assist with a document review.

Lining up a shadowing opportunity is not much different than lining up an informational interview. Do any family members, friends, former employers, co-workers or professors know lawyers or non-lawyers with interesting jobs? Are you involved with any social, athletic, extracurricular, or religious organization where other members have jobs that interest you? How about your doctor, dentist or hairdresser? Or, ask your school's alumni office and career-services offices if they can connect you with alumni in legal and non-legal fields.

If you're looking to speak with lawyers, call the local bar association for a list of their officers, and if you wish to speak with non-lawyers, contact any organization whose products or service interest you. Incidentally, don't start conversations by requesting to shadow them. Your contact will think you're nuts at best; a stalker at worst. Make the approach only after meeting with them. Most will agree to spending a few hours with you. Presuming you don't hinder their work or make a fool of yourself, the investment of a few hours will turn into a full day and a treasure chest of valuable experience and contacts.

The Case for Career Counseling

Career counseling has a surprisingly bad rap. Although it has many adherents, the majority of people we speak with think of it in the best case as a luxury and in the worst as a waste of time and money. But it's hard to see why. People consult counselors for financial issues, legal issues, marital issues. They hire nutritionists, personal trainers and spiritual guides. It's difficult to understand how your career (at which you will probably spend at least one third of your life) is any less important or deserving of attention.

As with anything else of great import, it can be extremely valuable to have an experienced professional help you when you're feeling stuck or dissatisfied with your work life. Given that people change careers an average of 12 times during their lifetime, it makes a lot of sense to get assistance from a qualified career development expert during some of those transitions. It's also not that expensive. Reasonable fees typically range from $100 to $150 per hour, and you can often (though not always) deal with most of your issues in a handful of sessions. (Warning: Avoid any counselor who insists on selling you a package of services or requires that you commit to multiple sessions costing thousands of dollars.) If you're concerned about the cost, think about it this way: Spending, say, $600 to figure out that you really don't want to be a lawyer is infinitely preferable to spending $60,000 on law school—or spending another five or 10 years being miserable in practice—only to arrive at the same conclusion.

The fact is, if you're unhappy in your current job or career, or unsure of what you want to do, a good career counselor can help you:

Clarify why you're feeling disenchanted or confused.

Define what you want in a job or career.

Identify your favorite skills and subjects, preferred work environment and career priorities.

Brainstorm and generate ideas for jobs and careers that meet your preferences.

Identify and explore new jobs and careers.

Meet professionals in the career fields that interest you.

Resolve issues that arise in your job search or career change.

Provide motivation and support throughout the career-exploration process.

Career Counseling Source List

Academic—If you're still in college, your school most likely offers free counseling in its career services office. Even if you've graduated, most schools offer alumni free or discounted access to these services. Likewise, any of the law schools to which you are considering applying will provide at least a little time and guidance to prospective students.

Private—The starting point, of course, is referrals. Ask friends, neighbors, relatives and discreet colleagues if they've ever used a career counselor or know of a good one. Beyond that, there are several reliable private sources for referrals, including the national network of law-related career counselors at www.DecisionBooks. com. Click on its Law Career Experts section for a regional guide to career consultants. Also, check out the National Career Development Association (www.NCDA. org), whose "Consumers and Job Seekers" link will lead you to a list of certified career counselors and tips on how to choose one. Finally, the appendix of *What Color is Your Parachute* includes a state-by-state listing of career development organizations and career counselors and guidance for finding the best one for you.

Thoughts on Choosing a Law School

There are plenty of books devoted to this topic, but as you do your research, we'd like you to remember one particular Choice Challenge that tends to influence law school decisions. Remember *anchoring*, the tendency to let certain facts or ideas unduly influence your decisions? Many law students (and their parents) tend to *anchor*—attach themselves—to law school rankings supplied by U.S. News and World Report. Even though the magazine's methodology and annual rankings have been roundly criticized, the data still wields great influence on students' choices.

We're not suggesting you ignore the magazine's rankings entirely, only that you be aware that *anchoring* can be problematic if it leads you to ignore other important considerations. For example, which law school will best further your career goals? This is important, because where you go could influence where you wind up. If you want to work for a large private law firm or a federal judge, for example, going to a top-ranked school can make it easier to open those doors because many of these employers care about a school's rank. But if you're not gunning for a large firm or a federal clerkship, you might be better served by going to a decent but less expensive school, especially if you're borrowing a lot of money for your education. Lawyers tell us that if they could choose again they would opt for a law school with lower tuition...in a less expensive city...over a higher-ranked school with higher tuition. Why? Because they would have incurred less debt and had more job options upon graduation. So do the math. If you think borrowing less money will increase your job options, and if you think you won't feel compelled to take the highest-paying job you find regardless of whether it interests you, give serious thought to attending a less costly school.

If you aspire to a public-interest legal career, going to a school that's truly supportive of its public-interest law students may be more helpful to you than merely going to a school with a higher ranking. Although a few of the more prestigious post-graduate, public-interest fellowships might consider your law school's rank, most public-interest employers focus on your work experience in public-interest settings. So find out which of the law schools you're considering have a public-interest advisor on staff, and which have special programs (loan-forgiveness and loan repayment-assistance) designed to help graduates in public-interest jobs repay their loans. Also, see which law schools help students secure funding for summer public interest work and offer clinical programs and special elective courses on public-interest topics. It can also be instructive to find out the percentage of that school's graduates who go onto public-interest careers.

It's also important to think about where you want to work *after* graduation. Some lawyers regret they didn't attend law school in a city where they wanted to live after graduation because they could have spent three years volunteering, working, interning, doing clinical assignments and establishing contacts in that legal community—all of which would have bolstered their summer and post-graduate job searches. One last thing to keep in mind when you're researching which school to attend: Seek out the widest, most divergent opinions. Ask attorneys and law students about the pros and cons of each school you're considering, and ask if they would choose a different school if they could do it over again.

On Matters of Money

We should really call this section, *Lessons Learned From Shelling Out Twenty Grand a Year For Three Years*. Why? Because so many lawyers express remorse about some of the financial choices they made during law school.

Whether you're paying for law school up-front or taking out loans, it's critical that you pay close attention to matters of money. Because experience shows that student debt will have the greatest impact on your job choice, and, as a consequence, you may enter law school with one career goal but—because of your debt load—you may have to find work in areas of the law that are far, far from your intended goal. Nor are things getting any easier. Law school tuition continues to rise dramatically—in recent years, law school students in some urban settings were buried under more than $100,000 in debt compared to $70,000 for some private schools, and $44,000 for some public institutions had. The sad fact is that too many law students don't pay attention to finances early enough. By the time they do, often as 3Ls, they're shocked at the amount of their debt and monthly loan repayments.

It brings to mind yet another Choice Challenge—**The Bigness Bias**, which helps explain why so many law students experience such nasty sticker-shock upon graduation. As its name implies, *the bigness bias* refers to our tendency to discount the importance of small numbers. For example, most of us don't think twice about spending a few dollars every day on coffee, snacks, restaurant meals, and other impulse items. But we're appalled when we annualize those innocuous expenses. We're not suggesting that you cut out snacking and an occasional lunch or dinner out, but it's crucial that you keep two important principles in mind as you make decisions about your law school finances.

Important Principle #1: Little Numbers Add Up. A classic example used by financial planners to illustrate this notion is the "latte scenario." It goes something like this: suppose you spend three dollars every day on a morning latte (e.g., cappuccino, espresso, chai). Shelling out a measly three bucks for your caffeine fix doesn't feel like much each time you do it, but—surprise!—it adds up to nearly $1,100 a year. Forgive the pun, but that's a *latte* money. When it comes to law school expenses, students are no different than anyone else in ignoring the way small expenses can spiral into substantial ones. Consequently, they wind up borrowing more money than absolutely necessary because they're spending just a little more here and there for rent, restaurants, car payments, cable service, cell phone plans and other expenses that add up over the course of three years.

One habit that contributes to the problem is something called *loss integration*. It refers to our tendency to discount smaller expenses—to *integrate* them—when we compare them to larger ones. So, if you spend $2,000 on a new wireless laptop, another 50 bucks for a three-year warranty doesn't seem like such a big deal. Or maybe you borrow an extra $2,500 to cover summer living expenses because it seems like a drop in the bucket compared to the $25,000 you've already paid for the school year. Falling for *the bigness bias* and *loss integration* are two weaknesses common to law students. After all, you're already shelling out all that money on tuition, how bad can it be if you borrow a little more? The fact is, such rationalizations set a domino effect into motion. In short, if you lease a fancy car, eat out frequently, splurge on vacations, or shop on borrowed money, you will wind up paying a lot more for your indulgences than you may realize. The key to overcoming this tendency is to examine every single expense separately, and ask: "Is this essential to my legal education?"

We're not saying don't ever reward yourself (law school is hard work). We're just encouraging you to find economical ways to do it.

Important Principle #2: Time Equals Money. It's also useful to understand how failing to take small numbers seriously can affect the amount of student loan interest. To illustrate the effect of time on money, let's take look another look at the latte scenario: Someone we know bought a $3 mocha nearly every day for 10 years for a total of $11,000. If he had purchased a simple cup of drip coffee (or even green tea), and had invested the savings in a stock mutual fund, that money could have grown to over $100,000 over 30 years, leaving him a lot wealthier (and probably healthier). That's the power of time on your money.

It's critical to understand how interest rates and loan repayment periods impact your bottom line—that is, how much you ultimately pay for your education. Here's an example: Suppose you borrow $50,000 for law school at 8.25% percent. If you repay that loan over 10 years, you'll pay $613 a month and your loan will have cost about $74,000 (of which nearly $24,000 would be interest). Now, if you double your repayment period to 20 years, you would pay only $433 per month, but the cost of the loan would soar to nearly $104,000 (of which about $54,000 would be interest, an amount equal to the cost of your education). Most law school students don't realize how quickly interest piles up until they've already borrowed and spent a pile of money.

Many lawyers we interviewed for this book admitted they would have made greater efforts to borrow less money and repay their loans in less time had they known how much interest would ultimately add to their loan repayments. We invite you to crunch the numbers yourself with one of the online loan calculators (see page x to help you find them). You'll see the stark difference between interest rates, the amount of money you borrow, and the amount of time needed to repay. In the meantime, here are some painless ways to minimize your law school debt:

Think small—Pay attention to little expenses and how they add up. The best way to do this, of course, is to make a budget and stick to it. Sure, it sounds nerdy (and it is) but it'll pay off in the long run by helping you avoid borrowing as much as you can, just because you can. At the very least, ask your law school financial aid office for tips regarding how to minimize your borrowing, and then make it your goal to live below the estimated cost of attendance that the law school provides you. This is one instance where it pays to be below average in law school!

Uncover hidden costs—When estimating their expenses, students often overlook obligations such as credit card debt, car payments and undergraduate student loans, as well moving expenses, security deposits and first and last month's rent. In addition to accounting for these expenses, be sure to budget for 12 months not nine. Your summer jobs may be unpaid, and your financial aid awards will only cover the nine-month school year.

Earn more—Get a part-time job during law school and apply for grants, scholarships and writing competitions. It's good for your resume as well as your bank account.

Wait and save—Consider working and saving money for a couple of years before law school, so you can borrow less money. This can make a tremendous difference in giving you more options when it comes time to choose jobs.

Use online calculators—When considering lenders and repayment options, use online calculators to find out how much your monthly loan repayments actually amount to with different interest rates and varying numbers of monthly payments. Compare the difference between government and private loans (which frequently offer different rates, as well as the difference in how much you'll spend over different lengths of repayment).

Books & Web Sites

The Law School Experience

Books

2002—*Law School Insider: The Comprehensive 21st Century Guide to Success in Admissions, Classes, Law Review, Bar Exams and Job Searches, for Prospective Students and Their Loved Ones*—Jeremy B. Horwitz. A detailed guide to getting into and making the most of law school and launching a successful career.

2000—*Law School Confidential: The Complete Law School Survival Guide by Students, for Students*—Robert. H. Miller. For prospective law students and law students. This guide provides strategies for getting admitted to and choosing a law school, as well as succeeding in law school and landing summer and post-graduate jobs.

1999—*A Woman's Guide to Law School*—Linda Hirshman. For women considering (or already in) law school. This book discusses which law schools are good for women (and which aren't), and how to succeed in law school no matter where you are.

Web Sites

ABA Career Counsel (abanet.org/careercounsel)—Useful tips, articles, and a Q&A web board for pre-law students.

Advice and financing resources for public-interest careers—Equal Justice Works (equaljusticeworks.org/finance), PSLawNet.org (pslawnet.org)

Findlaw's Student Resources Channel (stu.findlaw.com)— Offers law students and prospective law students advice on popular topics such as succeeding at law school academics, managing your legal career and passing the bar exam, as well as discussion forums and student message boards.

How to finance law school—The following sites provide a basic understanding of how student loans work and what they mean for your specific situation, and also offer online calculators to help you create a budget and manage your debt. Edfund's Online Financial Planning Guide (edwise.org), Students First (edfund.org/students/index.html), finaid.org, Nelliemae.com/calculators, and Studentaid.ed.gov/students/publications/student_guide/index.html.

How to humanize law school (law.fsu.edu/academic_programs/humanizing_ lawschool.php)—Articles, reading lists, discussion boards and other resources for prospective and current law students interested in making law school a kindler, gentler experience.

Law.com's Law Student Channel (law.com/jsp/students.jsp)—Features articles of interest to both law students and prospective law students (such as law-school news and the state of the legal job market) and other resources, including law "blogs" (focused on law school life).

On scholarships—FinAid! (finaid.org), Wired Scholar Sallie Mae (wiredscholar. com), FastWEB (fastweb.com), Scholarship Search (cbweb10p.collegeboard. org/fundfinder/html/fundfind01.html).

Vault.com's Law School Channel (vault.com)—For law students and prospective law students, this site contains law school message boards and articles on topics ranging from law school admissions to academics, as well as career advice. Type "law student" at Vault's search engine and check out the law student discussion.

WetFeet.com's Legal Channel (wetfeet.com/research/industries/law/law_articles. asp)—Helpful for law students and prospective law students, this site features articles addressing the issues on law school students' minds, such as academics and career success.

Legal Career Development

Books (General Legal)

2003/2004—*The National Directory of Legal Employers*. Providing basic information (practice areas, firm demographics, billable hour requirements, salary, etc.) for those interested in researching large and medium private law firms, this directory is available in most law school career services offices and online at nalpdirectory.com.

2003—*Ask the Career Counselors…Answers for Lawyers on Their Lives and Life's Work*—Kathy Morris and Jill Eckert. Tips, articles and exercises to propel readers towards a more satisfying professional life in, around or beyond the law.

2003—*The Complete Guide to Contract Lawyering: What Every Lawyer & Law Firm*

Needs to Know About Temporary Legal Services (3rd ed.)—Deborah Arron & Deborah Guyol. For lawyers and law students interested in freelance lawyering, this book explains how to determine if being a contract lawyer is for you and details strategies for establishing and building a successful contract-based practice.

2003—*Running From The Law: Why Good Lawyers are Getting Out of the Legal Profession* (3rd ed.)—Deborah Arron. For dissatisfied or burned-out lawyers (and confused law students), this book offers strategies and resources for job and career changes, along with case studies of lawyers who successfully left the law.

2003—*What Can You Do With a Law Degree? A Lawyer's Guide to Career Alternatives Inside, Outside & Around The Law* (5th ed.)—Deborah Arron. For lawyers and law students interested in exploring alternatives to legal practice, this comprehensive book offers extensive self-assessment exercises, strategies for marketing yourself to non-legal employers and managing your job search and a detailed appendix with job and career profiles and job search and career development resources.

2002—*The Lawyer's Career Change Handbook: More Than 300 Things You Can Do With a Law Degree* (2nd ed.)—Hindi Greenberg. For lawyers and law students interested in new jobs or careers, this fine book provides advice and resources for identifying and pursuing work that's a good fit for you.

2001—*Choosing Small, Choosing Smart—Job Search Strategies for Lawyers in the Small Firm Market*—Donna Gerson. For students and lawyers thinking small, a discussion of the pros and cons of small-firm practice and how to land a job and succeed in a small firm.

2001—*Full Disclosure: The New Lawyer's Must-Read Career Guide*—Christen Civiletto Carey, Esq. Advises recent law-school graduates on how to succeed at their first job, offering advice on issues such as completing assignments, dealing with partners and deriving job satisfaction.

2000—*Objection Overruled...Overcoming Obstacles in the Lawyer Job Search*—Kathy Morris. Covers common barriers to the successful lawyer job search and provides practical advice about overcoming the stopping blocks.

2000—*The Official Guide to Legal Specialties*—Lisa Abrams. Aimed at helping prospective law students, law students and lawyers understand what it's really like to practice in thirty major practice areas (corporate, criminal, public interest, intellectual property, etc.), this book includes an overview of each area of law and profiles of attorneys working in the various public and private practice settings within them.

2000—*What Law School Doesn't Teach You...But You Really Need to Know*—Kimm Alayne Walton. For law students and recent law school graduates, this guide offers tips for maximizing your law-school experience and launching a successful legal career. It includes tips on a wide range of topics such as dealing with billable hours, fitting into your workplace culture, navigating office politics and handling ethical issues.

1999—*Transforming Practices: Finding Joy and Satisfaction in the Legal Life*—Steven Keeva. For lawyers and law students interested in deriving more meaning from law (and life). This hopeful book includes profiles of lawyers who changed work habits and attitudes to better contend with the adversarial nature of legal practice and achieve greater career satisfaction.

1998—*America's Greatest Places To Work With A Law Degree and How to Make the Most of Any Job, No Matter Where It Is*—Kimm Alayne Walton. A valuable guide for prospective law students, law students and lawyers, this comprehensive book profiles law firms, corporations, government agencies and public interest organizations where the lawyers like being lawyers. It also provides extensive resources and strategies for finding and landing jobs with these and similar employers.

1997—*Alternative Careers for Lawyers*—Hillary Mantis. This book helps lawyers and law students decide whether to change careers or switch jobs, find new fields of interest, consider the financial ramifications of career change and land jobs in non-legal fields. It includes helpful profiles of attorneys who successfully switched careers.

1997—*Guerilla Tactics for Getting the Legal Job Of Your Dreams*—Kimm Alayne Walton. Terrific for law students and recent law school graduates, this comprehensive job search guide offers effective strategies for landing a legal job you'll like. It helps readers identify jobs of interest, make networking fun and painless, write effective cover letters and resumes and ace job interviews. Offers clever strategies for dealing with a low grade-point average and getting in the back door to a large law firm.

1996—*Six Months Off: How to Plan, Negotiate and Take the Break You Need Without Burning Bridges or Going Broke*—Hope Dlugozima, James Scott, and David Sharp. Great for anyone considering a career sabbatical, this book details how to identify, finance and actualize sabbatical opportunities (and eventually return to work). Includes case studies of professionals who used sabbaticals to jump-start their lives and careers.

Books (Public Sector and Public Interest)

2003—*Serving the Public: A Job Search Guide*—The 14th edition of Harvard Law School's public interest job search guide, this book helps law students and lawyers find public interest and public sector jobs. It includes listings of public interest and public sector employers, post-graduate fellowships, federal honors programs and entrepreneurial grants, and offers helpful advice regarding marketing yourself for public interest jobs, transitioning from private practice to public interest and financing summer public interest work.

2003—*The Great Firm Escape: Harvard Law School's Guide to Breaking Out of Private Practice and Into Public Service*—Aimed at lawyers interested in shifting from private practice to public service, this book includes tips on finding and landing public interest jobs and making the financial transition, as well as profiles of lawyers who successfully left private practice and established themselves in public interest careers.

2002—*Behind the Bench: The Guide to Judicial Clerkships*—Debra M. Strauss. For law students and recent law-school graduates interested in judicial clerkships, this book advises readers on how to target courts and judges, craft effective application materials, interview successfully and prepare for a clerkship once they land one. The book's companion web site (judicialclerkships.com/book. htm) offers additional tips and resources.

Web Sites

DecisionBooks (www.DecisionBooks.com)—Devoted to helping law students and lawyers with career decision-making and development, this site includes career counseling resources, online self-assessment tools and essays on myriad career development topics.

Equal Justice America (www.equaljusticeamerica.org)—This nonprofit provides funding for semester and summer public interest internships for law students at affiliated schools.

US Office of Personnel Management (www.usajobs.opm.gov)—Official job site for U.S. Federal Government job listings and employment information, where job seekers can search a database for government positions by agency, location and level.

Equal Justice Works (www.equaljusticeworks.org)—A non-profit supporting public interest-minded law students and sponsoring post-grad public-interest fellowships.

Findlaw.com (www.profdev.lp.findlaw.com)—Helpful reading for lawyers and law students alike, including a collection of articles regarding changing and landing jobs and achieving career satisfaction.

Idealist (www.idealist.org)—This site allows public interest-oriented job hunters to search thousands of non-profit and community organizations, find volunteer opportunities and view job and internship listings.

International Alliance of Holistic Lawyers (www.iahl.org)—A non-profit association of lawyers interested in increasing career satisfaction and transforming the nature of conflict resolution in the U.S. through annual conferences, retreats, and other events.

Local Bar Associations—Many state and local bar associations offer career development programs for attorneys, including workshops aimed at helping lawyers explore alternatives to legal practice. Contact your state or local bar association to see if they offer such programs.

Opportunity Knocks (www.opportunityknocks.org)—This public service career web site offers an extensive array of job listings with non-profit organizations as well as non-profit career resources.

PSLawNet (www.pslawnet.org)— Features an extensive database of semester, summer and post-graduate public-interest internships, jobs, volunteer opportunities and fellowships nationwide. Includes resources to help law students fund their summer public-interest legal work.

Renaissance Lawyer Society (www.renaissancelawyer.com)—A non-profit educational group dedicated to creating new models for legal practice by making the profession less adversarial and more fulfilling through conferences, retreats, and continuing legal education.

Books (General Career Development)

2003—*The Internship Bible*—Mark Oldman and Samer Hamadeh. Features extensive profiles of internships in a wide array of fields and advice on finding and landing the right one for you.

2003—*Job Hunting A to Z: The WetFeet Insider Guide to Landing the Job You Want.* A good guide for relatively new job hunters, this book offers tactics for identifying potential employers, getting your foot in the door, acing the interview and negotiating your job offer.

2003—*Vault Career Guides*—These comprehensive guides present an in-depth look at various industries (Law, Finance, Fashion, Media & Entertainment and Investment Banking, to name just a few).

2003—*WetFeet Insider Guides*—Offers detailed information about myriad industries and profiles major companies in each one.

2003—*What Color Is Your Parachute? A Practical Manual for Job-Hunters and Career Changers*—Richard Nelson Bolles. The world's best-selling job-hunting book, this classic guide provides time-tested strategies for figuring out what you want to do, where you want to do it, the person who has the power to hire you and how to get hired. The book's companion web site, jobhuntersbible.com, features useful career development and job search articles and resources.

2000—*A Foot in the Door: Networking Your Way Into The Hidden Job Market*—Katharine Hansen. Good for recent college graduates and people who fear networking, this book explains how to use networking to your advantage and how to do it effectively, how to conduct informational interviews and how to become comfortable with networking even if you're painfully shy.

2000 —*Hand Me Down Dreams: How Families Influence Our Career Paths and How We Can Reclaim Them*—Mary H. Jacobsen and Sarah Silbert. An interesting read for anyone making or reassessing their career choices, this book helps readers assess how their career decisions may have been influenced by family dynamics and expectations and take steps to identify and pursue their true aspirations.

1999—*The Career Guide for Creative and Unconventional People*—Carol Eikleberry. Useful for anyone who's interested in emphasizing creativity at work, this book explains how to identify potential jobs and careers where you can make a living using your creative skills. Includes stories of real people who successfully found work that allowed them to be creatively satisfied and pay the bills, as well as an extensive appendix describing hundreds of creative and unconventional jobs.

Web Sites

Collegegrad.com (collegegrad.com/careers)—Offers those new to the job market listings for entry-level jobs, internships and overseas opportunities.

Vault Industry Reports (vault.com)—Provides free online overviews of different career fields and "Day in the Life" profiles of those who work in them.

HotJobs.com—Offers job hunters a massive array of job listings in a wide range of occupations, as well as job search advice and online discussion boards.

Monster.com—Features a searchable database of job listings, as well as career advice and job profiles.

WetFeet Industry Profiles (www.wetfeet.com)—Includes overviews of myriad careers and "Real People Profiles" of the folks in them.

*W*e've always believed that you can tell a lot about a book's author (or authors) by its acknowledgments. In our case, you might assume that both Deborah and Gary have an over-developed sense of gratitude and an eagerness to credit all those who have helped us in this and various other endeavors. We can live with those assumptions.

Broadly, we would like to thanks the hundreds of lawyers, career counselors, lawyers, professors, lawyers, law students, administrators and lawyers we spoke to over the course of researching this book. We are continually amazed and humbled by the honesty with which so many people, friends and strangers alike, share their most intimate thoughts, triumphs, fears and failures. Their insights are invaluable.

This book, you may have noticed, is a collaboration, but our physical distance and general nature mean that much of what both of your authors brought to the project was the result of individual labors and experiences. As a result, we have individual acknowledgments to offer.

From Deborah . . .

To Jane Dystel, our terrific and talented literary agent who just happens to be a law-school drop- out. The world is certainly a better place as a result of her leaving law for literature.

To Victoria Zenoff, a brilliant career counselor and dear friend, for helping to spark my idea for this book. To Dick Bolles for inspiring me to begin writing it. And to Ted Weinstein for all the cheerleading along the way.

To the wise (and busy) women who made time to share their wisdom with me: Sue Aiken, Stacy DeBroff, Cheryl Heisler, Kathy Morris, Carol Vecchio and Wendy Werner.

To everyone (some listed here and some not, believe it or not) who supported this project in some way, shape or form: Meg Barnette, Robin Beers, Cindy Berg, Debbie Berger, Melanie Berkowitz, Dan Bernal, Jason Brandeis, Jen Buchanan, Randy Burrows, Andrea Burstein, Tara Casey, Rachel Callaghan, Michael Capozzola, Abbe Chant, David Chui, Meghan Cleary, Karen Coburn, Amy Cohen, Michelle Cotton, Krysten Crawford, Kathy Davis, Mary Dixon, Josh and Liz Engel, Darren Fancher, Eric Ferraro, Clare Gallagher, Irene Feldman, Will Fitton, Julie Fleisher, Brooke Foster, Catherine Crystal Foster,

SuEllen Fried, Emily Friedman, Robin Gerber, Donna Gerson, Brandt Goldstein, Leslie Gordon, Sarah Goulder, Kindra Gromelski, Lauren Grossman, Dan Gustafson, Elizabeth Hahn, Amy Hamill, Catherine Hamlin Amy Garland, Kim Hochman, Brooke Hodess, Michelle Holcenberg, Alexandra Jenkins, Tina Joh, Rose Jonas, Cheryl Kagan, Julie Kalk, Bob Kallen, Hal Kane, Roberta Katz, Lisa Keating, Pauline Kilijian, Nancy King, Joanna Krinn, Aimee LaFerriere, Jamie Lake, Karen Lash, Shauna Leff, Karen Leventhal, Lisa Levert, Megan Linney, Chris Loux, Nancy Lublin, Julie Lyss, Shelley Malin, Erika Maltzberg, Julie Mangurten, Julia Mariani, Zorina Matavulj, Tara May, Beth McCarty, Duncan McDonald, Andrea Michaels, Jennifer Michalski, Liz Mikola, Tracie Militano, Marcy Milman, Jeanette and Kevin Moore, Katie Morris, Lara Myers, Jessica Natkin, Julie Norris, Sandy Owens, Carlos Perez, Scott Plamondon, Leslie Platt, Richard Poland, John Pollack, Taylor Rabbetz, Megan Radeski, Andy Raskin, Kathy Reich, Pat Reilly, Julie Rich, Michael Rich, Krista Rosa, Wendy Rosenblum, Julie Obbard, Adam Rothwell, Emily Samose, Leslie Savin, Joe Scanlon, Maya Segal, Kelle Selcer, Dayna Shaw, Laura Klearman Silver, Jason Sklar, Randy Sklar, Susie Smith, Elaine Sosa, Debbie Stephens, Megan Sullivan, Karen Szeto, Jean Tang, Rachel Teisch, Jeff Thomas, Rebecca Tillet, Karen Tokarz, Traci Van Buren, Rob Victor, Kimm Walton, Lisa Waltuch, Fred Wasser, Julia Webber, Ken Weine, Tony Winnicker and Guy Zuzovksy. I also thank my fellow campers from Camp Parachute 2001, my colleagues at U.C. Hastings College of the Law (Denise Barnes, Elena DuCharme, Pat Gonzales, Tunisha Grant, Phil Marshall and Sari Zimmerman), and members of the Bay Area Legal Recruitment Association and the Northern California Law School Consortium. It took a village.

To Jenn Epstein, for all the tennis-court talks, and Leslie Koren, for all the symposiums. My life wouldn't be the same without them.

To my grandparents Gene and Sylvia Weissman, the greatest role models imaginable. (They also paid for law school.) Although this isn't exactly how they envisioned me using my law degree, they've embraced this decision—all my decisions—with tremendous pride and love.

To my father, Mel Schneider, for enthusiastically supporting all my endeavors and teaching me at an early age what it means to be an advocate. And to the memory of his parents and my grandparents, Gussie and Hascal Schneider.

To my sister, Elizabeth Schneider, who has always inspired me by making decisions based on her convictions.

Finally, and most importantly, to my wonderfully funny, incredibly supportive and very cool mother, Deanna Schneider, for decades of walking, talking, laughing and listening.

From Gary...

This book began because Deborah read another book I co-authored about Behavioral Economics. She was fascinated with the subject and impressed by the insights of the field's most original thinkers. I know the feeling, which is why I must acknowledge the brilliant efforts of Daniel Kahneman and (the late) Amos Tversky, and Richard Thaler. This troika of intellectual giants is most responsible for the acceptance of behavioral economics as serious science. I'm grateful for their scholarship and their kind help to me over the years. Any tenuous leaps in this book from their work (and the work of their peers) to our conclusions is our fault entirely.

To Tom Gilovich, who has taught me much about behavioral economics, psychology, decision-making, statistics and sports myths. Tom is one of the smartest people I know, and one of the happiest. You hardly ever see those two descriptions applied to the same person, which explains why I admire him so.

To Russell Roberts and Peter Keating, critical thinkers and excellent teachers.

To my colleagues at ESPN, specifically Neil Fine, Gary Hoenig and John Papanek, for their support (practical and theoretical) of my extracurricular interests.

To Jodi Kahn, Linda Eisner and Jason and Lisa Ablin, for their friendship and support, and to Nikki Weinstein, for the same.

To Lynn Goldner, and to Natasha and Eliza Poster, for their Wednesday-night solace.

To my siblings (Myron, Rhona, Larry, Howard, Jonathan and Barbara), my nephews and nieces (Ari, Elly, Yirmi, Adir, Sam, Zevvy and Aniel) and my mom (Irene) for their love and good humor.

And, finally, to David Kahn and Mark Eisner, who know me all too well and don't seem the least bothered by it.

Notes